Structural**Violence**

JOSHUA M. PRICE

Structural**Violence**

Hidden Brutality
in the Lives of Women

Published by
STATE UNIVERSITY OF NEW YORK PRESS, ALBANY

© 2012 State University of New York
All rights reserved
Printed in the United States of America

For information, contact
State University of New York Press, Albany, NY
www.sunypress.edu

Production and book design, Laurie D. Searl
Marketing, Fran Keneston

Library of Congress Cataloging-in-Publication Data

Price, Joshua M.
 Structural violence : hidden brutality in the lives of women / Joshua M. Price.
     p. cm.
 Includes bibliographical references and index.
 ISBN 978-1-4384-4344-7 (pbk. : alk. paper) — ISBN 978-1-4384-4343-0
(hardcover : alk. paper) 1. Women—Violence against—United States. 2.
Women—Violence against—United States—Prevention. I. Title.
 HV6250.4.W65P724 2012
 362.83—dc23

                                                                2011041967

10 9 8 7 6 5 4 3 2 1

How everything turns away
Quite leisurely from the disaster

—W. H. Auden, *Musée des Beaux-Arts*

His words signal deference to the uncapturability of the life it mourns. It is the deference that moves her, that recognition that language can never live up to life once and for all. . . . What moves at the margin. What it is to have no home in this place. To be set adrift from the one you knew.

—Toni Morrison, Nobel Lecture

This book is dedicated to the women in it.

Contents

Illustrations

Acknowledgments

In the course of research, I have been inspired over and over again by the courage, intelligence, and fortitude of many women, especially survivors of violence. I have learned enormously from their thinking and analyses. This book is built on the insights and experiences of activists and advocates in the struggle to stop violence against women. Of course, I take full responsibility for whatever I have gotten wrong.

The political concepts at the root of this book took form while I was a member of a center for popular education, the Escuela Popular Norteña. I want to thank my compañeras/os, in particular, María Lugones, Laura Dumond Kerr, and Julia María Schiavone Camacho. Our collaborative work, critical companionship, and conversations over the course of more than a decade were fundamental for me to think as I do and transform as (I hope) I have. The contribution and support of María Lugones, in particular, were inestimable at every stage of the process of this book. She helped shape my understanding of violence against women. She also read and commented generously on numerous versions of this text. I am deeply grateful to her. In EPN, Rafael Mutis, Rick Santos, Hector Mauricio Graciano, and Geoff Bryce offered a context in which to take in and think through critiques of violent masculinity by feminists of color. Over the course of years, in conjunction with the women of color in our collective, we developed techniques to work with men against violence against women of color. Other members of the collective who influenced my thinking include Aurelia Flores, Dalida María Benfield, Cricket Keating, Suzanne LaGrande, Mildred Beltré, Rob Gonzalez, Isabel Gonzalez, and Sarah Lucia Hoagland. Sarah's work has also changed how I think about resistance and agency under oppression, as well as my understanding of lesbian identity. Sarah also made extensive, and very helpful, comments on an earlier draft.

Many other activists have shared their time, acumen, and hard-won sagacity generously with me. Bertha Hinojosa, Caridad Souza, Veronica Frankel, and

Marta García each took time to speak with me of the struggle to stop violence against women in its variegated character, especially Latina immigrants, poor women, homeless women, and Latina lesbians. They have also added dimension to my critical take on the shelter movement and on law courts.

I would like to acknowledge my gratitude to Rozann Greco, Mary DeGroat, Kathy Pierre, Candis Henderson, Noelle Paley, Cheryl DeRosa, Felicia Jennings, and Nancy Jennings, who taught me about the intersection of incarceration and structural violence in women's lives. I learned a lot from Noelle and Rozann in particular, from working, writing, and thinking with them while engaged in advocacy for the currently and formerly incarcerated, often in very trying circumstances. In that spirit I would like to mark the countless other women and men, community members, and university students involved in the Broome County Jail Project and in the Southern Tier Social Justice Project.

I have benefitted from terrific colleagues and excellent students at Binghamton University. M. Sue Crowley and my colleague and *appa* Lubna Chaudhry, on top of years of productive dialogue, both read the manuscript and gave valuable suggestions. Lubna introduced me to the concept of structural violence.Rudiah Primariantari taught with me, and I learned a great deal from her about structural violence and the oppression of women in the global South. The Radical Interdisciplinary Dialogue, and then the Working Group on Methodologies of Resistant Negotiation in Binghamton, provided critical commentary and a receptive space to do interdisciplinary work, as well as a forum in which to rethink the possibilities of anthropology given deep challenges. Members included Kelvin Santiago-Valles, Gladys Jiménez-Muñoz, Risa Faussette, Kai Lundgren-Williams, Rudiah Primariantari, María Lugones, Julia Glanville, Tabor Fisher, Elizabeth Morrison, Manuel Chávez, Jennifer Lutzenberger, and Chris Cuomo. I thank generations of students, especially those women who shared their stories with me and gave me critical feedback.

A stay at the James Weldon Johnson Institute for Advanced Interdisciplinary Research, of Emory University, under the able, generous, and visionary stewardship of its founder and director, Rudolph Byrd, and its associate director, Calinda Lee, supplied a wonderful and collegial setting in which to finish this manuscript. Professor Byrd passed away as this book goes to press. His guidance, leadership, initiative, not to mention his good spirit, will be missed. We are impoverished by his absence. A generous leave provided by the State University system, with support from Deans Ernest Rose and Ricardo Lauremont gave me time and support to write.

Karen Wenzel taught me about the clandestine networks rural women use to survive violence. I learned more from Karen than from any other student I have ever had. May she rest in peace.

It was at Caitrin Lynch's invitation that I initially attended domestic violence court in Chicago. Michael Silverstein taught me how to study language and interaction, and Elizabeth Povinelli lent support at a critical juncture. Gary Wilder,

William Bissell, and Nicholas DeGenova gave early feedback to the writing and helped me navigate those years in Chicago.

Jonah Murdock made a home with me for the important first years of this research, a time that I regard with enormous tenderness and fondness. He also contributed important critical responses on several drafts of this manuscript, especially to my understanding of liberalism and the private/public split. Beth Murray also supplied crucial companionship, as did Zohar, my constant companion from early morning until late at night.

I would like to acknowledge the able and thorough assistance with legal research provided by Emily Rothenberg, especially in chapter 4. Professor Janet Dolgin recommended her to me and also gave me useful background on the law.

Ann Kibbey saw something worth publishing in the journal *Genders*. She gave me significant feedback on what became chapter 3. Eunjung Kim provided additional valuable comments.

Vivian Price's stalwart praxis continues to provide a consanguine model for how to bring together political commitment and scholarship.

Monroe E. Price and Aimée Brown Price have each provided me with a distinct model for how to live a scholarly life. From time out of mind I have watched them up close as they write, edit, develop ideas, and conduct research. The interplay of these two models has influenced the person and scholar I am. Monroe Price also made helpful editorial comments on several chapters.

This manuscript finally found a home at State University of New York Press. Andrew Kenyon and Larin McLaughlin were enthusiastic and encouraging from the start. Under their watchful eyes and good criticism, this manuscript became a book. In a similar vein, I would like to thank the entire editorial staff of the State University of New York Press, especially Laurie Searl. Ina Brownridge, director of multimedia resources at Binghamton University, provided expert assistance with graphics.

Finally, I would, with pleasure, mark my deep, abiding appreciation and admiration for Constanza Guzmán and her presence in my life (whether she is near or far) and her company, critical conversation, and love. Thank you, *mi amor*.

I am grateful to the *Domestic Abuse Interventions Programs* of Duluth for permission to reprint the "Power and Control Wheel" and the "Institutional and Cultural Supports for Battering." I also acknowledge permission to reprint illustrations in chapter 1 from the organization Peace over Violence (formerly the L.A. Commission on Assaults Against Women). "The Power Flower" and "The Triangle Tool" were originally published in Rick Arnold, Bev Burke, Carl James, D'Arcy Martin, and Barb Thomas, *Educating for a Change* (Toronto: Between the Lines, 1991). An earlier version of chapter 2 appeared in the *Cardozo Journal of International Law*. An earlier version of chapter 3 appeared in the journal *Genders*.

Introduction

Let's start with a room. It is small and closed—the size of a broom closet. In front of me is a thick plate of glass. The walls are white cinder block. The carpet is worn. I wait in a cheap plastic chair. I am in the visiting room at a county jail in upstate New York. In collaboration with the NAACP, I am interviewing people who have come forward with complaints about heath care at the local jail.

The woman on the other side of the glass is in her fifties. Let's call her Andrea Watson. The interview is going slowly. Many of the people we speak to are voluble. They want to tell us what's happening to them. This woman is rather distant and withdrawn. She stares off at some indeterminate spot beyond my left shoulder as she twists her cornrows between her fingers in what must be a habit, a gesture. She also shifts uncomfortably from time to time and rubs her shoulder gingerly. She tells me she thinks it was broken when the police arrested her because they beat her into submission and kicked her in the shoulder and ribs. She is in pain, but they will not take an x-ray of her shoulder, and now they have suspended her Advil, too. We have a mutual friend, someone I met through monitoring health care at the jail. She is speaking to me only because the friend has vouched for me. She won't talk to my students. Our friend tells me afterwards that this woman's sister died in this jail twenty years before. Her sister had a tubal (ectopic) pregnancy that burst, and she died of a hemorrhage when her transportation to the hospital was fatally delayed.

At the end of the interview, I put down my pen and ask her if there's anything I can do for her. "I've lost my glasses, and so I can't read. Call Jimmy and ask him to bring me my reading glasses." I learn later Jimmy never does bring the glasses. There she is, without her glasses, in her late fifties, nursing an untreated shoulder, bruised ribs, beat to the socks, sitting in a cell in the jail where her sister died twenty years earlier. Her relatives have not visited. This is happening now, in the town where I live.[1]

I take her as the starting point, because in this book I suggest that we need to redraw the map of violence against women. (Throughout this work, when I invoke

1

"we," I mean to include all who work to analyze and stop oppressive violence in its variegated forms. It is a heterogeneous "we," because people's perceptions are different; their ways of working to stop violence are diverse. Maintaining a sense of the plural, of the differences, is part of the project.)

What would it mean if *she* were the first person one had in mind in thinking of violence against women? For many touched directly by the criminal justice system, incarceration *is* uppermost in their mind as a form of violence against women. For most other people, women who are incarcerated occupy only the margins—of their nightmares.

Depending on their social location, people see different forms of abuse. This question of space and location is crucial. When one focuses on the spaces women are in, then one can see that women who work as prostitutes and women who are harassed and detained at the border face violence, though they are often not included in initiatives to stop gendered violence.[2] Institutions such as the border patrol and the police are sometimes indirect perpetrators, when they collude with batterers by doing nothing or sending women back to unsafe situations, including deporting them. Sometimes, however, agents of the state are direct perpetrators of violence against women: because of their position, they can physically or sexually assault women with relative impunity. Women at the margins experience violence generated by structures, institutions, and histories, which make their experiences irreducible to the commonsense notion that violence against women is basically a question of "domestic violence."

In this book, I challenge that narrow notion of violence against women. I follow women in their understandings of violence, and of violent spaces, to take up a range that includes not only interpersonal partner violence but also institutional and structural violence. Consequently, violence against women is revealed as a heterogeneous phenomenon. (Later in this chapter, I discuss how the analysis of spaces of violence is a method to uncover heterogeneity.)

Therapeutic models that address battering, self-help books, some shelters, the courts, federal and state legislation, empirical studies in sociology and even some mainstream feminist polemics reinforce the view that all women face the same kind of violence. They treat "violence against women" as synonymous with "domestic violence." From the Violence Against Women Act, to the "Cycle of Violence," from the Power and Control Wheel to the National Coalition Against Domestic Violence, from the movement to institute domestic violence courts to the shelter movement, the models that describe violence against women, the agencies and organizations that respond to violence, and even the everyday language most people use tend to reduce violence against women to battering tend, in short, to reduce violence to a common dynamic that cuts across social boundaries.

The thesis of this book is that this popular and institutionalized assumption of sameness masks violence against women that does not conform to the imagined norm; the assumption overlooks or suppresses public, institutional, and structural collusion with violence against women. It hides the heterogeneity of women's situations as they face violence. Rather than broaden understanding, the assumption limits the view of violence. It renders violence against the most socially marginal invisible or distorted. The purpose of this book is to articulate this flaw and demonstrate the implications for judicial intervention and other forms of public involvement.

Taking "domestic violence" as a stand-in for all violence against women is to take violence against monogamous (implicitly heterosexual) women as the *prototype*, to borrow Joy James' phrase (1996), and see all violence based on that prototype. The prototype is an abstraction. It excludes the experiences of women such as Andrea Watson. It also distorts accounts by women whose home does not conform to the normative model.

The dominant current in the work of criminologists, advocates, policy makers, psychologists, shelter administrators, and so on, has contributed to understanding violence as uniform and as domestic. They have incentive to do so. Agencies, funding sources, policies, models, and national studies have come to predicate their work on this normative understanding of violence. They promote a binary of "victim" versus "perpetrator." As they propose calling on the power of the state (in the form of prosecutors, police, judges, welfare office, and so on) to stop violence, they absolve the state as a force, sometimes a violent force, in structuring the lives of women. Evan Stark's solution to the "coercive control" of violence against women serves as an example of this trend: "In the world I favor, police, prosecutors, and courts would employ their considerable power of coercion to remove those who assault or entrap women from their society. Appropriate adjudication of domestic assault and coercive control cases requires a level of bureaucratic formalism that applies the same criteria to all battered women and perpetrators, albeit while considering variations in circumstance, motive, means, meaning, and consequence" (Stark 2009, 398). This law-and-order "sameness" approach has several problems. First, aided by the victims' rights movement and certain strands of the feminist movement to end violence, this approach promotes the punishment of "criminals" even without the cooperation of women who are survivors. Linda Mills sees mandatory arrest rules by the police, no-drop policies by the state, and mandatory reporting of suspected abuse by medical and school personnel as counterproductive (1999, 555–56). These measures are coercive and take decision making out of the hands of women. Mills characterizes these state interventions in cases of violence against women as themselves forms of "emotional abuse." If one considers the ways in which the coercive power of the state has been used on the poor and in communities of color, then one can see that sometimes the abuse is not only emotional.

This binary of battered women and "perpetrators" is also predicated on a simple dichotomy of innocence versus guilt. It leaves aside abused women who are criminally involved. Where do women in gangs belong? Undocumented women? Women who are involved in illicit drug trade? Where does Andrea Watson belong in Stark's schema? Is she a battered woman or a perpetrator in his schema? Or is she off the map of women who face violence and need safety and protection? Is it because she faces public violence, state violence (in the form of law enforcement or incarceration), and violence outside the private sphere?

As I show in the first chapter, the once-revolutionary work of the Duluth Domestic Abuse Intervention Project has come to exemplify some of these troubling tendencies. Despite its feminist grass-roots beginnings, its historical hostility to therapeutic solutions, and original transformative agenda, it has come to pioneer joint, interagency approaches to stopping violence through punishing perpetrators (*Blueprint* 2007). It has come to frame violence as homogeneous even as it allies itself with nonfeminist forces. Although the Duluth Project seeks to empower women, it bolsters approaches that involve the police, prosecutors, and other criminal justice agents and agencies to deliver swift punishment to perpetrators. In this kind of approach, the collusion of these same criminal justice agencies in harming women (especially women of color, immigrant women, sex workers, and other marginalized women) is ignored or suppressed in the name of the fight to stop a certain kind of domestic violence.

Our work on monitoring jail health care, in contrast, turns up many examples of institutional abuse. Women of color and poor white women are often victimized by sheriffs' deputies, jail guards, parole officers, members of child protective services, immigration agents (Immigration and Customs Enforcement), and so on. Sometimes, women suffer from interagency collaboration rather than benefit from it (see Bhattacharjee 2002).

Why is structural and state violence so often overlooked? It is overlooked in part because of the emphasis on sameness and on *domestic* violence in the movement to stop violence against women. Despite the apparently nonracist character of a position that sees all women—or any woman—as facing domestic violence, women of color have expressed skepticism of such rhetoric. Beth Richie describes the destructive consequences of the claim of sameness:

> [T]he assumed race and class neutrality of gender violence led to the erasure of low-income women and women of color from the dominant view. I contend that this erasure, in turn, seriously compromised the transgressive and transformative potential of the antiviolence movement's potentially radical critique of various forms of social domination. It divorced racism from sexism, for example, and invited a discourse regarding gender violence without attention to the class dimensions of patriarchy and white domination in this country. Put another way, when the national dialogue on violence against women became legitimized and institutionalized, the notion that "It could happen to anyone" meant that "It could happen to those in power." (Richie 2000, 1135)

When the struggle to stop violence against women moved to the mainstream and became institutionalized, she notes, it imported an image of commonality that eclipsed the character of violence against working-class women and women of color. Richie concludes that what looks like inclusion may paradoxically have a racist and a class component to it. For example, the mainstream antiviolence movement marginalizes efforts by communities of color to stop prison growth, to end racial profiling of men *and* women of color, to fight for immigrant rights and to stop detention and deportation of immigrants, including immigrant men. The dominant language continues to neutralize attempts to highlight other forms of oppression and how they intersect with gender violence.

Besides demonstrating the weight of difference in the study of gender violence, the following pages will include an exploration of this claim to "sameness" and its implications. Has "sameness" been institutionalized? How deep do the differences go? How can we frame violence against women in a way that embraces the most marginalized women's experiences of violence? How can we frame violence against women that is not predicated on claims of sameness? How can we do it in such a way that coalitions can still be formed?

In order to think about the exclusion and invisibility of the most marginal women, I want to put women like Andrea Watson at the center. What does she consider "violence"? Where can she go to be understood? These are questions I ask of her and of many other women. It is a significant challenge to take stock of the full range of forms of violence and build a movement based on fighting that entire range.

Centering the most marginalized women is an alternative to emphasizing commonality and sameness among women as the basis to build a movement to stop violence (see 1996; Richie 2000). Beth Richie exemplifies this strategy in "Queering Antiprison Work," her study of the violence faced by young African American lesbians serving time in juvenile detention (2005). Richie shows how "violence" looks to the women. In focusing on young African American lesbians, she notices how the mainstream LGBT movement and the antiprison movement each tends to overlook or ignore young African American queer women, especially those engaged in illegal activity. She argues that it is through putting the marginal at the center that a movement to end violence against all women is strengthened— not by focusing on commonalities, but by paying attention to differences, and emphatically those differences, such as race, class, and age that are used to isolate or marginalize some women. At the intersections of difference, she argues that it is a mistake to look for internal homogeneity even inside a group, because that will marginalize some *within* the group.

In a justly celebrated essay on intersectionality, Kimberlé Crenshaw prefigured Richie's concerns when she argued that anti-racist and feminist practices ignored the pressing, concrete problems faced by people who live at the intersections: "Although racism and sexism readily intersect in the lives of real people, they seldom do in feminist and antiracist practices. And so, when the practices expound identity as woman or person of color as an either/or proposition, they relegate the identity of women of color to a location that resists telling" (1991, 1242).

Twenty years later, feminist and antiracist movements and practices still operate to marginalize women of color and others who face intersecting oppressions. The political movements hide the particular struggles of women of color. These struggles include not just stopping interpersonal violence but also stopping the violence of oppressive structures that limit their lives in other ways as well.

The social structures that limit people's lives are themselves hidden. Lubna Chaudhry describes structural violence as:

> unequal life chances, usually caused by great inequality, injustice, discrimination, and exclusion, needlessly limiting people's physical, social and psychological well-being. These inequalities are the result of the exercise of power and coercion of dominant groups at the local, state, and global levels, and manifest themselves through economic, legal and administrative systems, legitimized through a superstructure produced by ideology, history, mythology, philosophy and religion. Structural violence is, then, rendered invisible, as it is perceived as the status quo, but it is experienced as injustice and brutality at particular intersections of race, ethnicity, class, nationality, gender, and age. (Chaudhry 2004; citations omitted)[3]

At the intersections, the violence is experienced as injustice; outside, from the standpoint of the dominant culture, the violence is often unseen as *violence* because members of the dominant culture have become habituated to the inequality, as in the violence of poverty or homelessness (see Galtung 1969; Mignolo 2008). Deep structural elements of the society mark some people as deserving worse treatment, or even mark some people as less human. The structures responsible for the violence are also responsible for cloaking the violence as violence. Colonialism, racism, and class difference are examples of structures that engender histories of difference, difference marked by violence. Attention to these structures requires attention to the histories. In order to see the violence, one must see the structures.

Stormy Ogden theorizes in this vein when she relates her own experiences of sexual and physical abuse, first at the hands of relatives and boyfriends, and then by the state (2005). She describes how she suffered incest in her youth, was raped numerous times as a teenager, and was introduced to drugs and alcohol in her early teens: "Days and nights consumed with alcohol, drugs, bars, and the back seats of cars, rapes, beatings, hospital visits for a broken arm, a gunshot wound, and to have an IUD surgically removed because I was raped with a cane. There were too many different men, too many empty bottles, and too many suicide attempts . . . At the age of twenty-two I was sentenced to five years in the California Rehabilitation Center at Norco. For me, imprisonment was just a new phase in the abuse" (2005, 60–61). Highlighting ongoing threats to struggles for native sovereignty, she concludes, "For the indigenous women of North America, sexual assault and imprisonment are two interlocking violent colonial mechanisms.

The criminalization and imprisonment of Native women can be interpreted as yet another attempt to control indigenous lands and as part of the ongoing effort to deny Native sovereignty" (Ogden 2005, 64). Ogden sees complicity among interpersonal sexual violence, ongoing colonial threat to native autonomy, and the criminal justice system. She places her own abuse within a history that predates her and forms part of structures that extend far beyond her own individual experience of violence. At the intersection of race and gender, Ogden's understanding is that the interpersonal violence is interconnected to larger structures of abuse.

Ultimately, this is not a book on battering. It is a book on how structures hide difference and how the differences can be recovered. I trace how the histories, discourses, and structures form and then transform the perception, conceptualization, living, legal understanding, and popular understandings of violence against women. The sense of violence itself is transformed so that to say "battering" reduces the scope and meaning. This book is not narrowly about battering because the sense of "violence" is transformed so that it is wider; not just wider, but every act has more than one meaning. The proposal is not just to make the category of "battering" more expansive and encompassing; "battering" loses its link with domestic space, but also loses its centrality as other forms of violence register. Institutions narrow the meaning of gender and of gendered violence. Outside the narrow conception of gendered violence, what structures and institutions occlude is not seen as gendered violence, but as something else. For example, many people see the skyrocketing number of immigrant detentions and deportations, and their disparate effect on women, only as an issue of Mexican or immigrant illegality and not also as an issue of violence against women.

BACKGROUND AND MOTIVATION

My analyses emerge in part from my experiences in participatory, or popular, education. I was a staff member of a center for popular education, the Escuela Popular Norteña, for ten years. Influenced by the work of Paulo Freire and Myles Horton, we worked in community settings, primarily in Latino neighborhoods, and focused on how to understand and resist interconnected oppressive forces in our lives. Throughout the 1990s, we developed workshops and retreats. During those years I learned much about the intersection of politics, race, culture, language, gender, class, and sexuality, in Tucson, El Paso, Northern New Mexico, Chicago, New York, Cleveland, Los Angeles, and elsewhere. The struggles were variegated but focused especially on violence against women of color. Through these years of political discussions, activism, and involvement, I developed an investment in stopping violence against women.

For example, the focus in chapter 2 on Latina women is an outgrowth of a popular education project in Chicago of which I was part. The project included a series of workshops conducted with a group of churches attended primarily by predominantly Mexican Americans, Mexicans, Latin Americans, and other Latinos. I began to learn how the complex interconnections among race, immigration status, family, the centrality of the church, the law, police, and the courts were lived by Latinas, especially women in situations of violence. This led me to meet many Latinas active in the multifaceted fight to end violence against Latinas.

On a more personal note, since the activism involved consciousness raising, it was in and through the activism that I came to see, vividly, how I was, or have been, implicated in the prerogatives of masculinity, the privileges of whiteness. I came to see this in concrete, detailed ways.[4] Indeed, reflecting on my social location is what motivated the research on which this book is based: I felt responsible to understand and stop violence against women.

My social location also has clear methodological consequences. I recognize that since I talk to women about harm, violence, and questions that are often tinged by shame, intimacy, and fear, the women I interview may not always speak candidly with me. In chapter 2, I refer to the need for a "theory of translation" to account for how an activist I am interviewing verbally maneuvers in order to head off certain interpretations I, a white man, may have of her, of her organization, or of violence in her community. Such a theory would account not only for what is said, but also what is left unsaid. At the same time, since I encountered many women in the context of political work, they were more forthcoming than they would be with a stranger. I have tried to provide enough context so that the reader can examine my account critically: are the women I interviewed frank with me? When are they dissimulating? How do they translate their experience to this white man? What might they hide? Have I interpreted their accounts well or poorly? And so on.

Consciousness of social location and its implications comes through cultivating perspective on my own comportment—how I appear from several different points of view. As I move about the world, I have the perception—which may be partly an illusion—that I can move about in relative freedom, relative freedom from harassment by men or by the police. My motility is not particularly contained or restricted; I occupy a lot of space easily and fluidly. I am confident of my ability to navigate through everyday life, financially and materially secure. Although Jewish, I understand myself as an insider to whiteness. I grew up with people taking care of me, of my material needs, cleaning up for me. These seem to me to be aspects of my experience relevant to this study. The intersubjective politics of my position as located in struggle gives me a perception of the dominant politics at work around me such that I experience the world in the way that I do (see Lugones and Price 1995).

I see political engagement as crafting a subjectivity that can shift in and out of dominant and outsider perceptions. Shifting back and forth in perception does not happen alone. My perceptions, identity, ways of thinking and feeling develop in company, intersubjectively, as I change my habits of everyday life, thus, my attention, focus, the people with whom I make sense, with whom I transgress norms, and so on. I slide in and out of awareness of my complicity in the small ways in which I uphold the fabric of everyday life. Struggle with people located outside of dominant structures is crucial to my maintaining a critical awareness of how I may collaborate in their exclusion.

By writing in this way, with this ambivalence about my own participation, I note the ways in which I have come to understand things about myself and about other people who have been motivated by the insights and challenges of women, especially women of color, who resist domination. Developing with clarity the way in which I believe cultural domination is processual and interactional prepares me to transform my practices. I also take this writing to be a process of revealing some of the ways discourse organizes space, sensibilities regarding communication, and certainty about who one is and can be.

The political involvement paralleled my research. I have been conducting research on violence against women since 1992. I studied for my doctorate in a department of anthropology. However, influenced by feminist and antiracist activism and scholarship around me, I decided for intellectual, ethical, and political reasons I wanted to study contemporary political and cultural questions close at hand rather than overseas. At the invitation of one of my classmates, I began to sit in with her on domestic violence court in Chicago.

I found unnerving the relentless parade of women testifying to horrific violence. The court proceedings themselves were curious: I had trouble at first understanding why judges ruled the way they did based on the evidence before them. Listening to women's testimony in court, I was struck almost immediately by the tremendous heterogeneity of women's domestic situations, the great differences in the lives they led, and the contrasting tendency of the courts to frame all of that violence as the same—as simple cases of "domestic violence," against all evidence to the contrary. I continued to do fieldwork and participant observation in courts in New York and in Chicago from the mid-1990s onwards.

In order to supplement what I was witnessing, I conducted interviews with lawyers, activists for battered women, counselors, and shelter workers. I reviewed theories on violence against women, the current social science literature on domestic violence, models, statistics, and national surveys of, on, about violence against women. In the mainstream research I found a similar tendency to presuppose commonality; a lot of the work in this field, which includes scholarly literature, legal practices, psychological models, and activist work, is premised on the idea that whatever the differences among women, they have something in common: they face violence. The implication is that this violence is always the same. This sameness clause occurs on a very deep level and is a prevalent notion.[5] In some cases, despite much evidence to the contrary, this "sameness" claim is put forward by women who have faced violence, often as a bid for inclusion in the movement to stop violence (I discuss this at length in chapters 2 through 4).

I use many of these texts, from quantitative studies of domestic violence to mission statements by community-based organizations, theoretical models, websites, and court procedures in issuing orders of protection, as evidence for the argument that the "sameness" approach has been institutionalized. My analysis is based in part on examination of these channels because I want to show how difficult it is to take on institutionalized violence against women when violence is generally represented as private, as individual, and as simply physical.

As time went on, and as I interviewed and participated in more political education projects with women of color, I began to appreciate the extent to which many women of color attributed violence directly or indirectly to social structures (racism, class oppression) or to the state (border agents, the police, the law courts themselves). Taking in these perspectives and analyses, my frame for violence has undergone a deep change.

In the last few years, listening, reading, working with women of color and others in developing workshops and conferences, I have come to appreciate that violence against women must be framed within larger forces and structures that punish and abuse women, especially women of color. In particular, the analyses of women of color associated with the national organization INCITE! have been key. INCITE! is an umbrella organization of self-identified radical women of color. The book titles by authors associated with this movement reveal how they link interpersonal violence with state-sponsored and structural violence: *Global Lockdown: Race, Gender, and the Prison-Industrial Complex; Compelled to Crime: The Gender Entrapment of Battered, Black Women; Killing the Black Body: Race, Reproduction, and the Meaning of Liberty; Policing the National Body: Race, Gender and Criminalization in the United States; Conquest: Sexual Violence and American Indian Genocide.*[6] These titles reflect an effort to frame violence against women as a consequence of structural forms of oppression (like race and class) and institutional forms of domination (through law courts, medicine, some shelters, the prisons, and even fighting overseas wars). The women of INCITE! theorize the interconnections between interpersonal and societal violence, public punishment and private battering, colonization and sexual assault, medical control, the war on drugs, anti-immigrant policy, and abuse of women.

In 2004, I founded and began directing the Broome County (New York) Jail Health Project, an ongoing participatory research project under the auspices of the NAACP. We document abuse and neglect of the health of people incarcerated at the Broome County Jail, in central New York, which is where I live. I collaborate with local community members, people currently or formerly incarcerated at the jail, their families, and students to document the testimony of incarcerated people in response to their requests and to advocate for them. We have interviewed more than one hundred people on their experiences in jail or prison and the challenges they face once they are free again. Many of the people we have interviewed are women who suffer or experience a wide range of health care concerns, such as pregnancy, yeast infections, urinary tract infections, venereal disease, seizures, osteoporosis, menopausal and postmenopausal needs, hormone replacement needs, high blood pressure, diabetes, and untreated traumatic injury (See Paley and Price 2010). The medical care is generally atrocious; the treatment brutal and cruel. We have also interviewed and work with many women who have loved ones who are incarcerated. This project has given me a practical sense of how private and public violence feed into one another, interweave, generate crises in the lives of women, especially poor white women and women of color, and in that sense entire communities. It has given me a clearer and more detailed sense of state violence (in the form of prisons, the parole office, police profiling of women of color) and interpersonal violence (rape and battering).

The activism, scholarship, and teaching nourish each other. This writing emerges from that history.

METHODOLOGY: ALTERNATIVE COGNITIVE PRACTICES AND THE ANALYSIS OF SPACE

I draw on participant-observation, on interviews I and others conducted, as well as published texts by women who disrupt the narrative that conflates violence against women with domestic violence. Drawing on what women say counts as violence is part of the method, but it's also part of the politics: contributing to building a movement based on difference, on the details of women's lives rather than on abstractions.

But what methodology focuses on women who occupy a location that "resists telling" as Crenshaw puts it? How does one open oneself to Stormy Ogden's account of the way interpersonal and state violence are linked to colonization? Putting the most marginal women at the center is a strategy. However, a strategy alone is not enough without a methodology.

I have come to believe that the stubborn persistence of narrow and abstract views on violence against women is in part a result of how the structural forces organize cognitive processes. By cognitive processes or practices, I mean the attitudes and expectations that constitute our attention as selective, that underlie our perceptions, evaluations, and choice of action (see Lugones and Price 1995). The narrow view of gender violence—that violence against women is synonymous with domestic violence and all domestic violence is the same—is a result of selective attention. The selective attention is simultaneously and systematically inattentive to the desires, needs, plans, and experiences of women outside the mainstream: violence at the hands of police, sex work, forced sterilization, deportation.

Attention, Marilyn Frye once commented, has everything to do with knowledge. "If one wonders at the mechanisms of ignorance, at how a person can be right there and see and hear, and yet not know, one of the answers lies with the matter of attention" (Frye 1983, 120). The selective attention that reduces all violence to sameness is anchored in three cognitive practices (See Lugones and Price 1995).

1. The tendency to perceive and make judgments of reality with *certainty*.

2. The impulse to reduce reality to simple, simplistic, or simplified formulas and formulations.

3. The urge to look for commonality, common denominators, or universals (in this case, among women).

Early on, for example, I noticed how many people I encountered in my everyday life, when they learned of my research topic, eagerly shared their ready-made theories of violence against women, whether or not they had any experience or expertise. Unprompted and unsolicited, people would explain to me what the problem was, who was battered, why, the etiology of violence, why women stayed. These were often (though not always) framed in general terms—overarching, simple formulations, one-liners, in effect, couched in universal theories of women, of human nature, male nature, the organization of the domestic sphere. These commonsense views are reflected in women-blaming clichés and rhetorical questions, such as "Why doesn't she just leave?" This is evidence that the cognitive practices I refer to are present at a popular level, among experts and nonexperts alike.

The cognitive practices also form the basis for psychological models, such as Lenore Walker's Cycle of Violence (1989), the practices of various men's groups, strategies put forward by the shelter movement (see chapters 1 and 2), therapies of self-help, and so on. Most social scientific studies of domestic violence strive towards clear and simple explanations. In the logic of dominant social scientific studies, simplicity and parsimony of explanation are cast as virtues. Such studies tend to assume, furthermore, normative understandings of "the home" what it means to be a "woman," what counts as "violence." They dismiss the possibility of multiple realities, simultaneous enactment of different conceptions of culture, understandings of how to relate to each other, and fundamental aspects of identity such as gender. The expectation of certainty rejects the possibility of more than one account; alternatives are discounted as false or distorting.

Instead, I am arguing for a cognitive shift away from simplicity and certainty, and away from the search for commonality and universality. In fact, the reduction to simplicity can itself be violent. The cognitive shift to seeing difference among women at the intersections requires an interpretive stance that is avowedly partial. The epistemology of complexity and uncertainty refer to accessing meaning across worlds of sense or understanding. Living with uncertainty, living with and within complexity, and living with a deep appreciation for conflicting perspectives is a prerequisite for open-ended understanding. It takes time to unravel why people are saying what they are saying or why they are acting the way they are. Even then, one never feels on unshakable ground. Meaning changes from cultural framework to cultural framework. The shift is to:

1. Seeing with complexity.

2. Interpretations in which uncertainty and tentativeness are embraced.

3. Understanding open to difference and not just commonality.

We don't, in other words, always have to strive to find "common ground." Violence has many manifestations with many meanings. Seeing the possibility of deeply diverse meanings of violence involves moving onto uncertain analytical ground. Taking up this latter group of cognitive practices, one is in a good position to perceive the many histories of violence and struggle. The history of the penal system, slavery and the slave trade, the history of immigration, of threats to native sovereignty, of colonization, all become relevant to understanding violence against women. These many histories engender many consequent meanings of freedom, mobility, autonomy, integrity, self-worth, and dignity.

With these cognitive practices, one sees not only differences at work—one can see how dominant institutions and models and discourses steamroll the differences, narrow the view of violence, ignore, exclude, and distort outsiders. One can hear the silenced voices through attending to the complexity at the intersection of gender and other axes of difference. In particular, one can see how dominant institutions, such as the courts, impose a simplified and abstract notion of "the home" onto women's heterogeneous accounts of violence. The cognitive practices lead one into the variegated meanings of violence and its social effects.

ETHNOGRAPHY OF "ABSTRACT" SPACE

I have proposed drawing a new "map" of violence against women. While the cognitive practices are tools to perceive anew, the descriptions and analysis of the *spaces* where women encounter violence is a device to understand and represent the differences. I anchor my account in women's descriptions of the spaces they inhabit and derive from those descriptions a sense of the differences among women. That is, I start with the descriptions rather than with categories (such as "African American women"); I interpret difference based on the *descriptions* and not on categories whose explanatory value is assumed. To put it differently, I uncover the meaning of difference by working through women's particular accounts rather than assume that the given markers of difference (such as race) reveal difference in a way that is self-evident or self-explanatory.[7]

The courts, mainstream social scientific studies, and models of violence against women homogenize violence by presupposing the space of the home as a uniform container. These mainstream attempts to construct the spaces of violence as homogeneous are in contradiction to the multiple lived experiences of space.

Space appears as homogeneous as a result of cognitive operations and social processes that together produce what Lefebvre has termed "abstract space." Abstract space is the chief and dominant organization of space under capitalism. It is marked according to Lefebvre by a geometric gridlike sameness and an emphasis on vision to the exclusion of all other senses (Lefebvre 1991, 285ff). Space is at once guaranteed as objective, geometric, rational, and given. It is capable of being subdivided on blueprints, of being monitored.

As I look at women's descriptions of space, I uncover difference. As I look at the dominant imposition of space, I see violence framed in terms of a homogeneous private sphere. One significant distinction among women has to do with how different women stand in their relation to structures like the U.S. border, the criminal justice system, or access to good doctors. Paying attention to space reveals the heterogeneity and unveils the importance of larger structures that are hidden. The masking of the heterogeneity is linked to the masking of state and structural violence.

Attention to women's descriptions of space in the study of violence against women has therefore several advantages. The accounts of space are imbued with different meanings; the spaces themselves have different histories that lead one to appreciate the importance of group difference. So analysis of space is thus an antidote to the urge to simplify. It leads us to see the contexts in which women live, struggle, and survive. Attention to space in the study of violence against women: dismantles the fiction that women's experiences of violence are homogeneous; suggests the importance of structural forces and cultural differences in understanding women's accounts of violence; reveals that social institutions are sometimes responsible for violence against women, even as they cloak or steamroll the differences in women's situations. To analyze abstract space as it is produced is to engage in a multifaceted investigation into discourse. The space we inhabit is the outcome of social processes, but it has come to be naturalized as a uniform container (Lefebvre 1991; Goffman 1971). What appears as prima facie natural, given, objective, is a consequence of a given set of social relations (Lefebvre 1991, 49; Harvey 1990, 223); hence, it is not part of the natural, inevitable, or irreversible furniture of the world. It is produced not only in the epistemology of architects and designers who look down from on high at their projects (de Certeau 1984; Soja 1989). It is also—and here's the rub—evidenced in the quotidian practices of lower level bureaucrats, civil servants, judges, social workers. One can see the reinscription, the imposition, the contribution to abstract space in the turn of mind, the judgment, the rulings, the modes of framing, in the imaginations of space, that are brought into being by people situated differentially within institutions of power. It is within the latter cluster of activity, how abstract space is imposed, that I plot the way in which space is imagined, and imagined as homogenized—and, as imagined, comes to have a certain efficacy in organizing social life. In other words, the imposition of abstract space is highly consequential in the ordering of our social lives and how we understand our social lives—the ideologies we hold.

This side of the story, then, is based on the notion that the thousands of daily decisions made by legions of people in their every day—quite apart from the planners and policy makers—uphold and advance the homogenization of space. The ideologies of space that people hold and articulate function in organizing space. In this book, I focus on the way in which abstract space promotes a set of beliefs so that it acts as a functional ideology that stipulates the lived experience of space for people in its domain.

Focusing on the ideology of space provides another side of the story, however. Taking stock of the construction of space in women's descriptions of violence is a methodological tool to reveal the particularity of each woman's experience. By analyzing space I draw out the sense of expanse and enclosure in the descriptions of locations. Space refers to how any site—the street, a bedroom, a doorway—is imbued with meaning by social actors. The method of looking at space allows for a detailed understanding of the violence that specific women face—how each depicts different spaces through which she moves, which are the spaces of danger and which of safety, which are spaces of intimidation and which of nervous anticipation, where she can go and where she can't, where she feels she needs to stay, where she feels accompanied, which are spaces of the unknown and which of the intimately familiar. Analyzing space reveals significant differences among women's experiences of violence. When understood in terms of space, the differences can be rightly understood as deeper than mere difference of circumstance. Because the differences are deep rather than circumstantial, the violence is itself different from case to case. Understanding violence as fundamentally homogeneous when the differences between women are deep fails to address violence, a phenomenon that is polymorphous. The law has failed to describe the polymorphic character of violence.

Deep difference in the experience of violence is such that to understand the violence one needs to understand the difference. That is, the difference makes and marks a difference in sense. A circumstantial difference leaves the sense of the violence untouched. Differences tend to be understood as circumstantial from the standpoint of abstraction, but this is an interpretation of the situation underpinned by the logic of homogeneity. From the perspective of women's concrete spatiality in violence, one can see the qualitative differences among women's experiences of violence. The differences are not extraneous to the violence in each case.

I have found that differences between women that are more substantial and enduring than those of happenstance are difficult for courts to incorporate or even perceive. On one level, this is treated as a virtue of the jurisprudence: the law does not discriminate between people based on their gender, race, or social class. Treating all similar cases similarly is the principle of precedent. But what makes one case similar to another? Which differences count? Are the differences deep or circumstantial?

Analysis of space provides a key. That a person is white, or Latina, or HIV positive, or works as a prostitute taken as a descriptor, a feature of the circumstance of violence, ought not to make a difference in rulings on battering—unless the difference it makes is crucial to understanding the violence (the very thing that is the subject of the ruling). I attempt to show that if courts do not take up women's perspectives on violence, then the law courts do not resolve the problem of gendered violence at least in part because they presume that all forms of battering of women are cast from a common mold. Devising meaningful solutions for women requires insight into what types of spaces offer haven and what sites produce terror for particular women. Solutions that do make sense, that are intelligible in the light of these findings, conflict with the assumption that the problem can be understood as simply a problem of domestic violence, taken as a unitary phenomenon.

One additional consequence of the attention to space is that one can see that the way women live, think, act, describe, and move is not congruent with the way they are imagined to, given the domestic/public split. In other words, this split, though consequential in how women are regarded, judged, constrained, imagined, does not meet up with women's actual experiences, senses of self, felt spheres of influence, authority, in the way that is imagined.

Throughout this book, then, one can see that the logic of the split between the domestic and the public is important in conceptualizing the problem of violence against women. To presuppose this split would be to go along with certain slippages that are highly consequential. To take the most obvious example with which I began, "violence against women" is often turned into "domestic violence," which excludes certain women. It also miscasts what "domestic violence" may mean for some women. Annanya Bhattacharjee has reviewed cases of immigration agents who raid the homes of immigrants (2002). In these cases, "the home" is a site of domestic violence, but the violence is state violence. Thinking of these cases, she asks what it would take to include an *immigration raid* in the picture of "domestic violence." It would mean challenging a dominant perception of who the agents are of "domestic" violence and, perhaps, even what the "home" is.[8] (I return to this theme in chapter 6, "Why Doesn't She Just Leave?").

QUALITATIVE EVIDENCE VERSUS STATISTICS

The women whose voices feature in this book are treated as theorists in the sense that they reflect on the world and on the events they have lived through. They do not simply tell their experience without interpreting it; they give an account of its meaning, its significance, and sometimes why it happened. They lead me to interpret their accounts within theoretical frameworks, sometimes of their own coinage and sometimes ones I introduce. In this sense, I try not only to be a faithful scribe, but also to provide an analysis.

Women's voices erupt through the text of the subsequent chapters. They make their presence felt; they surround the reader even as they surround me as a writer and researcher. Their voices, insights, observations, testimonies disrupt attempts to oversimplify their experiences. Conducting the research for this book, living with the words of women testifying to violence, has been harrowing; it has meant living in a reality where one senses the enormity of the violence while living simultaneously a mundane everyday life that cloaks it. Living in two or more realities simultaneously in this way is exhausting. The writing strategy will be successful if it communicates those multiple realities, one invading the other, and if the corresponding atmosphere is claustrophobic.

Some of the most important forms of violence, such as those glimpsed in this chapter and those that follow, are not generally counted in national studies or even methodologically perceived as incidences of *violence* by most mainstream researchers. But understanding violence requires more than counting the number of punches, or bruises.

Feminists have put on the map psychological abuse, intimidation, and stalking as significant forms of abuse. Women describe the psychology of terror, of the anxiety and apprehension. They describe the influence of oppressive structures on their day-to-day lives.

In this study, I assume that violence against women is prevalent in the United States. This premise is based on my seasoned assessment. It is informed by the movement against violence against women. The National Crime Victimization Survey, Centers for Disease Control and Prevention, the National Institute of Justice, the U.S. Department of Justice, and the Bureau of Justice Statistics (as well as countless academic researchers) regularly track statistical trends in violence against women. They register figures in the hundreds of thousands in the number of cases of rape, sexual assault, and intimate violence against women.

In marking the scope of the claim that violence against women is prevalent, I will only occasionally rely on statistics to support my claims. Most of the time, I rely on qualitative research by myself and others. In trying to bring forward qualitative evidence, the following should be born in mind about the limits of quantitative data:

1. *Unreliability of quantitative measures of interpersonal violence:*[9] Violence against women is notoriously underreported. Conventional social scientific instruments for counting violence are often flawed: if the statistics rely on self-reported incidents through telephone interviews, then one must consider that many women might be reluctant to be forthcoming (Is the batterer home? Why should she trust a stranger on the phone? and so on). If the data rely on the FBI's statistics or the Bureau of Justice Statistics, then they were often initially recorded by police officers responding to calls. But why would I trust the police as data collectors? Why would I trust the FBI, or any other government office, in tracking violence against women? Why would I necessarily make their criteria mine?

2. *Violence is measured too narrowly:* statistics on violence against women most often only capture discrete acts—blows, kicks, specific

examples of sexual assault, and more recently, by asking if a woman has been stalked. Not all violent acts are easily quantified. Statistics that focus on a researcher's own definition of violent acts do not necessarily capture how a person is uprooted or ground down, how a woman's life is made smaller or stunted. In the chapters that follow, women give many examples of "violence" in their lives, although they may not count as abuse for the courts, for the National Institute of Justice, or for the National Crime Victimization Survey. Women who are isolated, women in prison who are forced to undergo strip searches on a regular basis, sex workers sexually assaulted by the police, and undocumented women detained and deported as they are violently uprooted from their lives do not generally make it into the indices of violence against women.

3. *Who counts as a woman subject to violence?* I follow Elizabeth Schneider's (1992) observation of feminist organizing in maintaining the tension between living in a society in which many, many spaces are violent toward women (and others) even while marking—without marking off—a class of women as facing violence. Schneider resists referring to certain women as "battered women" by pointing out that "battered" is implicitly offered as a descriptor or quality.

CHAPTER SUMMARY

In this introduction, I have suggested that we need to take stock of the full range of women's voices in order to develop a range of responses. Attention to space dismantles the fiction of homogenous space. However, as one looks at institutional responses to violence against women, then one can see that institutions dealing with violence homogenize it: violence against women is constructed as the same, requiring a sameness of solutions.

Chapter 1 anchors this book by showing one way this happens. In chapter 1, I examine the social history of one of the most important tools used by the movement to stop violence against women. The tool, or model, is called "the Power and Control Wheel." I trace how antiviolence activists first designed the Power and Control Wheel as a tool for participatory education. The activists who invented the Wheel were trying to link private and public violence. At some point, however, their work became co-opted to a certain extent by oppressive economic and organizational forces. The diagram was transformed once it was appropriated by shelters, social work organizations, court-mandated groups for men who batter, and others. As it became institutionalized around the country, the Wheel was used in a way that *masked* the link between public and private violence. It was also used in a way that made diversity in the experiences of gendered violence harder to see. In short, it was altered as it became popular throughout the United States and became institutionalized in many antidomestic violence programs. In fact, the Duluth Project now uses the Wheel to *facilitate* interagency collaboration, among prosecutors, social services, shelters, and police, even though it originally was used to *critique* state collusion with batterers.

I center the most marginalized women as a strategy (see Richie 1996; 2000). In the next chapters, I analyze the discourses of women excluded from the mainstream. As they strive to describe the violence they face, they register their ambivalent responses to state solutions and to the mainstream movement to stop violence against women. What tactics and rhetorical strategies do they use to be recognized?

My work in Latino communities forms the basis for the analysis in chapter 2. I focus on an interview I conducted with a Latina activist to address the institutional complexity faced by immigrant, often undocumented Latinas, when they are in the grips of violence. In her discourse as in her life, she weaves her way through many of the institutions I will explore in the next chapters, including the law courts and shelters. She shows how the violence faced by many Latinas is structured by immigration law.

Women who work in prostitution employ a variety of rhetorical strategies to challenge violence seldom recognized by outsiders or by the courts, the police, and so on. In chapter 3, I examine a great range of views by sex workers of what they count as violence. I also look at the obstacles they see to being heard in their accounts of violence, since the accounts of prostitutes are so often discounted or ignored. In particular, I take up whether the concept of a "counterpublic sphere" is useful for thinking about prostitutes' speech on violence as political intervention.

In chapter 4, I start with a specific case of a white woman assaulted by her former lover, another lesbian. She reports the assault to the police. For turning in her lover, she is taken to task by her lesbian community. I take up the complicated rhetorical strategy she employs in court and in her written account, which catches her in a contradiction: she claims her experience is the same as that of heterosexual women who have experienced violence even while what she says underscores how different her experience is from those of heterosexual women. Putting her account in conversation with lesbians of color, we can see that her impulse to couch her experience in terms of "sameness" may be in part due to her inattention to forms of racism experienced by lesbians of color.

Having established in these chapters the differences in women's experiences and understandings of violence, I will show how the state updates, upgrades, and modernizes its mechanisms or infrastructure (Gilmore and Gilmore 2007) in order to discipline women and marginalize women of color, even as it cloaks these structural and institutional mechanisms. In the following chapters, I return to the institutions, models, and mechanisms that hide, flatten, and homogenize difference.

In chapter 5 I analyze domestic violence courts, since they are a key forum for framing violence against women. Though their motives and intentions differ, many women turn to domestic violence court because it offers some promise of rectification. I focus on the logics that ground women's narratives of spaces of violence and how they not only counter the logic of the legal decisions made by the judges in their cases, but also how the women's narratives are not recognized as driven by alternative understandings of violence. Using the text of courtroom interactions is my way of explaining the gap between the understanding of violence by the court and the point of view of the women who come to court. In privatizing violence, the courts and other agencies mask the role of state power itself: how health and welfare agencies, and not least the courts themselves, sometimes collude with violence against women or otherwise create violent situations for women.

Chapter 6 begins with the oft asked question, "Why doesn't she just leave?" I note that the question presupposes a logic of abstract sameness of social space. When space is homogenized, violence is homogenized. This insight is gained by spending time on different women's accounts as a way to uncover the multiplicity of spaces they are in. As one asks "Why doesn't she just leave?" one sees that it is a different question depending on the relation between the woman and the space.

In the conclusion, I assess possible responses or solutions, given the analysis of the previous chapters.

CHAPTER ONE

The Power and Control Wheel

From Critical Pedagogy to Homogenizing Model

In this chapter, I examine the social history of one of the most important tools used by the movement to stop violence against women. The tool, or model, is called the "Power and Control Wheel." Activists and advocates at the Duluth Domestic Abuse Intervention Project (hereafter the Duluth Project) devised the Power and Control Wheel as a tool for participatory education, but it was altered as it became popular throughout the United States and became institutionalized in many antidomestic violence programs.

From the beginning of the second wave of feminism in the early 1970s, feminist activists made the connection between violent relationships and the institutions that supported violence against women. Ellen Pence, a well-known activist associated with the Duluth Project, describes the unwillingness to yield a social and political analysis of violence against women.

> The battered women's movement has, since its earliest days, identified battering not as an individual woman's problem, but as a societal problem linked to the oppression of all women in our society. Institutions in our communities were engaged in practices that blamed women for being beaten. Early organizers in the movement challenged mental health centers who claimed women were sick, police who charged that women were provocative, courts that refused to acknowledge that women's bruises were the result of criminal behavior . . . and an economic system and a community . . . over and over again reinforced a batterer's power over women. (Pence et al. 1987, 5)

The political project of Pence and others was to raise critical understanding among battered women of how institutional, structural, economic, and cultural forces are implicated in violence against women. The activists who invented the Wheel were trying to link private and public violence.

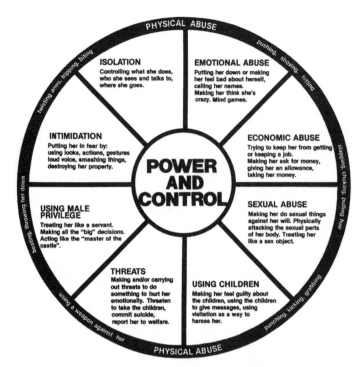

FIGURE 1. Power and Control Wheel.

At some point, however, part of their work became co-opted by oppressive economic and organizational forces. As one counselor in New York told me in an interview, "We follow the 'Duluth Model' of Ellen Pence. If you want funding in New York, you must use that model." As it became institutionalized around the country, it was used in a way that *masked* the link between public and private violence. It was also used in a way that made diversity in the experiences of gendered violence harder to see. Success in one set of terms—public recognition, increased funding—has resulted in a failure to sustain its more ambitious political critiques. Though originally open to a diversity of understandings of violence, including the collusion of a range of social and cultural forces in violence towards women, it now seems generally to be used to provide a template to describe violence against women as if it followed a single pattern. Pence, one of its authors, seems to have congealed in her views. "The ones that are on there I think are core tactics that almost all abusers use" (quoted by Pheifer 2010).

The story of the Power and Control Wheel shows how grass-roots, democratic research can be used to analyze and fight against oppressive forces, in this case against a largely invisible and diffuse war against women. The other side of the story, however, is that one must be vigilant to insure that politically liberating practices remain so.[1]

The perils of institutionalization are not lost on the founders. In a training manual to combat domestic violence, Ellen Pence and Bonnie Mann express an unwillingness to surrender a collective and collectively renewed political, social, and cultural analysis of the circumstances of battered women. "Over the past ten years the nature of women's groups offered by shelters and battered women's programs has evolved from a cultural and social analysis of violence to a much more personal psychological approach. Our own experience fits this pattern" (1987, 47). How did their work move from social analysis to psychologizing individual women?

In the introduction to this work, I argued for the need to dismantle the fiction that women's experiences of violence are uniform. As one looks at institutional response to violence against women, one sees that these institutions tend not to see—in fact tend to erase the differences. In particular, the social, cultural, and structural forms of violence are often the most elusive. In this chapter I describe one place the differences are erased: in some strands of the movement to end violence against women. In a later chapter, I take up the role of the courts in this process.

One cannot presume to measure for all time the efficacy of a particular tactic or strategy independent of how it is practiced, by whom, and with what sort of institutional backing. Apparent confinement can be refuge. What looks like refuge is sometimes confinement. What something *means*, what it stands for, and how it is used changes through time and context. Stuart Hall:

> The meaning of a cultural form and its place or position in the cultural field is not inscribed inside its form. Nor is its position fixed once and forever. This year's radical symbol or slogan will be neutralized into next year's fashion; the year after, it will become the object of a profound cultural nostalgia . . . The meaning of the cultural symbol is given in part by the social field into which it is incorporated, the practices with which it articulates and is made to resonate. What matters is not the intrinsic or historically fixed objects of culture, but the state of play in cultural relations. (Hall cited in Giroux 1992, 187)

POWER AND CONTROL WHEEL: METHODOLOGY AND CRITICAL PEDAGOGY

To get a handle on some of the complexity of liberation and collaboration, radical action and conformism, the new and the old, I will first interrogate the critical pedagogy of the Power and Control Wheel. As the staff of the Duluth Project first conceived it, the Wheel has two parts (figure 2) (Pence et al. 1987, 31ff). I have seen the first part of the Power and Control Wheel in practically every

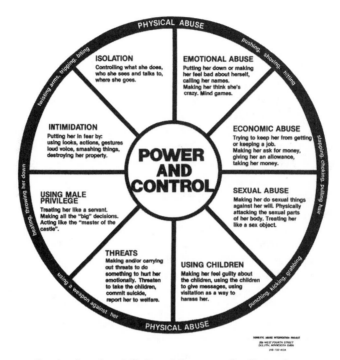

Institutional and Cultural Supports for Battering

Tactics of Power and Control	Institutional and Community decisions which support individual batterer's ability to use abusive tactics (police, courts, media, medical, clergy, business, education, human services).	Cultural Values and Beliefs that support batterers.
Physical Abuse		
Sexual Abuse		
Isolation		
Emotional Abuse		
Economic Abuse		
Minimizing and Denying		
Using Children		
Threats		
Using Male Privilege		
Intimidation		

FIGURE 2. Institutional and Cultural Supports for Battering.

program I have been to or heard about, including several versions in Spanish. It has been translated into forty languages worldwide, including Maori, Hungarian, and Icelandic. But generally speaking, the entire two-tiered approach, used as an educational tool, has been absent. The second part of the code, *that part that seeks to uncover and describe institutional and cultural collaboration with the batterer*, is often eliminated.

The Wheel was developed from a specific methodology that drew heavily from the Brazilian educator Paulo Freire.[2] His contribution is a pedagogical theory to develop a "critical consciousness." A critical consciousness of domestic violence, for example, would be one in which a battered woman can situate individual abuse within greater societal processes of oppression and domination. The Power and Control Wheel works as a pedagogical tool for the analysis of violence, an analysis that then passes into wider consideration of institutional and cultural supports for battering.

In reviewing the code and method, I will pay special attention to *how* it instigates a critical appraisal of domination. That is, I would like to look at its methodology for uncovering violence.

BACKGROUND AND HISTORY

The Duluth Domestic Abuse Intervention Project was begun in the late 1970s by a group of battered and formerly battered women, each of whom had survived battering in the absence of a formal shelter or hotline. They formed a women's group to begin to discuss and develop responses to the violence each had experienced. They also began an educational campaign to provide information to the community on violence against women. As they flourished as an organization, they perceived a need to develop new educational methods. "The neighborhood-based education groups were well attended and very successful. However, after several years, we felt increasing discomfort with the process we were using. Our lecture/discussion format provided information but did not truly involve women in the process of discovery. There was an imbalance of power in our 'giving' women information and their receiving it. We began to experiment with Freire's teaching methods" (Pence et al. 1987, 1–2). It was through Freire's methods that they moved away from simply providing information. The methodology as they practice it begins with surveys and interviews with battered or formerly battered women. "Each year since 1981 we have conducted a survey of women, asking what kinds of issues they want to discuss in groups. These surveys are crucial to the educational process. No matter how many women come to the doors of our programs, we cannot assume that we know what they want from groups unless we ask and listen to their responses" (1987, 7). The process of surveying women is ongoing and intrinsic to their method. Focusing on battered women, the project members solicit thoughts, questions, and concerns from women in bars, around a kitchen table at a shelter, on benches waiting for court hearings, in the hair salon. Through this process, they amass qualitative data for analysis. The thoughts and concerns voiced are not only descriptions of their experience, nor are they confined to specific instances of abusive behavior. They include questions, reflections, opinions, dilemmas. Some samples from their surveys follow (1987):

> How do I deal with the fact that I don't like my son because he is like his father?
> He doesn't hit me, but he break things, smashes walls, and says he isn't a batterer.
> Sometimes emotional abuse is worse than physical abuse.
> Does alcoholism cause battering?
> Why do I feel guilty about staying with him?
> Why do I feel guilty about leaving him?
> He keeps accusing me of being a lesbian.
> We've been to three different marriage counselors, and they all encourage us to do things I'm scared to do.
> How do you deal with his threats to commit suicide?

The body of texts that they solicit serves as the material from which they abstract "themes." Themes stand for the basic characteristics of one's situation put in terms of a general context of domination and oppression. Thus, the theme contains recognizable elements, since it was generated through interviews, but at the same time, it has been put in a larger social and political framework. Pence explains:

> Themes broaden the base of a single issue. The facilitator looks for themes in the survey that allow her to pose a problem, the analysis of which will help the group make connections between seemingly isolated concerns. For example, specific abusive behaviors appear on the list twelve times. These behaviors are repeatedly mentioned in our surveys. This suggests that battering consists not only of physical abuse and threats, but also of abusive acts which reinforce the physical violence. If we examine each of the acts individually we may be misled as to its intent, cause, and impact. (Pence et al. 1987, 9)

Discovering recurrent motifs, the project members conceptualize themes that are intended to generate critical connections among moments of behavior that had seemed random, inexplicable, and hard to conceptualize as abuse. By this method, for example, the abuser who verbally degrades someone, denies her perceptions, breaks things, and punches the wall could be revealed as inflicting abuse. Themes provoke discussion and insight among women into what counts as abuse and how abuse is linked to other phenomena. The discussions also have the consequence of breaking isolation between women.

The project members select or devise codes that can be analyzed from three perspectives: "personal, institutional, and cultural."

> When the design team has decided that the theme is generative—that it allows for discussion on all three levels—the next step is to develop a code. A code is a teaching tool used to focus group discussion. It can be a picture, a role-play, a story, a guided meditation, a song, a chart or an exercise. The code provides a reference point for discussion and analysis . . . In designing a class the group facilitators prepare for their roles not by outlining a rigid structure that routes discussion from Point A to Point B, but by working to understand an issue more fully, so that as women we are able to make connections in our lives between our personal experiences and the world we live in. (1987, 10)

While the facilitator has determined the code, the character and direction of the process of analysis are open-ended. Within its original practice, then, the code is one step in an entire pedagogic and theoretico-political enterprise.

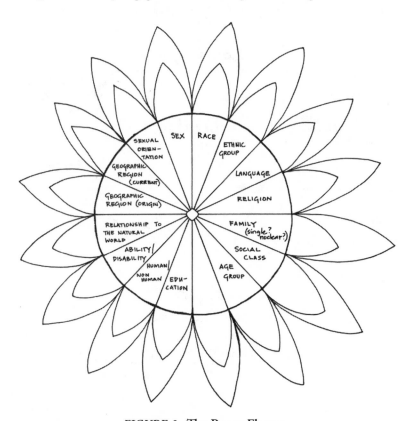

FIGURE 3. The Power Flower.

A facilitator commented on how the process of isolating codes made her change how she "reads" the world: "When I first started working on this curriculum I'd be hearing songs on the radio or seeing scenes in movies and on TV as possible codes. Suddenly everything had the potential to be a focus for discussion in a women's group" (Pence et al. 1987).

The Power and Control Wheel is an example of a code. Twenty years later, in 2010, Pence described the process: "So we went to all three of those groups over several months, and kept developing this thing over and over and we'd bring our little designs in, we had a lot of different designs to it and finally we came up with the one where we put the 'Violence' around the outside and all the other tactics on the inside. We were trying to make it like a wheel where the violence held everything together. These tactics were . . . all part of a system" (*Power and Control* 2010). The Power and Control Wheel is one example of a code, one example among many (figures 3 and 4 show examples of other codes).

In the second part of the workshop, women furnish responses to a chart that asks them to think of instances in which social institutions and cultural mores support the violence. As it is conceived, women see how social institutions, such as the welfare office, housing officials, and cultural forces (such as traditional

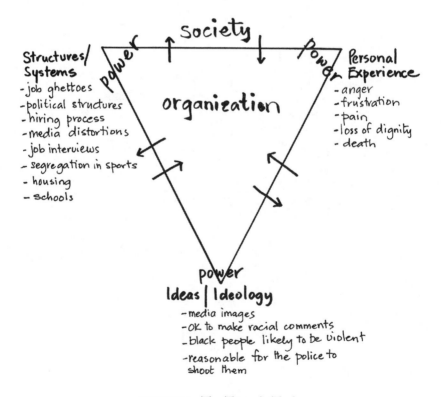

FIGURE 4. The Triangle Tool.

hierarchies within a community) collude in abuse. (Figure 2 shows the two charts in tandem.)

Here is a list of responses solicited from the part of the workshop that looks at institutional and cultural support for battering (1987).

> Pastors tell women it is their role to be subservient to their hus-
> bands; even if the husband gets "carried away," the wife owes him
> forgiveness.
>
> Marriage counselors ignore the man's use of violence or equate it to the
> woman's yelling at him.
>
> Judges lecture women during protection order hearing, stating that they
> too are part of the problem, or they issue mutual restraining orders
> when the woman hasn't used violence.
>
> Judges order women into counseling when they have not used violence.
>
> Judges refuse to enforce their own court orders requiring counseling or
> no contact with women.
>
> Courts threaten lesbian battered women with the loss of their children
> when they ask the court for protection.
>
> Doctors prescribe Valium to women who are suffering emotionally from
> battering, ignoring the reason for their suffering.
>
> Welfare workers allow themselves to be used to harass women by fol-
> lowing up on false reports from batterers of welfare fraud and child
> abuse.

Social structures (the law, medicine, organized religion) and bureaucratic institutions (the police, law courts, social service providers) are mapped onto personal experience. Places assumed to be safe can be refigured through this process. The police are no longer necessarily just protectors, but they are put into the context of their collaboration with the batterers. Cultural practices are interrogated for the ways in which they buttress violence against women. It depicts systematic oppression.

One of the virtues of the two-part schema is that in the first instance, the pedagogical device is intended to solicit the unique instances of abuse and to pro-voke reflection on distinctive, individual behavior. In the second step, the personal characteristics of the batterer and the battering situation are placed in a way that motivates connection and reflection on their full sociohistorical scope. The pas-sage from detail to larger sociopolitical systems and structures undermines the privatized nature of abuse. Through critical consciousness, the battered woman comes to see that the personal is political.

CHARTING OPPRESSION

The Wheel provides an arresting view of space. It is a powerful and excellent tool for critical analysis. One shelter worker commented to me in an interview,

"Women had such a powerful response almost always. It was like, oh my god, this is my life. They just immediately began describing stuff that is just like that" (fieldwork interview). Part of its genius and power is to provide a narrative, to see how behavior that looks at first to be nonabusive functions as part of an abusive pattern. The picture it draws is cohesive: the parts derive their significance and their strength from their interrelation. Like the spokes that represent them, each form of violence reinforces the control, while the whole system is in turn held together by physical and sexual violence. "At the hub of the wheel, the center, is the intention of all the tactics—to establish power and control. Each spoke of the wheel represents a particular tactic. The rim of the wheel, which gives it strength and holds it together, is physical abuse" (Pence et al. 1987, 11–13).

In a recent interview, Ellen Pence comments that in retrospect the Duluth Project should have distinguished the *purpose* of the abuse from its *consequences*:

> I always interpreted it as that women were saying that men desired power and control, and when I did my men's groups I would say that I would always think that you were desiring, but I never heard the men say that. And that's when I started to understand the difference between feeling . . . entitled to that control and desiring it . . . Like as a white person, me feeling entitled to certain space, it wasn't the desire to dominate people of color, it's two different things . . . So I ended up not thinking that men wanted power and control, I ended up thinking and realizing, I think, that they felt entitled to it. Which is a different way of talking to men about it then. (2010)

The difference is between positing a universal psychological dynamic and looking at concrete experience:

> The Power and Control Wheel . . . said, "When he is violent, he gets power and he gets control." Somewhere early in our organizing efforts, however, we changed the message to "he is violent *in order* to get control or power." The difference is not semantic, it is ideological . . . By determining that the need or desire for power was the motivating force behind battering, we created a conceptual framework that, in fact, did not fit the lived experience of many of the men and women we were working with. Like those we were criticizing, we reduced our analysis to a psychological universal truism. (Pence 1999, 28)

The Duluth Project distinguishes staying close to the real lives of men and women from the impulse to reduce the dynamics of battering to a universal psychological model. The pedagogy rejects assuming uniformity and universality and imputed psychological states. This contrasts strongly with the universal models we have already discussed, such as Lenore Walker's "Cycle of Violence" (1989). As we shall see below, the Duluth Project explicitly contrasts itself with Walker's influential theory.

Another quality of the resulting device is a focus on domination to the exclusion of a battered woman's resistance.[3] The pedagogy develops *critical* perspective, but it would have been useful to see more of a focus on the language of *possibility* (Giroux 1992, 19ff). A critical language remains within the paradigm of oppression, while a language of possibility elaborates individual and collective resistance, possibility, and potential.[4] To its credit, the workshop discussion does ask women to name an action that they have taken to stop violence or abuse. "This demonstrates that as battered women we have never become total doormats, that we have in fact acted and can continue to act to protect ourselves" (1987). Oppression is never complete. The pedagogy points women in the direction of having them enunciate forms of resistance, mostly individual forms of resistance, but also collective. Some examples they draw out of their workshops include the following (1987):

> hanging up when he calls so that he can't emotionally abuse me by calling me names or playing mind games with me;
> getting a protection order;
> asking my employer to move me to another office where I'm more protected from his harassment;
> talking secretly to a friend he has refused to allow me to see to let her know what's happening.

RISING TO THE CONCRETE

One thing that needs to be emphasized is that the Wheel was never intended to be a "map." The space of the Wheel was not intended to be the *equivalent* to the spaces that women occupy. It is not even a *description* of those spaces in the normal sense. It is an attempt to grasp those spaces and to interpret them, to re-present those spaces to battered women, so they talk about the abuse they have experienced. The strength of the methodology is measurable in its flexibility in apprehending action in its larger cultural context, located in history, at the same time as not losing sight of the specificity, the singular. Pence comments:

> A woman in a violent relationship is not allowed to step back and look at her life for what it really is. Her abuser imposes an interpretation of her reality that protects his self-interest. He works to prevent his partner from thinking about herself as a person separate from him. With few exceptions, batterers attempt to cut women off from other people, places, ideas, and resources that would help her understand what is happening to her . . . The expression "can't see the forest for the trees" describes what it is to be like in the midst of a bad situation trying to make a good

decision . . . One of the most dramatic things a women's group does for a newcomer is help her to step back and see more of her life, and from that place to make decisions in her own interest. (Pence et al. 1987, 15)

The purpose is to provide a technique, a catalyst, a challenge, to battered women to draw connections. In this sense, the intent of the method is not to abstract from the concrete but to supply the concrete with meaning, to motivate in women a theoretical turn on their own situations, to order the endless flow of the incremental phenomena of the everyday by reframing it. It is striking in its ability to organize frequently encountered tactics of batterers in a way that is animating, thought-provoking, inviting.

Violence against women can be painted as if it exists only in closed spaces and as a matter between two people. Gendered violence can be theorized as private, domestic, spousal, and always the same. Or it can be seen as multifaceted, manifold, and propped by massive, bureaucratic organization, extending into structural mechanisms of governing. Defining the relevant space for analysis of violence is central to how the violence is understood. If the space is homogeneous and imagined to include only the private sphere, the violence will be viewed only as private.

The Power and Control Wheel and its companion, the Institutional Supports for Battering chart, ingeniously challenge the privatization of violence. Since they correspond to the private and public respectively, they appear to assume the split between the private and public spheres. But they then show the tie between the private and the public. This is an astute method for troubling the private/public split that grounds the privatized nature of abuse.

However, using the Power and Control Wheel by itself, one is left with only the private dynamic of the couple in the home. One person uses physical and emotional abuse to control his or her intimate. Only by using the second chart, Institutional and Cultural Supports for Battering, can one tie the private to the public—or more accurately, who is implicated in maintaining intimidation. This might include friends who don't ask questions, agents of the law, the law itself, emergency room staff, religious authorities, neighbors, kin, and so on. I emphasize this because the depoliticization of the Power and Control Wheel hinges on this separation of one diagram from the other. "Battering not only consists of seemingly isolated acts of individual abusers. It encompasses a much larger system of actions of abusers and of the community institutions which support women abuse" (Pence et al. 1987, 31).

Though the method breaches the private/public split, it is nonetheless premised within the split. Other forms of violence that involve different relations of power that already occur against the grain of the private/public split are not incorporated into this schema, such as violence against sex workers or domestic workers. Its conceptual exclusion of other forms of spatiality reveals the formulation as abstract: it proposes a generalized template through which to read violence according to a unified and uniform map.

"THE WHEEL IN MOTION"

Is the Power and Control Wheel homogenizing? Does it contribute to the product of making violence against women uniform? Does its pedagogy hide difference or reveal it? The Wheel was designed by battered women in Duluth after interviewing battered women in that particular locale. A schema like the Power and Control Wheel is thus limited in its very design to engaging that particular group of women. The particular aspects of (some) women's lives in Duluth, the resources available, and the way in which gender is configured there all serve as the material for the construction of the code.

Elsewhere, or for women located in a different structural position (for example, undocumented women or women who are incarcerated), a different code would need to be invented through a similarly rigorous analysis of the local conditions of women's lives. Part of this is due to the fact that systems of sexism, racism, colonization, and homophobia combine in a range of ways and need to be examined in a way that is attentive to different locales. It makes sense to use the Power and Control Wheel in Duluth with the women on whose lives it is based. Nevertheless, some of the Duluth Project's literature has broader aspirations. The author-activists remark that some of their work "offers a framework for discussion of how the abusive tactics of batterers are *the same* as those used against poor people, people of color, women, and all other oppressed people in our society" (Pence, et al. 1987,26; emphasis added). This is an unsubstantiated generalization. This way of putting things does not allow for analysis of the fact that some white middle-class women mistreat women of color who clean their houses, for example. Both groups of women are oppressed as women, yet the white women are clearly not oppressed in the same way that the women of color are in that situation.

So we can fairly ask whether the entire critical method is used as a process in other places. Educational codes produced according to this method are bound to the time and place of their origin. Also, they are supposed to be used as a *generative moment*. As a code, the Wheel is intended to provoke reflection rather than curtail it. If the process is not used elsewhere, then we can ask what work the Wheel is doing, how it is used, by whom, with whom, how, and why. Although the Wheel is flexible, it can be used in a way that stops or stunts discussion among battered women.

As it has traveled, by and large, the Wheel has become a model rather than a device to provoke analysis. The Wheel has made its way into shelters, antiviolence projects, and websites. The following section has some examples.

***

The Minnesota Coalition for Battered Women published a pamphlet entitled "Understanding Battering," in which they reproduced the Wheel. They introduce it with the caveat, "This model was developed for use primarily with white, heterosexual battering, so other types of controlling behavior may be more common in other groups." In the passage, the Wheel has already changed from a *technique*, enmeshed in a particular process and method of popular education to become a *model of* domestic violence. Although the same pamphlet emphasizes that the "model" be used "as a starting point only," it is already on the road to being ossified.

Nothing in the original methodology commits them to exclude women of color and lesbians of any color. The process of conducting interviews and isolating resurgent themes does not necessitate exclusion of certain groups of people. Moreover, since the code is used to provoke critical analysis, it need not provide a perfect description of violence. In any case, "white, heterosexual women" is not an internally homogeneous group.

María Lugones has addressed this question of work by white women which "leaves women of color out." "White women used to simply and straightforwardly ignore difference. In their theorizing, they used to speak as if all women *as women* were the same. Now white women recognize the problem of difference. Whether they *recognize* difference is another matter . . . It is interesting to see that the acknowledgment is a noninteractive one" (Lugones 2004, 85; emphasis in the original). Lugones argues that some white women have come to acknowledge a problem of working politically or writing as if all women are the same, but without taking up the question of difference, interrogating it, seeing how difference works not in isolation but in terms of how women of color and white women are connected with one another.

The MCBW booklet offers a disclaimer qualifying the relevance of the Wheel for nonwhite, nonheterosexual women but offers no guidance for those outside of that circumscribed domain nor insight regarding what others ought to do. The disclaimer, as Lugones points out, is a technique for evading substantive engagement with the question of difference. After the disclaimer, nothing again indicates that difference has been recognized (see Lugones 2004, 85).

One way to have solved this dilemma would have been to present the Power and Control Wheel as a code embedded *within a methodology*, instead of as a model. From a technique used to provoke women into critical analysis of their situation with their batterer and in the wider society, the Wheel has become a description of violence. Its detachment from the interview process marks the passage from its dynamic potential to its ossification.

In particular, in the new version, a particular solution is proposed: *escape*. Escape implies individual movement away from a situation. To describe abuse as "building barriers" to a woman's escape or safety is already to advance the solution of leaving. This proposal of escape to safety is important. But escape is not a possibility for all.

Which leads one to ask: what happened to the chart that asked women to interrogate the institutional and cultural supports for battering? It has disappeared. One of the persistent motifs of the passage of the Wheel is how, as it has been institutionalized, it has lost its partner. The second chart, far less popular, was precisely that chart that violated the private/public split of domestic violence and showed how outside spaces also support abuse. With it, "escape" could no longer be the clear end-all solution for all women. The relation it drew extended to provoke institutional and cultural critique.

"QUÉ OPCIONES TENGO?"

Even while the Power and Control Wheel is sometimes asserted to apply only to white, heterosexual couples, it is also employed elsewhere unproblematically to define violence involving women of color and lesbians of any color.[5] For example, the Wheel has been frequently translated into Spanish for use with Latinas (see figure 5; also see my interview with a Latina activist in the next chapter). I take as the example the pamphlet "Cómo sobrevivir la violencia doméstica: Una guía para capacitar a mujeres maltratadas," compiled by "Peace over Violence" (formerly the *L.A. Commission on Assaults against Women*). The words are translated into Spanish, although the Wheel remains the same. The original methodology, the process of conducting interviews, isolating themes, and so on, can apply to many different communities. But the Wheel taken alone surely is not intended to match *any* form of violence against women forever. The Duluth Project insists that conducting surveys annually is crucial. "No matter how many women come to the doors of our programs, we cannot assume that we know what they want from groups unless we ask and listen to their responses" (Pence et al. 1987, 7). The Wheel is the result of the process of conducting surveys. It should not to be reemployed uncritically.

In these new contexts, however, the Wheel is presented in such a way that subverts the original intent of the methodology. This in itself might not be a problem; time and context change, and one may rework tools, words, and so on, in a new context to revivify them. In this case, however, the Wheel has been represented in a way that is opposed to its original design. It does violence to women's experiences and is misleading. "Aquí le explicamos lo que es la violencia doméstica y qué recursos existen para ayudarle a protegerse a si misma y a sus hijos. [Here we explain to you what domestic violence is and what resources exist that can help you protect yourself and your children]." While I appreciate the activists' efforts in naming abuse, I worry that there is something vaguely patronizing in "explaining" what domestic violence is to Latinas. Raising consciousness among Latinas is important; however, the *Rueda* names *for* Latinas what violence is, instead of soliciting them to name it in their own terms. The purpose of the guide is consistent with the way that the Power and Control Wheel is presented. "La Rueda de poder y control" (diagram 5) is introduced as a *description* of violence. "Este diagrama representa todas las formas en que su compañero violento abusa de usted para mantener control sobre su vida. [This figure represents all the ways in which your violent partner abuses you in order to maintain control over

La rueda de poder y control

Este diagrama representa todas las formas en que su compañero violento abusa de usted para mantener control sobre su vida.

Por lo general, el nivel de violencia aumenta con el tiempo y los golpes se hacen más y más frecuentes. Una vez que su pareja comienza a tratarla así, es muy raro que el abuso deje de suceder a menos que haya algún tipo de intervención.

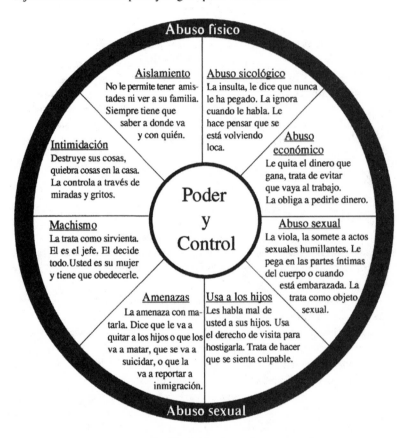

Abuso físico

Aislamiento
No le permite tener amistades ni ver a su familia. Siempre tiene que saber a donde va y con quién.

Abuso sicológico
La insulta, le dice que nunca le ha pegado. La ignora cuando le habla. Le hace pensar que se está volviendo loca.

Intimidación
Destruye sus cosas, quiebra cosas en la casa. La controla a través de miradas y gritos.

Abuso económico
Le quita el dinero que gana, trata de evitar que vaya al trabajo. La obliga a pedirle dinero.

Poder y Control

Machismo
La trata como sirvienta. El es el jefe. El decide todo. Usted es su mujer y tiene que obedecerle.

Abuso sexual
La viola, la somete a actos sexuales humillantes. Le pega en las partes íntimas del cuerpo o cuando está embarazada. La trata como objeto sexual.

Amenazas
La amenaza con matarla. Dice que le va a quitar a los hijos o que los va a matar, que se va a suicidar, o que la va a reportar a inmigración.

Usa a los hijos
Les habla mal de usted a sus hijos. Usa el derecho de visita para hostigarla. Trata de hacer que se sienta culpable.

Abuso sexual

FIGURE 5. La rueda de poder y control.

your life]." Rather than a starting point, the diagram purportedly identifies all the ways in which the reader is battered. "This diagram represents all the ways . . ." Such a purpose can only exclude certain experiences of violence that exceed the model and mold others to conform to it.

The construction of violence does not always translate so easily across race and gender lines, particularly when the batterer is himself or herself in a subordinate position with respect to race and class. What might appear on the face of it as a tactic of control might be displaced rage or motivated by the pleasure one takes in being cruel or in inflicting pain, for example.[6]

For the dynamics of abuse, it may make a difference that the actors are Latino. Depicting the dynamics of battering as universal is helped along because the second diagram of the Duluth Project, the Institutional and Cultural Support for Battering, has disappeared. (Domestic) violence among Latinos is painted as homologous with any other precisely because the "institutional and cultural relationship to battering" among Latinos is not represented; it is conceptually excluded.

The proof? The text goes on to ask "¿Qué opciones tengo?" (What options do I have?) (figure 6). The options include: "centros de terapia," "la policía 9-1-1," "ordenes de protección" which offers the unlikely description and promise, "Son documentos de la corte que especifican que el agresor no debe acercarse a su casa o lugar de empleo, que no debe llamarla ni hostigarla. Si tiene una orden de protección y su agresor la viola, llame a la policía . . . deben arrestarlo. [They are court documents that specify that the abuser may not go near your house or place of employment, that he is not allowed to call or harass you. If you have an order of protection and your abuser violates it, call the police. They are obligated to arrest him.]" Not so much optimistic as misleading in its description, orders of protection can stipulate or proscribe any combination of those actions, or none of them. That orders of protection are in any case ineffectual is repeated over and over by women in the movement. A shelter advocate commented in an interview:

> You know, when you called yesterday you came here and you wanted to talk about the orders of protection . . . Listen, I've been here for nine years and let me tell you, the orders of protection are bullshit. Absolute bullshit. This is what I tell women when they come in here: [she holds a piece of paper in two hands and places it across her mouth] "Fuck you bitch." Does it stop that? [she punches the paper, rather alarmingly, and I am taken slightly aback, as it flutters down behind her] Does it stop that? It is one tool in your toolbox, I tell the woman [she takes the paper and neatly puts it down in front of her], along with new locks [she takes the 3M pad and lays it beside the piece of paper], a divorce order [she lays down a stapler]. These are all tools. The order by itself is just a piece of paper. (Fieldwork notes)

An order of protection, in other words, may not provide the protection it promises. The narrative of police responsiveness is, if not fictional, at least excessively hopeful. The pamphlet presupposes that the women are documented (legal residents), since it recommends that the women have their legal papers when they leave. It also presupposes that the women will be able to communicate with the police: "Si no le quiere ayudarla, ¡insista! Es su derecho. [If (the police)] do not

¿Que opciones tengo?

Líneas de ayuda para mujeres golpeadas

Servicio las 24 horas para mujeres golpeadas que necesitan apoyo e información. Su llamada es confidencial. (Teléfonos en la pág. 15).

Refugios

Casas donde se ofrecen servicios de emergencia a mujeres golpeadas y a sus hijos. La estancia es de hasta un mes. La dirección es secreta para que su agresor no pueda encontrarla.

Grupos de apoyo mutuo

Mujeres golpeadas se reúnen con una consejera para dar y recibir apoyo moral. Algunas han dejado a sus golpeadores mientras que otras siguen con ellos.

Centros de terapia

A veces hay programas de consejo en español para mujeres golpeadas en clínicas comunitarias. Llame a una línea de ayuda para mujeres golpeadas para el centro más cercano.

Tratamiento para hombres violentos

Estos programas tratan de ayudar a golpeadores a resolver sus problemas sin violencia. Por lo general, sólo después de un año de tratamiento una vez por semana se pueden ver cambios en el comportamiento del golpeador.

Asegurar su casa

Asegúrese de tener cerraduras fuertes en las puertas y ventanas de su casa o departamento.

Cambiar de residencia

Si su golpeador la ha amenazado, o si teme que un día la golpee o la mate, un cambio de residencia y teléfono es una opción.

La policía 9-1-1

Si su pareja le ha golpeado, ha cometido un crimen. Llame a la policía al 9-1-1. En Los Angeles deben arrestarlo si Ud. tiene heridas visibles.

Ordenes de protección

Son documentos de la corte que especifican que el agresor no debe acercarse a su casa o lugar de empleo, que no debe llamarla ni hostigarla. Si tiene una orden de protección y su agresor la viola, llame a la policía...deben arrestarlo.

Ayuda legal

Hay agencias que le ayudan a obtener órdenes de protección gratis. También se pueden obtener divorcios a bajo costo. Las líneas para mujeres golpeadas le darán una referencia. En la página 15 aparecen los teléfonos de varias agencias.

Clases de defensa personal

Aquí le enseñan a tener confianza en si misma. Adquiere habilidades para defenderse efectivamente de un asalto de un extraño o compañero.

Familiares, amigos y vecinos

A veces puede recurrir a una hermana, comadre o vecina. Quizá tiene pena o piensa que no la comprenderán, pero a veces nuestros seres queridos son los que más nos quieren ayudar. Pídale a sus vecinos que llamen a la policía si ven a su golpeador cerca de su casa.

Visitas supervisadas con los hijos

Si él tiene derecho de visita o si comparten custodia de los hijos, usted tiene el derecho de pedir un arreglo que la proteja de él, como visitas supervisadas por un amigo, un familiar o una trabajadora social, o en un lugar público.

FIGURE 6. ¿Qué opciones tengo?

want to help you, insist! *It is your right*]" (emphasis in the original) (figure 7). They also tell battered women that they can make a citizen's arrest of their assailant, which the police are obligated to respect. It advises this as if a battered, undocumented Latina in Los Angeles were in any position to insist on anything from an L.A. cop.

The pamphlet rests upon a narrative of citizenry and nationhood (De Genova 2005; Calavita 2007; Berlant 1997). From the standpoint of space, the fact that many Spanish-speaking Latinos cross *la frontera* illegally cannot be overlooked, especially if recommending that they look for assistance from *la policía*. Methodologically, the suggestion that women go to the police or the courts is only made possible *because* they do not ask women to consider the institutional and cultural supports for battering.

N. lives and works in California. She is being harassed and stalked by her exlover who is undocumented. N. calls me to ask me what she should do. Among other things, I give her the phone number in the pamphlet "Como sobrevivir la violencia doméstica." She calls the number and the person who answers recommends that she call the police, get a court order, leave and stay with friends, and seek counseling. Option one is unacceptable because she is not prepared to turn her exlover, an undocumented lesbian, over to the police. Moreover, her neighbors in this largely immigrant neighborhood are suspicious of the police and the law; they would shun her if she called the police into the neighborhood. If she were to get a court order, she would be forced to come out as a lesbian, which she does not want to do. She cannot afford to leave her home; she has made her life in the community, and to leave would be to leave everything. She does not want counseling because there is nothing wrong with her. "I was mistreated," she says, "I do not need therapy."

The advice she is given is consistent with that offered in the booklet: seek an order of protection, call the police, get therapy. In developing a protocol for responding to violence against women, the authors of the pamphlet clearly did not have women like N. in mind. They have not taken stock of the notion that some battered women do not want to turn their batterers over to the police, that the court system is not an acceptable option for them. The advice is not based upon, and thus does not touch down well on, the circumstances, the lived spaces of the intended audience.

As I argued above, the Duluth Project has tried to stay clear of universal psychological models. Pence remarks, "The process of education must constantly compare theory to the real experiences of women so that we do not operate from false assumptions" (Pence et al. 1987, 22). She is concerned that the popular pedagogy and its methods can become separated from their grounding in the circumstances in which women find themselves. She continues,

> Such assumptions lead us to actions which do not result in changing the system. *Perhaps there is no better example of this than the Cycle of Violence*

La ley en California

En California el "castigo corporal marital," o sea, la violencia doméstica, es un crimen. No tiene que estar casada con el agresor para que la proteja la ley. Si tiene moretones o huesos quebrados la policía puede arrestar al agresor por felonía. El estado levanta cargos contra él y usted es un testigo.

En la ciudad de Los Angeles, si usted tiene heridas visibles, la policía tiene que arrestar. Si no hay suficiente evidencia para arrestar, la policía hará un "Reporte de violencia doméstica." Es importante como evidencia si algún día vuelve a suceder.

Si no arrestan al agresor, Ud. puede hacer un arresto de ciudadano (no tiene que ser ciudadana). Diga que desea hacer un arresto de ciudadano, él policía llenará un formulario y deberá arrestarlo.

Si se lo llevan y tiene miedo de que regrese a lastimarla, el policía puede ayudarle a obtener una Orden de Protección de Emergencia después de horas hábiles. Si no le quiere ayudar, ¡insista! Es su derecho. El día siguiente podrá conseguir una orden más duradera. Utilice las referencias en este libro.

Si viola la orden, ¿qué puedo hacer?

La policía debe arrestar si se viola la orden de protección. Llame al 9-1-1 y dígales que su golpeador está violando la orden y que Ud. está en peligro. Bajo la ley, la policía debe responder lo más pronto posible a llamadas de violencia doméstica, especialmente si existe una orden.

ORDENES DE PROTECCIÓN

La orden de protección ordena que el golpeador no la llame o se acerque a su casa o trabajo. Se fija una cita para que un juez evalúe la situación. Si el juez cree que usted está en peligro se extiende la orden por 2 ó 3 años.

Según la orden, usted tampoco debe contactar al golpeador. Es importante no hacerlo. Si decide volver con él, hay que ir ante el juez para anular la orden. Si usted le hace una trampa para que viole la orden y se dan cuenta las autoridades, es muy posible que no reciba la ayuda que necesita si algún día corre peligro.

La defensa personal y la ley

La ley en California dice que uno puede usar "fuerza razonable" para defenderse. Esto es el nivel de violencia requerido para defenderse de un ataque o para salvar su vida.

Bajo la ley, no se puede reaccionar injustamente (pegarle a alguien que le pide la hora), o usar fuerza excesiva (usar una pistola contra un agresor que no está armado) o tomar venganza contra un agresor.

En ciertos casos una mujer que usa una pistola contra un agresor sin armas ha usado "fuerza razonable" si no tenía otra opción y temía por su vida.

Si lo lastimo al defenderme, ¿pueden arrestarme?

Sí. La ley que obliga a la policía a arrestar cuando hay heridos puede ayudar a mujeres golpeadas que han sido lastimadas por sus compañeros. Pero, si una mujer lastima a su agresor al defenderse, puede ser arrestada.

Si la arrestan porque lastimó a su golpeador, asegúrese de que el policía lo indique en su reporte. Obtenga tratamiento médico y explíquele al doctor como fue lesionada.

Se considera "razonable" porque los hombres suelen ser más fuertes y más grandes que las mujeres.

FIGURE 7. Es su derecho.

theory[7] and the many theories that have in the past few years dominated the work with batterers, resulting in hundreds of men's groups forming around the country which focus on teaching men who beat women into submission to reduce their stress level, to cope with anger differently, to express feelings differently rather than working with batterers on issues of power and dominance. These theories focus on the psychology of battering rather than on the political and social context of battering, and they analyze battering piecemeal. Our failure to deal with the full social and historical context in which battering occurs will result in a faulty agenda for our work. (Pence, et al. 1987, 22; emphasis added)

The pamphlet juxtaposes the Power and Control Wheel with the Cycle of Violence chart. This is despite Pence's firm distinction between the psychologizing of battering and investigating its full sociohistorical content. According to Pence, the two methods contradict one another. At the very least, they are not in communication with one another. One has a psychologist's pedigree and sees women as the victims of learned helplessness whose view of the situation has become distorted as their agency is mitigated. The Duluth Project sees women as able to take action through critical analysis.

The pamphlet advocates therapy: "En la terapia la mujer explora sus sentimientos acerca del abuso que ha sufrido. [In therapy, the woman explores her feelings about the abuse she has suffered]." As I have shown, from the outset the Duluth Project has positioned itself as antagonistic to therapy.

The booklet from Los Angeles draws disparate elements into narrative relation. All of the various components conspire to draw attention to private spaces, while social institutions figure as sources of succor and support for the battered woman. So, it speaks of "la ley en California" (the law in California), by referring to the "castigo corporal marital" (corporal punishment within marriage). It speaks of the need to formulate "un plan de escape," which as I have argued, implies a focus on violence that is confined to the private sphere. This description, based on the private/public split, excludes the public aspect of abuse.

This is not the only Spanish-language version of the Wheel in use. Another organization adapted the Wheel for use with Spanish-speaking immigrant women ("*Formas en las que la mujer experimenta el abuso doméstico*") (see Futures without Violence 2011). Although this Wheel depicts in painful detail the violence to which immigrant women are subject by their partners, it sidesteps identifying the larger institutions and structures with abuse or support for abuse, and instead renders institutional violence as a taken-for-granted background for intimate abuse. Thus, sections of this revised Wheel read: "Threatening to report you to the INS to get you deported"; "Threatening to withdraw the petition to legalize your immigration status"; "Hiding or destroying important papers (i.e. passport, ID cards, health care card, etc.)"; "Threatening to report her children to Immigration." It is important work—identifying and connecting these forms of abuse. But the Wheel does not discuss how the background legal structures, tough immigration laws, the immigration agents themselves, the detention and deportation process, and nativism and xenophobia are significant sources of harm for immigrant women. They are presupposed rather than discussed as part of the process of consciousness-raising. In other words, the Wheel does not countenance the gendered effects of U.S. immigration policy that directly or indirectly harm women. (I explore this more in the next chapter.)

CONCLUSION: FROM METHOD TO MODEL

I could multiply the examples: the Power and Control Wheel has been used to work with batterers; with lesbians who face violence; to stop violence against children, teens, elders, deaf people, military spouses, and women in relationships with police officers. In each case, the violence is painted as private. When they are used, they usually have two qualities in common: (1) the violence occurs in private spaces and the violence is interpersonal rather than structural or institutional; (2) private spaces are all the same insofar as they conform to the dynamics of Power and Control. The diagram erases the particular forms violence takes, whether lesbian battering, police brutalization of prostitutes, or the terrorizing of undocumented immigrants. It erases the role of the state in upholding violence.

This chapter gives one history of the construction of sameness. As I have shown, the Duluth Project assembled a diagram as a visual technique—a code— to get women to talk about the abuse they had suffered. Influenced by Paulo Freire, the Duluth Project was a process of popular education predicated on developing in women a critical turn of mind. It has been recuperated by organizations in a way that severs the link to structural and institutional violence. These organizations put the Wheel forward as a formal and unchanging *definition* of *battering* (now only within domestic spaces) rather than leading to a critical *analysis* of *violence*. The rigidification it has undergone is more glaringly the case once one sees how it is applied equally and uncritically to battered Latinas in Los Angeles, men who batter in rural New York, and lesbians who are battered in small towns in Ontario. In each case, *applied* is the correct word: the systematic critical engagement between a diagram and people's experience is nowhere in evidence. People who experience gendered violence that is not *domestic* violence are not on the landscape. The diagram is used to describe violence as domestic violence with a uniform, flattened pattern. The *process* has fallen by the wayside. In this way, the institutions I have looked at have each turned this model into an instrument of the normalization of violence. By portraying the spaces as private and monolithic, the accompanying violence within those spaces is correspondingly seen as unchanging. This is even more the case once the exercise that examines the institutional and cultural support for battering is cropped.

Everything is in place for each of these institutions to represent battering as private, isolated, and everywhere the same.

Methodologically, philosophically, and politically, the original diagram was intended to instigate the contrary—to violate the private/public split and to urge women to meditate on the connections or disjunctions between various women's situations and in that context to assess the consequences of battering in cultural and sociohistorical terms.

Tracing the passage of the Wheel has been my technique of studying institutional response to the multiplicity of violence against women. I have also traced its route from the grassroots, where women are organizing, to institutionalized control or co-optation of the Wheel. As popular education, the methodology focused on the grassroots and on continual engagement with women's lives. The first Wheel was designed to solicit women's voices.

The research can—should—be a key ingredient in a political project. Unfortunately, "research" too often connotes either academics gathering data for their own ends or an organization undertaking a self-evaluation to satisfy a funding agency. I am referring instead to the need to undertake ongoing *participatory research* with people most affected by a particular problem, where the knowledge and the insights stay with the community—especially those most affected within the community—to raise consciousness and to change oppressive relationships.

Since 2007, the Duluth Domestic Abuse Intervention Project has collaborated with the city of St. Paul in a coordinated civic response to violence against women. The "Blueprint for Safety" uses, "interagency policies, protocols, case processing procedures, and information sharing to (a) maximize the ability of the state to gain a measure of control over a domestic violence offender; (b) use that control to intervene quickly when there are new acts of violence, intimidation or coercion; and (c) shift the burden of holding the offender accountable for violence or abuse from the *victim* to the *system*" (*Blueprint* 2010, 7). The *Blueprint* emphasizes collaboration among shelters, the police, and prosecutors. It promotes punishment and other criminal justice solutions to the problem of violence against women: "In the criminal justice field, it is widely believed that sure and swift punishment is more important than severe punishment. Research into domestic violence shows this to be particularly true in confronting this crime. Evidence suggests that building sure and swift consequences into the infrastructure of case processing can reduce recidivism in some cases and the severity of ongoing abuse in others" (*Blueprint* 2010, 7).

One could argue that the Duluth Project's current interagency collaboration is a far cry from the early days of the Duluth Project, which promoted a critical view of the state and a Paulo Freire-style of consciousness raising and grassroots organizing among women. The "Blueprint for Safety" promotes collusion with state agencies. However, Ellen Pence has described the Blueprint for Safety as "The Duluth Project on Steroids." But does the city-wide collaboration the Blueprint envisions represent a feminist advance—the institutionalization of a radical attempt to stop violence against women? Or does it mark a historical departure for a feminist organization dedicated to the radical proposal that violence is embedded in structural and cultural supports for violence?

I tend to think the latter; in this case, feminist activists have allied themselves to agencies with no commitment to feminists or feminist values. Kristin Bumiller has pointed out something similar in the project to eradicate sexual violence. "The state's interest in controlling violence is powerfully driven by social control priorities; for example, intimate partnership violence is 'of interest' . . . for the purposes of containing crises and managing harm, not to address women's systematic oppression" (Bumiller 2008, 12–13). Bumiller adds that the state has tried, especially in recent years, to limit its responsibility for women made homeless as they flee violence. The pact with state agents, in other words, is Mephistophelian.

My support for the Power and Control Wheel is qualified. If it's not used as part of a project to identify and eliminate institutional and structural supports for battering, its effectiveness is limited, even in its own terms: the goal of stopping violence against women. I argue this since, as we shall see in the next chapters, prosecutors, the police, and so on, are entirely implicated in violence against women.

Despite my skepticism, I hope in this chapter to have given a framework and the material for a balanced and circumspect evaluation of the fate of a radical political project. I have also indicated some of the dangers of institutionalization.

CHAPTER TWO

Difficult Maneuvers

Stopping Violence against Latina Immigrants in the United States

I am interviewing a well-known local Latina advocate in a spacious, modestly furnished office in a community center on the South Side of Chicago. I met Juana Liliana[1] as I was doing popular education in Chicago with other members of the Escuela Popular Norteña, a center for popular education, and collaborating with local church groups to design workshops. The project was influenced by Paulo Freire's methods of consciousness raising and the *comunidades de base* of liberation theology from Latin America. This work led me to her door.

A seasoned feminist firmly seated within a grass-roots organization in a predominantly Mexican community in Chicago, Juana Liliana illuminates the way she and other women maneuver, position themselves, and see the character of the violence they face, the needs they have, the support they want. She speaks at length of the specific challenges she faces supporting Latinas, often poor immigrants from Latin America who speak little English and have scant knowledge of the U.S. legal system. It is this latter group—immigrant Latinas—on whom we focus.

In her discourse as in her life, Liliana weaves her way through many of the institutions I will explore in the next chapters, including the law courts and shelters. She also discusses how her organization responds to lesbians, prostitutes, and especially undocumented women who face violence. She shows how the violence faced by many Latinas is structured by immigration law. In all of this, Liliana situates herself and her work within a nest of questions of racial, class, sexual, and linguistic differences, as well as differences in immigrant status among people living in the United States.

The interview lends insight to the tangle of problems generated within the multifaceted movement to stop violence against women. In this way, we can use this interview as an entry point to larger questions of structural violence, homogeneity, gender, and institutional power. At times, she tends to simplify and homogenize women and the violence they face; at other times, she resists and challenges that impulse.

BACKGROUND: IMMIGRANT LATINAS IN A STRUCTURE OF VULNERABILITY

Immigration law has put many women in a structure of vulnerability. The history of immigration law in the United States has reflected at least two oppressive forces that are in tension: the needs of capital and the desire to maintain white hegemony. On the one hand, capital has required and relied on a ready pool of labor, sometimes drawing on a large number of migrants, especially in the industrial and agricultural sectors. In contrast, immigration law has often been a process of legislating xenophobia, fueled as it has been by nativist fears of losing white Protestant hegemony (see Haney López 2006; Takaki 1998). These two forces, or needs, have combined to drive immigration policy. Over the past centuries, legislation has taken various forms of restriction on who may enter and who may naturalize. Depending on the period, the restrictions have taken the form of placing quotas based on the applicant's country of origin, on racial rules on who may naturalize (López 2006), and on other agreements, understandings, or administrative limitations on who may enter and under what conditions. For example, the Chinese Exclusion Act and the "Gentlemen's Agreement" with Japan of 1907 significantly restricted the number of East Asian immigrants for many decades (see Hondagneu-Sotelo 1997). Nevertheless, during the nineteenth and twentieth centuries, in times of severe labor shortage, the United States admitted large numbers of Asians, Mexicans, and others to build the transcontinental railroad, to farm and harvest, and to do factory work. The restrictions on the Chinese led to a predominance of male Chinese workers to the almost total exclusion of women. During the middle of the twentieth century, the massive *bracero* program imposed severe restraints on the rights of Mexican guest workers to organize or to move freely (*Harvest of Loneliness/Cosecha triste* 2010). Even as the United States continues to rely in significant respects on noncitizen labor, the last decade has seen a resurgence of hostility to and fear of immigration and immigrants, especially migrants from Mexico and Latin America. Mexicans have come to be seen as the prototypical "'undocumented'" workers (De Genova 2006);[2] immigrants, especially undocumented immigrants, are painted as criminal, even terrorist (see, e.g., Hagan, Levi, and Dinovitzer 2008). One consequence has been a slew of regressive legislation aimed at restricting immigration and militarizing the U.S. border, especially between the United States and Mexico.

Apparently gender-neutral legislation can have a disparate effect on women (Lindsley 2002). Syd Lindsley reads the fear of invasion by immigrants to the United States as driving legislation that is an "assault on immigrant women as reproductive agents" (Lindsley 2002, 176). Pointing out that the contemporary wave of immigration is mostly women, she argues that legal restrictions on spousal immigration affect women disproportionately since women more often receive sponsorship through a spouse or relative, whereas immigrant men are more likely to receive citizenship through other means (181). Over the last fifteen years, new state legislation and municipal ordinances across the country exclude undocumented people from social services, housing, access to education, and even medical care. Women and children especially rely on these important forms of social support; indeed, these restrictions arguably violate their human rights. The fear of immigrant women producing children has been a central preoccupation in the xenophobia reflected in these laws that restrict immigrant women's rights. Lindsley concludes that "laziness and criminality are thus rhetorically pinned on immigrant women." They are viewed as parasitic and opportunistically taking the goods and services paid for by hard working (American) taxpayers. "In an ideal union between capitalism and white supremacy, immigrant women and men of color can continue to provide cheap, surplus labor, while remaining comfortably outside the realm of full citizenship. Thus, capitalist development can be preserved while the imagined white national identity can remain intact" (Lindsley 2002).

What is the experience of living "outside the realm of full citizenship"? Latina activists have ably taken up how the vulnerability is lived and experienced by immigrant women. They have provided an eloquent record of the experiences of immigrants, of entering a racialized state, of navigating the world of work and public life in a time of strong anti-immigrant discourse. For the purposes at hand, I will focus on the experiences of immigrant Latinas who face violence, though of course many other groups face similar challenges. For immigrant Latinas, interpersonal violence and structural forms of violence, including the law, are sometimes mutually reinforcing. The legal and social structures make them vulnerable to economic exploitation, mistreatment, and sexual abuse.

Immigrant women are often at increased risk of isolation, especially if they are recent immigrants, if they are undocumented, or if they are not familiar with existing resources. "[W]hen you are working with a Latina," Liliana commented in our interview, "and most of our clients are . . . first-generation immigrants in this country. They are isolated. They don't have income; they don't have any support system. They are economically dependent." Immigrant women may fear authorities, including the police and the courts. The police often question Latinos' and Latinas' immigration status. Another Latina activist comments, "I have been doing immigrant rights work for over ten years, and I can't tell you how many immigrant women suffer from domestic violence and never report their batterers to the cops because most of the time the police ask the batterer *and* the woman about their immigration status" (Saucedo 2006, 136; emphasis in the original). In some areas, including where I live in upstate New York, the police and the sheriff turn undocumented people over to immigration authorities (Immigration and Custom Enforcement).[3] We have interviewed women and men at our local jail who were picked up on any number of charges, including noncriminal violations of the law (such as speeding), and then turned over to immigration officers. The nativist Right continues to experiment with regressive legislation; for example, a recent law (April 2010) in Arizona undergoing court challenge requires police to ask for papers from anyone with whom they have made legal contact and suspect is an illegal immigrant. Annanya Bhattacharjee has noted that the interagency collaboration between police and border agents has increased during the past ten years. She sees this as pre-existing September 11, 2001, but intensifying thereafter (Bhattacharjee 2002a).[4]

Immigrant women face violence at the border itself. Border guards and other immigration officials have sexually harassed women. Women may also face racial or ethnic profiling by border officials, forced to submit to humiliating body searches or questioning, depending on where they are from or how they appear. Sylvanna Falcón has studied documented cases of rape at the U.S./Mexico border by border officials and concluded that "rape is routinely and systematically used by the state in militarization efforts at the US-Mexico border, and provoked by certain factors and dynamics in the region, such as the influence of military culture on Border Control agents . . . Many women who cross the border report that being raped was the 'price' of not being apprehended, deported, or of having their confiscated documents returned. This price is unique to border regions in general" (Falcón 2006, 119, 120; also see Schmidt Camacho 2010, 282–85 on *feminicidio* and border rape).

Challenging these forms of violence means challenging the state. "If they decide to prosecute, women who have been sexually assaulted in the US-Mexico border region confront not only an individual, but directly challenge several powerful institutions—the [Immigration and Customs Enforcement], the US government, the US legal system . . . Human Rights Watch, Amnesty International and the state advisory committees to the US Commission on Civil Rights have all concluded that no useful mechanism exists for victims of human rights abuses to lodge complaints against border agents" (Falcón 2006, 122, 125).

In this context of heightened vulnerability, as we shall see, Juana Liliana's position resists simple categorization. To take one prominent example, she knows that in her largely immigrant community, people are intimidated by the law, by the police, the courts, and this is a consequence of the structure of immigration law itself and how it renders them vulnerable to abuse. Still, in order to stop violence against women, she relies on these institutions, and sometimes even on how they intimidate immigrants.

Through the details of the way she talks, one can read a set of attachments, motivations, desires, investments. Through the way she talks to *me* we can begin to consider the context of the exchange, an exchange that really merits a theory of translation: How does she maneuver in order to head off certain interpretations I, a white man, may have of her, of her organization, or of violence in her community? What does she want to communicate to me?

Sameness and Difference

Liliana began the interview by taking the position that domestic violence is always and everywhere the same.

JL: [I]n general this works across all social, economic, races, ethnicity, classes, everything. Because domestic violence cuts across this way [cuts air with hand, horizontally]. But when we are working . . . I always like to say that the only color that domestic violence knows is the color purple. Those are the . . .

JP: The welts?

JL: The welts, the bruises, the black eyes that we see in our clients.

Why does Liliana say that "the only color domestic violence knows is the color purple"? Why the emphasis on sameness? In the interview, Liliana's motivations were ambiguous at times. Was it a question of trying to anticipate a racist reading I, the interviewer, might have of violence in Latino communities—an association of Latinos with violence? Perhaps she was worried that I have a stereotypical sense of Latino men as violent, as more misogynist than white men, as more controlling or cruder. As she remarked to me later, "They can be very . . . I don't want to say 'macho' because we don't have a monopoly on machismo." Thinking of communication as translation would be a way to acknowledge the different social worlds we inhabit, even if those social worlds are linked to one another (Lugones 2003a).

But as we shall see, after emphasizing commonality among women, Liliana goes on to show how Latinas who face violence are in a more precarious position than other women. The inner tension in her position is important. Liliana walks a difficult line between attention to difference and particularity while at times suppressing all differences between women, especially among Latina women, in her discourse. One can see the tension when for example she employs a generic pronoun, "she," as a stand-in for all Latina women who face violence, even as she is commenting on the specific circumstances that face (really only some) Latinas. That is, Liliana tends to appeal to an archetypal "Latina" to explain the experiences and predicaments of Latinas in the grips of violence.

On another level, her comments also betray an ambivalent relationship with the women's movement to end violence and the feminist movement more generally. Even as she employs the vocabulary and the logic of the feminist movement, she also clearly articulates her perceptions of the shortcomings of a movement that does not enfranchise the needs of Latinas. This ambivalence shades at times into a critique of social service (which she does not differentiate strongly from feminist activism) that is not friendly or receptive to Latinas. Nevertheless, she identifies as a feminist, and she frequently uses turns of phrase from both the feminist movement (she refers to violence against women as an issue of 'power and control') and from social work (e.g. she refers to the women she sees as "clients"). Feminism and social work administration, for example, are intertwined in her narrative of the origins of her organization (cf. Schneider 2000; Pleck 1987; Schechter 1982).

Why Doesn't She Just Leave?

Many women who face violence are asked, almost routinely, "Why didn't you just leave?" I explore this question in a later chapter. For Juana Liliana, "leaving" a situation of violence is inevitably tied to a woman's legal status as an immigrant. Undocumented women are especially vulnerable, of course. For example, she sees undocumented Latinas who were hostage to their husband's threats. "So when we talk about the immigration, the man will say that if you call the police I will tell them that you don't have any documents, don't have any papers, and they will immediately arrest you and deport to Mexico, and you'll never see your children again. What does that do to the woman? She freezes. And in reality she fears more the immigration services than she does the fists of her husband or partner. Because what she hears is only what he tells her." Undocumented immigrant Latinas have of necessity a different spatial sense from that of other women, especially vis-à-vis spaces of safety and danger. The abusers threaten them with the police, or use the prospect of deportation as a way to abuse and control them. Latino men are in a position to do this because of the gendered structure of immigration and its consequences for whom Latinas can trust, and how restricted or unrestricted their spaces are. Pointing to an example of a border guard whose helpful attitude to migrant women was a prelude to his sexual assault on them, Falcón observes, "Legal documents quite literally control the lives of immigrants, so when a US official 'seems' helpful regarding matters which may determine your future, it adds another layer of vulnerability" (2006, 123). In effect, abusers and border officials may collude in creating an ambiance of fear, isolation, and confinement by exploiting women's immigration papers. Liliana comments, "A lot of time he has papers because he came ahead of time or he fixed his papers. But he has this control over this woman. And he will say, one of these days and one of these days [I will get you immigration papers], but he knows this is one way of keeping her there."

Immigration papers and the gendering of how they are distributed becomes one of the major themes of Liliana's discourse. They allow men to work, to go out of the home, while Latinas who lack them have a space that is much more restricted. Nevertheless, while undocumented women are sometimes domestic captives to men who control immigration papers, they do challenge that organization of space and are sometimes successful in restructuring it.

> I have cases of very brave women. I remember a case when he had all the documents locked in the basement in the room. It was during the time of the IRCA [Immigration Reform and Control Act of 1986]. Her children were very afraid she was going to get sent back to Mexico; they were very afraid what are we going to do without our mom. And she would come and tell me that he tells me that he is going to send me back to Mexico, and my kids are very afraid. She was not very concerned

about herself. She was concerned about her children. But one day he left the padlock open, and she went into the room, and she brought all the papers to me, and we made xerox papers of everything, and she got hold of another agency, and she was able to obtain legal residency. Just to let you know the power and control of immigration.

Liliana centers the violence not on the body but rather in holding her *papers* captive, thereby terrorizing her and her children. The violence is one that is both a form of psychological terror and also a way of having control over her body because of the threat of deportation. This can have the implication of making her fear leaving, fear approaching authorities, since she risks being turned over to the immigration officials. So the state is complicit in confining them. Liliana continues, linking their immigrant status to class and to education in keeping many Latinas hemmed in.

They use that as a very important tool to keep the women under them. We were talking back about a woman who has no documents. We have to link that to economic dependency. A large majority of our clients are uneducated, they have no working skills, and they are homemakers. And again because he might not let them improve their lives.

They [the men] are the breadwinners, and they depend on him 100 percent for survival, economic survival. Then, to that we add . . . women south of the border who do not apply for public aid. If they come with two or three children born south of the border and one child born in this country, and she applies for public aid, she goes going to get aid for one child but not for the other three. So how's she going to survive with what she gets for one child when there are four or five in the household? And that keeps her in the abusive relationship.

To tell you the truth, we have had cases where we have had no choice but to send the women back to the abuser even if she wants to leave. Because how is she going to survive, how is she going to feed those kids? There is no money, no income. If she has no papers she can always work underground and get whatever they want to pay here.

J: Really being exploited.

A: Really being exploited. And if she has a number of kids how is she going to move about to get a job? So it is really difficult to be independent. Economic independence. And I always say the way to be free of violence is paved green. Not green the color of the lawn, but the color of money. If she has money, most likely she's going to say well, it's going to be difficult, but. Remember all of the things that I am telling you she wants to be sure she wants out of the relationship. Ultimately it's up to her to decide. So, economic dependency. I know you went like this when I said we sent her back to her abuser. They say a woman comes here and talks about her case; she is not working. She doesn't want to or can't go on public aid, or if she can she can go for one child, and he is the breadwinner. So the only thing if she wants to . . . the only thing we can offer her is an order of protection.

Liliana locates poor, immigrant Latinas as ensnared in a complex web of economic dependency, a shrinking welfare state that in any case discriminates against immigrants and abusive men who use their undocumented status to control them. Their quarantine in an abusive relationship is buttressed if they have children, especially children who are not eligible for aid. To those who would ask, "Why doesn't she just leave?" Liliana remonstrates by locating Latina immigrant poor women at the conjunction of economic vulnerability and an ambiance of intimate terror around the issue of their status as undocumented, where the public sphere holds enormous pitfalls.

When you are working with a Latina . . . and most of our clients are . . . it's changing a little bit, but most of our clients are first-generation immigrants in this country. They are isolated. They don't have income, They don't have any support system. They are economically dependent. They bring their culture. And immigration plays a very important role for the Latinas. And when I am talking about Latinas immigration plays an important role for those from south of the border, Mexico, Central America, South America. Thinking about the culture and the . . . isolation . . . when you have a support system, you feel there is someone to hear you. That's why it's a good thing that we are here. They know that we are going to listen to them in their own language. They know that most of us are first-generation immigrants, that most of us know the shock of coming here. So they feel comfortable talking to us. We do understand them. So that is the cultural part. The isolation. The fact that for many Latinas, when they say my husband abuses me, from Colombia or Mexico, anywhere south of the border, probably for lack of laws in those countries to protect victims of domestic violence, then we say, well it's bad luck. *Te tocó un golpeador.* I remember hearing this in Mexico. He was a batterer, so that was your bad luck. So they had to take it. That was the cultural part. Then we can take the religious part. That is, they are Catholic or any of these other newer religions. You have to take it. You cannot get a divorce. *Es el deseo de Dios.* It is God's wishes. You have to bear your cross, and that kind of thing.

Passing from one country to another, women are not cognizant of the changed cultural mores, according to Liliana. They are not only physically isolated, but they are also unversed in Anglo culture. She thinks that Latin American culture teaches a fatalistic attitude towards abuse, and contains within it a complementary Catholic teaching that bolsters accepting one's lot in life. All of these constituent elements brace the home of the undocumented woman and obstruct and impede immigrant, poor Latinas from leaving an abuser. According to Liliana, her Latina organization provides company in the shock of displacement since the members are themselves immigrants. She sees her organization as providing an oasis of linguistic and cultural understanding. This itself transforms the meaning of the spaces of physical and cultural isolation and makes them easier to bear. In fact, it may be that "leaving" is not always the individual and collective goal so much as transforming those spaces of terror.

The Power and Control Wheel and the Cycle of Violence

Liliana describes her primarily Latina clients in ways that distinguish them from other women. However, she does have a tendency to employ jargon that tends to eclipse how a woman's immigration status structures her relationship to violence. Liliana frequently employs the term "power and control," a phrase that resonates with feminist language to describe violence (I explored the Power and Control Wheel more fully in the last chapter). "Immigration plays a very, very important role. I say that the immigration part is again the issue of power and control from the abuser. And abuse is an issue of power and control. When a man abuses—I'm going to say a man because 95 percent of the abusers are men, and 95 percent of the victims are women—They use the power and control." Liliana has an eye for how larger structures are part of the context of violence—in this case, how immigration law and enforcement are used to abuse women. She bridges the language of "power and control" with the situation in her community by linking power and control to the centrality of immigration. She uses the article "the" in the final sentence, "They use *the* power and control." She handed me a copy of the Power and Control Wheel that had been translated into Spanish (I have reprinted a Spanish translation in chapter 1).

Liliana goes on to invoke Lenore Walker's Cycle of Violence. This drew my attention because as I mentioned in the last chapter, the explanation offered by Walker's cycle of violence is antithetical to the logic of the Power and Control Wheel, although each is used widely in feminist antiviolence work. The Cycle of Violence is a sociopsychological explanation of domestic battering. It argues that a more or less standard script exists: "the tension-building phase"; "the acute battering incident"; and the "tranquil, loving" (or at least nonviolent) phase that follows (Walker 1989). Walker's language emphasizes common patterns. For example, she argues that batterers always try to isolate the women they abuse. "This increasing isolation is common to all battered women; the effect it has on exacerbating her already-established psychological terror cannot be stressed enough." Some feminist critics have argued that Walker overgeneralizes to the exclusion of women whose situation does not fit the norm. For example, not all women who face violence face increasing isolation; but even if they did, the character of that isolation, who they are isolated from, how, and what that means, is diverse. In other words, describing "isolation" as a tactic of abuse leaves aside some of the most important questions: what are the various structures that isolate different women, and what are the diverse meanings women attach to the isolation? Feminists have also argued that the Cycle of Violence takes away women's agency. In Walker's view, women caught in the cycle of violence feel or perceive that they have no control:

> Although the battered woman sees it as unpredictable, she also feels that the acute battering incident is somehow inevitable. In this phase, she has no control; only the batterer may put an end to the violence. The nature of his violence can be as unpredictable as the time of its explosion, and so are his reasons for stopping it. Usually, the battered woman realizes that she cannot reason with him, that resistance will only make things worse. She has a sense of being distant from the attack and from the terrible pain, although she may later remember each detail with great precision. What she is likely to feel most strongly at this time is a sense of being psychologically trapped. (Walker 1989)

As we saw in chapter 1, the Duluth Project invented the Power and Control Wheel as a methodological tool to generate critical discourse among women on the violence they experience and link it to institutional and cultural critique. The two models are incompatible because the Cycle of Violence provides a psychological explanation of why (all) battered women stay with their batterer. The Power and Control Wheel, instead, encourages women to explore different facets of their experience of battering, develop insights, and come up with solutions. Its approach recognizes oppression of women by social institutions.

In taking up the Cycle of Violence and the terms of Power and Control, Liliana draws an abstract, generalized situation of abuse. In the following, she highlights emotional abuse by referring to cases where physical abuse has stopped due to court intervention, and emotional abuse has taken its place.

A: Well, you know, because then the Cycle of Violence.

J: The "honeymoon stage"?[5]

A: The honeymoon stage. Which, you know . . .

J: Isn't always there anyway, but they used to have it sometimes, but now don't have it ever. Is that right?

A: Then what happens—in some cases, and please, I am not talking about *all* cases—but there will be the Cycle of Violence; there will be just the part of tension and abuse, and it doesn't need to be physical abuse. It will be tension and emotional abuse, real emotional abuse.

Liliana strikes a similar note to Lenore Walker's discourse in other ways, as well: "When you are working with Latina . . . when you are working in general with battered women, I think its number one that women suffer from low self-esteem. If your self-esteem is not intact, it's more easy that you can take abuse than saying, 'Hey wait a second. You are not going to hit me.' So that is a commonality among battered women."
Lenore Walker:

> The typical battered woman has poor self-image and low self-esteem, basing her feelings of self-worth on her perceived capacity to be a good wife and homemaker, whether or not she also has a successful career outside of the home. Although she is more liberal than her mate in her sex role attitudes, she behaves in stereotyped, traditional ways in order to please the batterer, who generally holds extremely rigid and traditional values regarding home and family life. She may believe that she is the one at fault for not stopping her batterer's violent behavior; consequently she suffers great guilt. (Walker 1989, 102–03).

Liliana's position is complicated, however, and defies simple resolution. It is not as if she appropriated Walker's theory whole hog. Though she sees commonalities, she also sees differences. For if she finds the vocabulary, models, and paradigms of non-Latinas to be adaptable to her work with Latinas, she certainly does not see them as readymade for them. Her language is at all times clarifying the unique positioning of Latinas. Moreover, she also points to the ways in which Latinas and Latinos are excluded from or mistreated within existing institutions that respond to violence. Thus she says of programs for abusive men:

> Then we have another handicap: there are no services for abusers in Spanish. So, we are working with the women; we are empowering the women; the women are feeling much better about themselves. They are saying, "¡no me pegues! [don't hit me!]." No, this is not going to happen. And I will take you to court again, because we are working with her in group and individually. And he gets nothing. We need to work with women to get them to this level [puts hands at parallel level from floor].
>
> J: Equal to the men?
>
> A: Equal to the men.

She is not objecting to programs that are monocultural in the sense that they were developed and are intended to fit all abusers, all situations of abuse, irrespective of the specific history of the violence and its meaning across different cultural frontiers. What she takes issue with is the fact that the programs are mono*lingual*. However, a bilingual program could still be mono*cultural*: A particular project may have all its materials in Spanish but still be based on a model of violence alien to the particular community, or one that imagines all violence as cut from a common cloth.

Law Courts and Legal Institutions as Multivalent Forces on Immigrant Lives

Most of Liliana's work deals directly with institutions that are organized to protect women from violence. She articulates a complicated relationship to law courts and government authorities, at times remarking on how little confidence she has in them. Other times, it is clear that she sees the law courts as a workable, if problematic, institution for stopping violence against women, specifically the working-class immigrant Latinas who are her clientele.

For her, some of the most important things the law court provides are orders of protection. She places these at the center of her work, as the primary method for remedy.

> A: [T]he only thing—if she wants to—the only thing we can offer her is an order of protection. At least she will be sending him the message it is not okay for you to batter me. The law in Illinois protects me and says you cannot hit me.
>
> J: Can she get an order of protection even if she is undocumented?
>
> A: When Harold Washington was mayor he put an order in place where the police [have] no business asking a victim of domestic violence—asking anyone—what your legal status [is] here. Before they used to.
>
> J: There is no connection between the police and [immigration enforcement]?
>
> A: No. They don't need to ask. The courts don't need to ask either. We had only two cases. One [was] where the woman went to domestic violence court, and immigration came trying to arrest her. And that was when there was all this IRCA [Immigration Reform and Control Act]. I remember. I do a lot of public policy through different networks and councils. We . . . talked to Mr. Meyers, and they didn't promise anything in paper. But he said we will be very careful when we know there is domestic violence. So we haven't had any more problems in domestic violence court. This was about seven years ago. So she can get an order of protection.
>
> J: Is that part of the education that you can get an [order of protection], and it doesn't matter that you are undocumented?

A: We tell them that during intake. What I am telling you is very much the same that I would be telling a client.

While Liliana is sensitive to the vulnerability of Latinas, her response discloses how enmeshed she is in working with the police, immigration, and customs enforcement, and the law courts. One can scarcely help noticing the world of difference between "[immigration officials] don't need to ask," and "they don't ask." Earlier in this chapter I cited the activist Renee Saucedo, who comments precisely on how often police *do* ask, as well as a recent law in Arizona that requires them to. In any case, her response does not particularly take up the popular perception among Latinas of how they feel marked in certain spaces as vulnerable because they are undocumented, how they construct spaces of danger and of safety. Indeed, given the nature of the informal agreements she has established with immigration authorities, it would seem that Latinas' fear of *La Migra* is justified. Her answers reflect what she takes to be (informal) policy. However, as Annanya Bhattacharjee commented above, the last few years have seen increased interagency collaboration in apprehending immigrants who have overstayed their visas, who have been convicted of a crime, or who are undocumented (2002a).

We then talked more of the perception that Latinos and Latinas have of authorities, such as the courts, the police, and immigration authorities.

J: People have said to me that Latinos are for good reason [more] worried about the police than about the battery, and more than that, they are worried about their man. The police aren't the best thing for them. They don't want to be beaten; they don't want the batterer to go to jail for a long time.

A: They think that going to jail is the ultimate thing, but in reality, not too many abusers go to jail.

J: It never happens.

A: It happens. In all the years and I have been going to court, and my advocates go to court, have been going to court, and that is many years, I have had one guy go to jail, for the weekend, and that is because he had a job.

There is more than one reason. One, there is a fear of Immigration. That the police [are] going to arrest and deport them. The second reason is that they are ashamed. Battered women usually think it is their fault. They are ashamed. . . . I don't want him arrested. I am so ashamed to take him to court, and I don't want to call the police. And many women come here because they don't want to see the squad car by their house. So they come here and say, "I would feel more comfortable if you would

call the police for me." Number one because of the language, because
of the advocacy, and because they feel safe here. Many times we have a
police car in front of the agency.

For Latinas, the police conjure conflicting responses. At once they are a source of
tremendous fear, a public sign of shame, and are, or might be, protectors. Liliana
does not expressly acknowledge how these associations with the police conflict.
Why would a Latina who worries that "the police [are] going to arrest and deport
them," take comfort in seeing a squad car outside of the organization's offices where
she is going for refuge? Yet Liliana implies that many women feel safer *because*
the police car is in front of the agency. Her strategy relies on Latino immigrants'
lack of familiarity with the system. At times, though, she herself fluctuates on the
sort of recourse the court system provides. She says, for example, "[W]e teach her
how to use the order of protection. Anytime he disobeys the order of protection,
she should call the police. She should hold him accountable. If it's not her, it's
the judge who will hold him accountable." Earlier, she had remarked emphatically
that judges rarely incarcerate batterers. She must therefore either be speaking to
fears that Latino men have (such as the false belief that the judges will hold them
accountable, punish them, etc.), or she is herself vacillating. We continued:

> A: [I]f she goes back to him and has the order of protection, he's getting
> a message: I cannot batter her.
>
> J: Do you really think it is effective? Some people say it is just a piece
> of paper . . .
>
> A: It is effective in some cases. If he wants to batter her or punch her or
> kill her, it's a piece of paper. But for some, especially Latinos, they fear
> the system too much. It plays both ways. They can be very . . . I don't
> want to say "macho" because we don't have a monopoly on machismo.
> But they feel, "I know what I'm doing." But they also fear the system.
> You should see them. They don't know the system. If they know the
> system, then it's very . . . they know how to manipulate the system.
> They know that they are not going to be put in jail. They know they
> can delay the trial . . . [W]hat we see with the men and women, they
> respect the system—in general Latinos, and again we are talking about
> first-generation Latinos. A great percentage of them fear the system and
> respect the law. They know for example that in Mexico, if the police
> arrest you, they beat the . . . they beat you up. No questions asked. They
> don't want that to happen. And many of them are undocumented. They
> don't want to make waves.

In a very specific way, Latinas who are battered by immigrant Latinos have
something in their tool chest that most other women do not have: the fear that

many immigrant Latino men have of the courts. "When we see a woman get an order of protection, and they go back to him, to live with him, and he feels, now she's got me. And they feel emasculated. Because now there is this paper they gave us in court, and now she is the boss. They feel very threatened. So the physical abuse may stop because they know he can be taken back to court. And the judges are pretty good, you know they threaten, "The next time I see you back in court you are going to spend a year in jail, blah blah, blah." It doesn't happen, but they hear it." An order of protection served to recent immigrants is likely to intimidate, Liliana suggests. Having a detailed, insider's sense of the knowledges, the competencies, the fears Latino men and women have of certain spaces, Liliana operates with acumen and savvy both in the legal system and outside of it. She accesses Anglo power in a way that many non-Latinos cannot in order to stop men in her community from battering women.

Nonetheless, she is cognizant of how Latino men are taken advantage of because of their fear and apprehension.

J: [S]ometimes you say we send the Latinas back to the batterers because that is the best for them, so maybe you could talk about other things that you do?

A: For example, I am a Latina. I am a woman's advocate, but I am a Latina's advocate. Let's put it that way. I don't go to court anymore because I coordinate, and I don't have time. But I resent when I see these lawyers, especially the ones around the neighborhood, that exploit Latinos. Let's say there is a case of domestic violence, and he is making $4.25 an hour, and he is the breadwinner of this family, and he receives a summons and is served with an order of protection and knows he has to go to court. And he is very scared, and he will go and talk to one of these attorneys. And these guys will say, "Well, I can take you to court, but it will cost $500." Now these lawyers will not tell the guy you qualify for a public defender. I don't really need to go with you to court. I don't need to take your money. Go to court and establish that you need a public defender, and they will represent you for free. I resent when I see these lawyers, and they are taking money from hombres Latinos just because they are Latinos. To me, it is very difficult, because I am supposed [to be] advocating for the women. But in many cases I talk to the guy, and I say, "Look, Señor, you don't really have to pay for an attorney." Then they don't really trust the public defenders because they think they are all vendidos [sell-outs], okay? *Todos los abogados son vendidos.* [All lawyers are sell-outs.] And the public defenders in domestic violence court are great. They are better than the state's attorneys. I am putting him in better hands than I have my client [laughs]. But I will not in any way don't think Latino—Latina—when I see the abuses that they suffer, because I am a Latina! Number one, she is my number one priority. But I will also, in many cases, I have advocated for men, and I have told them you don't have to pay for an attorney. And I have called the attorney. That puts me in a difficult position because I am supposed to be working with her, for her.

As a Latina, she is concerned when she sees them taken advantage of, not by the court, but by unprincipled lawyers. Still, as a feminist and a Latina, she wants to stand by Latina women.

It would be a mistake, then, to see Liliana as glibly exploiting the fear and unfamiliarity of Latino men to stop them from abusing women. As a Latina, she situates herself as their ally to prevent them from being manipulated by unscrupulous lawyers. She seems to minimize the immigrants' fears as naïveté. She regards them as responding to a set of conditioning forces that exist other places but not within the United States. "They know for example that in Mexico, if the police arrest you, they beat the . . . they beat you up. No questions asked." She implies that this is a belief about authorities immigrants import with them uncritically from Mexico. At the same time, though, she betrays an insight into how abusive the spaces of the U.S. law courts can be to *any* Latino. "I remember the first time I went to court it was like, what the hell is going on here, you know. I was mistreated. And I spoke English. And these women most of the time don't." Although much of her language is cast in the idiom of social welfare worker, insider to the system, or a helper to the recent immigrant client, she experienced the racism of the courts and expresses a deeper solidarity and identification with Latinos than a social worker might otherwise claim.

Similarly, Liliana invested a great deal in keeping women within the Latino community if possible.

> J: I talked to other Latina activists or other Latinas who work with battered women, and they said . . . that there's a lot of racism in the shelters. And the fact that it takes women out of the community, and it makes them very vulnerable, and even if they are isolated, they are still in the community otherwise, and this takes them out. And maybe people just don't speak Spanish there.

> A: Well, that's a problem for us. We will not, unless it's a matter of life and death . . . We only place her if she's not in danger where there is bilinguals there at all times. Where we know she is not going to be the only Latina, and she is going to be able to find a sense of shelter within the community.

> J: So, that's a possibility.

> A: But not only shelters. We only refer to two shelters on a regular basis. There are other shelters, but we try not to send those women there.

She tacitly acknowledges the women's vulnerability not just in the courts but also in the shelters. I was struck by how disinclined she was to send women to shelters that do not attend to the needs of Latinas—she alludes to shelters where there are not bilinguals at all times, where Latinas are not able to find a sense of haven or company.

Latina Lesbians

Even if she wants to find sanctuary for Latinas within the community, this does not apply to *all* Latina women. Liliana does not explicitly exclude Latina lesbians from her analysis, but her institutional approach to them tacitly does. In response to questions about same-sex abuse, she remarked:

> We don't see [abuse by lesbians of lesbians], as a rule. We used to have a poster downstairs—I went to a homophobia training, and they said one of the things you have to have downstairs is a poster that says same sex violence is not permitted, or I don't remember. At least that, for someone who does not identify, knows she is a lesbian, she knows I am welcome here. And it was up for years. And then when they remodeled downstairs, and they repainted, it went. But I don't see it. But if I have, to me it is the same. Domestic violence is domestic violence . . . I know a good number of Latinas who are lesbians. I know they are very active, and I know that there is violence amongst same gender, same sex. But we don't see it here. Not that they don't exist.

Here she appeals to a logic of sameness; now, for her, domestic violence is domestic violence, and it is irrelevant if the person is a lesbian. But this appeal to sameness is inconsistent. Despite the "sameness" approach with respect to Latina lesbians, for other women she does draw distinctions between forms of violence, where they occur, the sorts of recourse different women and men have, and in what spaces they are heard and understood or erased and mistreated. As she talked of Latina women generally, her remarks were marked by abundant detail and a thorough eye for their quotidian practices, their fear of being deported, the way they attended to men, their responsibility to children, their choices between "career" and homemaking, and so on. Her approach incorporated this detail.

Her appreciation wavers when it comes to lesbians. Lesbians are considered as generic battered women, whose lives as lesbians are irrelevant, *particularly* their sex lives. "But I am not here to talk about your sex. I am here to discuss your domestic violence. I mean they might volunteer, but I am not going to ask them. It is a very delicate question." Liliana is willing to talk about race, about class, about immigration, religion, and how violence is gendered. Still, when it comes to sexuality, difference is neutralized. Sex is not what she is there to talk about.

However, one wonders whether this is true: would she be so squeamish in talking to straight women about sex? Sexual abuse?

Although she fights to keep other Latinas in the neighborhood even if they face violence, keeping Latina *lesbians* in the community does not seem as important to her. "But there is Horizons [a gay and lesbian center located geographically outside of the Latino community]." Latina lesbians facing violence have other places to go than to her organization. Should they identify as lesbians, they can go to Horizons, a place for lesbians, far outside of the community on the other side of town. And she does not seem to worry as much if Horizons has bilingual services.

Liliana's "solution" is predicated on a split: the Latina homoerotic subject is split between the implicitly heterosexual Latina community which Liliana tries to make safe for implicitly heterosexual Latinos/as, and an LGBT movement that is supposedly elsewhere, outside the community. In chapter 4 I return to this forced split between communities of color and the LGBT movement and explore the implications for women of color who face violence.

Liliana does have a complex approach to questions of culture and violence in the context of heterosexual Latinas living more or less conventional monogamous lives. For Latina lesbians, however, her explanation loses this complexity as she appeals to pat psychological explanations. This suggests that she lacks any other explanation or insight. Her sense of competence regarding relationships or locations she does not know or understand is maintained by making appeal to any of a set of theories (the Power and Control Wheel, the Cycle of Violence). They function as a stand-in for the sort of knowledge she evinces when it comes to immigrant Latinas. Unfortunately, these theories have sameness woven in them, yet that is what makes them useful to fill lacunae of knowledge. With lesbians, she assumes she knows a lesbian when she sees one, but then she does not have any explicit, articulated insights that reveal an understanding of violence in lesbian relationships. In that case, she "covers up" through invoking the models, her agency's poster, alluding to her "training," and finally through referring lesbians to more "appropriate" agencies.

Latinas in Prostitution

So although she makes generalizations about Latina women, the generalizations cover women who are married and live with an abusive man. Outside her ken are not only Latina lesbians but also Latinas who work as prostitutes.

J: How about prostitutes? Or is it mainly married women?

A: We don't see . . . I remember seeing, working with clients who were like bartenders. They probably were doing some kind of prostitution. They were battered by their spouses. No, nothing I could tell you.

J: Not a clear thing that is happening.

A: No.

But where are sex workers in the community supposed to go? To be fair, her position is common enough. Another activist, a white woman I interviewed, comments:

J: Is it your sense that a lot of prostitutes are going to shelters?

A: That's not my impression.

J: That's not your impression.

A: No.

J: Your impression is they're not.

A: Yes. There's one specific place for prostitutes in Chicago, [name of center]. It's the only place I know that specifically says we are here to help prostitutes. It's the only place I know that specifically reaches out to that woman. I mean domestic violence programs, like shelters, are dealing with someone who has been abused, or is some way related to that, having a kid, living together, in a relationship I guess is what I mean. I think what a prostitute is experiencing [is] a kind of violence that is different in some way. I think maybe sex abuse programs might keep more of those women. I guess. I think. (From field notes)

Liliana's organization is highly attentive to difference and to cultural, institutional, and structural forces that are violently imposed on Latinas. Nevertheless, her work ignores and ultimately excludes some Latinas whose lives do not conform.

CONCLUSION

Juana Liliana occupies multiple positions. Hers is not unitary. This makes it fruitless to attempt a definitive explanation of her stance. A better metaphor (though it's not simply a metaphor) would be of constant movement, inside and outside of institutions, inside and outside of the logic of particularity, appropriating generalized schemas that she both follows and subverts. She has a deep sense of the Latinas with whom she works, a sense of how they perceive the home, how they function within it, how they approach the law court, and how the boundaries of the community are marked.

She gives fabric to the claim that immigration law forms the experiences of many immigrant women. Apparently gender-neutral immigration policy has a disparate affect on women, especially in how it structures their experience of violence.

However ready and studied is her eye for the particular predicaments of Latinas from that community, she nevertheless appeals to dominant normative models of violence when it comes to the marginalized *among* Latinas. This appeal mutes the otherwise subtle account she gives of how Latinas perceive the police, the law courts, and the immigration documents that sometimes make them hostage to the home. When they do not impose homogeneity on women, these models arm her with a cognitive device to exclude Latinas whose sexual practices do not conform to the perceived norm of heterosexual monogamy, such as lesbians and women in prostitution. She considers them either the same as heterosexual women who face domestic violence or outside of the group of women with whom she works.

The point of this exercise has not been to arrive at a final assessment of her position in order to accept or reject it. Rather, a detailed examination lays the groundwork for understanding what sorts of interventions are possible, where interventions meet actors in their complicated, multistrand beliefs, postures, practices, actions, perceptions.

Putting at the center the voices of women at the intersections has several advantages. One is that it compels focus on very distinct accounts. In drawing out representations of spaces of terror, a focus on the marginalized reconstructs what counts as violence and how it is experienced, even if such accounts are against the grain of the dominant common sense or point in unexpected directions. In this sense, the focus on space also leaves a great deal of theoretical room for reformulation of what gendered violence is and how it is enacted.

Taken in its entirety, the focus on women at the intersections points to coming up with many solutions, not just one. The critical aspect of this work derives from a commitment to construct analyses and solutions that end violence that are not based on false beliefs regarding the experiences that women voice, who the women are, how individual women's identities change and evolve, and how this affects their conception of the violence they face.

CHAPTER THREE

Speech at the Margins

Women in Prostitution and the Counterpublic Sphere

A lot of men enjoyed bringing me in as a third party with their wives. Usually what would end up happening is we'd watch some pornographic film, say, and then he'd say, "All right, I want you to do that to my wife." Now, in these instances, I felt the wife was the victim, and that I was there to hurt the wife. I felt there was a real power play there, where the man was obviously saying to the wife, "If you don't do this, I'm going to leave you." I mean there were great overtones of manipulation and coercion.

—Giobbe 1994, 124

Depending on how they are socially positioned, different women face distinct forms of manipulation and coercion. In the epigraph for this chapter, the narrator, the wife, and the actors in the pornographic film encounter varying shades, forms, and tonalities of power and violence against them. Among other things, they stand in different relation to the law, to safety, to convention. Paying attention to difference allows us to extract the various meanings of the same space for each of the women. Seeing more than one meaning is a precondition to analyzing the differences in the violence.

This would help us to forge a multifaceted movement against violence against woman that emerges from women's activities and analyses. Solutions need to speak to the particularities of women's situations and their ways of responding to them. By putting the most marginalized women at the center, we can broaden the narrow view of violence. Women who live outside of the dominant norms, such as women in the sex industry,[1] face violence that is publicly disavowed.

This chapter focuses on their accounts of violence. The aim is to explore two related themes: first, a range of views of what counts as violence to women who work as prostitutes, and second, the obstacles they have to being heard in their accounts of violence.

Women in prostitution do not, of course, all share the same notion of sex work, exploitation, what counts as violence, choice, the law, solutions, and so on. As we shall see below, some women who work as prostitutes use the language of choice and decision making to describe a woman's agency in prostitution (including the choice to prostitute or engage in other forms of sex work). Others reject this as limited by the framework of a liberal understanding of agency and the contract in favor of an account of prostitution that emphasizes systematic and structural sexual oppression of women. Still others have argued that "the argument over whether sex work is *either* exploitative *or* liberating is a ridiculous one . . . and has little relevance to the complex, contradictory, and widely varied experiences of sex workers" (Lerum, 1998, 8, cited in Rabinovitch and Straga, 2004). Hedging on whether women who work in prostitution "choose" to, Rosen and Venkatesh (2008) characterize as 'circumscribed choice' the decision to prostitute, given the often meager alternative economic opportunities they see. In the following, I will try to situate the position of each speaker since it affects what he or she views as violence.

Many of the women I discuss below situate their positions within the debate on whether to legalize prostitution and the related debate of whether to decriminalize it. But exploring this debate is not the focus of this chapter. Nevertheless, the terms of the debate are present throughout, since one's position on legalization tends to have a bearing on her understanding of the violence involved in sex work. Those who see prostitution as inherently coerced, violent, and degrading (Giobbe 1991), usually argue that prostitution should not be legal. Others see that blanket condemnation of prostitution as "infantilizing" women who do decide to engage in sex work (Agustín 2007). Those who argue that prostitution is largely undertaken as free choice (e.g., Agustín 2006) tend to believe that women should be allowed to practice sex work. Some have tried to reconcile these positions by seeing sex work as exploited labor—that is, as work that is both chosen *and* violent (Hernández-Truyol and Larson 2002); for them, working as a prostitute could be likened to working in a sweatshop: prostitutes ought to be able to press legal claims if they are due wages or forced to work in unsafe conditions, even as their employers (pimps, johns) should face legal sanctions for exploiting them (Hernández-Truyol and Larson 2002, 212). In each case, the legal remedies match their account of whether women choose sex work and whether sex work is inherently violent.

Aside from how one constructs the "choice" involved in sex work and the position one takes on whether to legalize prostitution, many studies have shown that a majority of women who have worked in prostitution report having been sexually or physically abused (see e.g., Farley and Barkan 1998; Rafael and Shapiro 2004). In one study of Native American women in prostitution in Vancouver, the rate of abuse was as high as 90 percent (Farley and Lynne 2005).

I focus on the question of harm. Any sex worker can be harmed, even if that work is understood to be undertaken freely. I want to take up what women involved in sex work—some of whom are unknown, some of whom are highly politicized, some of whom write, publish, and lecture—say about the brutality they face.

I remember interviewing a woman at a county jail. She had previously been imprisoned for robbing johns at knifepoint. But on other occasions she'd been beaten by clients. One threw her through the window. She told me that the police had beaten her. Now, it is an open question how she had come to work as a prostitute, whether she thought of it as free choice or as coercion, or whether she had any alternative source of income (cf. Rosen and Venkatesh, 2008). But in this chapter, I want to ask—what counted as violence in her life? Where could she go for support?

The most marginalized of women face forms of violence that exceed the conventional notion of domestic violence. Moreover, they may speak about that violence in different venues, to different people, and they may be heard and perceived differently from women who are battered in the home. Their accounts of violence are marginalized or erased by the mainstream. What then of the communicative sphere in which a woman speaks? Does the space in which she communicates make room for her understanding of violence? Is there a space, or are there spaces in which violence against women can be explored that do not exclude some women but at the same time are not predicated on the view that they face the same violence as women in the home? When confronting structures of oppression that hit some women harder than others, such as women who live outside the law, what are the terms in which a political movement could be grounded that do not erase or exclude, rank or simplify?

Evading or not recognizing the ways in which state and structural violence is implicated directly or indirectly in violence against women allows one to frame violence as "domestic." When violence is framed as "domestic" it becomes harder to see the deeper differences among women, especially social outsiders. Women who work as prostitutes, lesbians, women racialized as nonwhite, immigrant, undocumented, and working-class women are normally excluded from mainstream analyses of violence, especially those that have as the implicit model middle-class, heterosexual marriage. They may never go to court, and if they do, their testimony may not be heard.

What tactics and rhetorical strategies do they use to be recognized? As it turns out, even women who give every indication of their difference sometimes claim identity and commonality with others. I want to consider this claim to sameness and identity across difference as a political question. The solution is to fashion political responses that are expansive enough and nuanced to speak directly to the most socially marginalized women, while also providing a framework that takes stock of why and when women claim the violence they face is the same as that faced by battered women in the home, even when it does not seem to be the same. I do not simply dismiss this claim to "sameness." They may claim sameness for a number of reasons.[2] More generally, focusing on the words of women who work in prostitution also helps challenge what solutions there are, or might be, to the abuse of women.

Yet this assumes that people are willing to listen. The speech of women who work in prostitution lacks credibility for many people. This is particularly true when they testify about the violence they face. It is often difficult for others to perceive violence against prostitutes as something real. Crossing spaces and having the weightiness of one's words, one's credibility, even one's identity change fundamentally is a recurrent theme in the accounts of women who work as prostitutes. Many argue that they frequently have the experience of going from places where they might be raped to places where their words count as nothing and where prostitutes are seen as nothing but criminals and liars. The risks they run in each of those spaces are complex, so they need to maneuver. As we shall see, many women describe this contradiction in which they are caught when they speak as prostitutes.

Women who work in prostitution employ a variety of rhetorical strategies to challenge those contradictions, or in some cases finesse them. I will take up their public speech and the barriers to their speech being public, and specifically the blockages to their speech in the traditional public sphere. I would like to explore in what transformed sense of public would violence against prostitutes be understood, and what understandings would be had. I will examine whether the category of a "counterpublic sphere" is a useful one to think about prostitutes' speech on violence as political intervention. The term "counterpublic" was coined by critics of Habermas' category of a "bourgeois" public sphere. Most theoreticians of the counterpublic see it as a useful communicative sphere for oppressed or excluded groups.[3]

Some versions or accounts of the counterpublic sphere are not helpful because they are predicated on sameness of experience or common experience of oppression. But many women who work as prostitutes point to the significant differences *among* prostitutes as well as the differences between them and battered women who are not prostitutes. These women argue that prostitution has its own hierarchies—streetwalkers are more vulnerable than other prostitutes to attack and to police harassment. A precious few women in sex work have a public platform through which to air their views, but the vast majority do not; this itself suggests a hierarchy. Other important hierarchical differences, such as hierarchies resulting from racism, are also operative and make some lives more perilous than others.

Because of the chilly reception women face when as prostitutes they testify to violence, listening is very much at stake in this chapter. I first locate myself as a "critical listener" to women testifying about violence and describe my motivation and methodology. Then, much of the substance of the chapter is devoted to prostitutes' own accounts of violence against them. Finally, I argue for a version of a counterpublic sphere that can make space for the discrepant understandings and interpretations different women have of the violence against them. Nevertheless, I do not think that even this modified basis is sufficient to take up the range of voices and the tactics women employ since, as I pointed out above, most women in sex work do not necessarily speak within a public sphere about sex work. I end by gesturing towards the enormous and effervescent realm of activity contesting domination (Scott 1985; Lugones 2000) that captures voices not expressed within any version of a counterpublic sphere and indeed highlights the limitations of the conceptual approach of the counterpublic to capturing women's testimony about violence against them.

LOCATION, METHOD, VOICE

Occupying the position of critical listener, I try to pivot the center of my own previous perceptions in order to develop new ones.[4] The effort to put myself in the picture is also intended to mitigate the possibility that this work participates in putting women on display. I have tried to cultivate an ear for the speech of women who work in prostitution, for their understandings of freedom, decision making, and their glosses on the consequences of being perceived as prostitutes. This "ear" is against the grain that men have been groomed for. In positive terms this writing seeks to forge or bolster communicative links. Such writing entails, moreover, breaking with the putative "voice from nowhere" typical in the social sciences, by positioning myself as engaged in a communicative posture of listening.

Methodologically, I have taken published accounts by women involved in sex work as the medium through which I read their words. Most, if not all, of the citations that follow were intended as public or semipublic utterances. I have drawn on published interviews with women who work as prostitutes, political platforms put forward at whores' congresses, speeches, published accounts, and position papers. This selection is not necessarily representative. But it does serve as a point of entry into the possibilities and perils of public testimony to harm.

Most are polemical in the sense that the women are moved to speech in order to articulate a critique, justify a stance, or contribute a critical insight. While they may not fully represent the views of less-known women, the vast majority of sex workers who do not publish their views, they nevertheless lend insight into to sorts of harm to which sex workers are subject. I have also complemented their comments with evidence from sociological studies (Rafael and Shapiro 2004; Farley and Barkan 1998; Farley and Kelly 2000).

As I interpret those voices and words in the following I will strive to give a sense of the context in which each position emerges and through what forms of mediation I encounter their respective texts. Though they have all been written down, most of these utterances have the character of oral speech because many of them were originally interviews or public speeches.

Throughout this exercise, one may fairly ask how and whether my intentions are working in conjunction with theirs. I am not the direct addressee except insofar as I encounter these texts as a reader in a public. In this way I seek to prepare the groundwork so that my own epistemological orientations and rhetorical strategies can be interrogated. My goal is to explore and widen the communicative realms where women can speak and be understood, including women who are otherwise marginalized or actively muted. This is the justification for trying to bring them into dialogue with one another in the context of this chapter.

LISTENING DIFFERENTLY

I want to work at just such a shift of interpretive framework. The shift in interpretive framework is part of the methodology. Part of my own socialization into gender in my childhood and adolescence included ingesting pornography. That is a highly conventional form of socialization for young men, gay and straight, in the United States. The "words" of sex workers in that context were, and are, heard, marked, as erotic utterances. As the communicative sphere was framed, speech was for male arousal. That's what it meant. That was its function (Dworkin 1989; MacKinnon 1987).

I put "words" in quotation marks because I do not presuppose that the pornographic material was in fact the sex workers' own words. Indeed, that (often male) cultural transcript for pornography designs and polices what is erotic, puts words in sex workers' mouths in short stories, novels, captions, videos, and so on. The words come from the pornography industry. At the very least, the institutional location and power of the porn industry from which the utterances emanate cast a doubt on the status of those words and their authorship. This is not to undermine the arguments offered by women writing about the experience of phone sex operators as a powerful experience of control and sexual agency (see Hall 1995). But if men were to understand the words as directly issuing from the imagination of other men, would the turn on need to be understood differently?

I want to decenter the understanding, the framework for interpretation of speech acts as eroticized, fetishized, or commodified, really a solidified presupposition about what speech by sex workers is for, what it is about. Listening to their voices, reading their words, involves not only hearing them differently. I take it as charting an alternative course for my location in a sexual economy. That refusal, that no saying, to (putatively heterosexual) male consumption of sex worker's speech, is a no saying to that way of hearing, reading women's speech. In that spirit of charting a way of seeing, hearing, and acting that stands against violence against women, I work to listen to sex worker's voices.

FRAMING THE VOICES OF PROSTITUTES

Hearing women who work as prostitutes as credible would require framing prostitutes' speech as the speech of active subjects (Lugones 2005) rather than as commodified (Marino 1994). Evelina Giobbe, a former prostitute, puts quite starkly how deeply prostitutes are evacuated of agency and of identity: "To be a prostitute is to be a blank screen upon which men project and act out their sexual dominance. Thus the word 'prostitute' does not imply a 'deeper identity'; it is the absence of an identity: the theft and subsequent abandonment of self. What remains is essential to the 'job': the mouth, the genitals, anus, breasts . . . and the label" (Giobbe 1991, 35). Giobbe opens the space to question of how one can work around and through the absence of an identity. This is consistent with her political position that prostitution is intrinsically exploitative and harmful to women.[5] She points to the contradiction of speaking when one is negated as a speaking subject, when one is treated as surface, as image. But in speaking, she also exemplifies how resistant utterances can build towards new, alternative social forms and meanings.[6]

In other words, in speaking, Giobbe must hold out the possibility that prostitutes' voices could have credibility. Listening, reading her words—Giobbe's work opens up new vistas for communicative exchange. Instead of hearing her words as eroticized (see Hall 1995) and commodified for heterosexual male consumption, Giobbe's words are arresting, challenging. Though describing prostitutes as blank screens for heterosexual male fantasies, her account ought not be taken as merely providing a description. Instead, her words gesture towards a reconstruction of the terms of discursive exchange where she is no longer taken as a blank screen but is rather a full agent of social change. Part of the speech act, part of the work it is doing, is to beckon to others to join her in solidarity. I interpret her as deftly, paradoxically departing from and breaking up that perception that reads or projects prostitutes as blank screens even as she signifies that serving as a blank screen marks the limits of, and stands in place of, an identity.

Many women who work as prostitutes have the perception that the public believes that all prostitutes are liars. The International Committee for Prostitutes' Rights World Charter at the Second World Whores' Congress reflects this belief in the statement. Under "Violations of the Human Rights of Prostitutes," one reads, "Freedom of expression and to hold opinions. The word of prostitutes is generally assumed to be invalid in public, for example as evidence in court. The opinions of prostitutes are rarely given a hearing, even in relation to their own lives. In private, prostitutes are often used as police informants and as counselors to male customers. In public, be it on the street or in court, their testimony and opinion are silenced" (1994, 141).

The activists draw attention to the hypocrisy of the private/public split as it applies to them. Publicly their voice has no authority: their testimony is disbelieved. On the street, they are silenced. In private spaces, they serve as johns' confidantes or as police informers.

This crazy-making, fragmented reality has even darker implications once one considers all the forms of violence they face. Within the spaces that prostitutes occupy, the violence is variously erased or permitted institutionally. As one woman comments in an interview, "I can't tell you the countless times I've heard police say that a prostitute can't be raped. It really upsets me. I think a lot of men believe that. It's totally ridiculous. I've had friends who've gotten hurt. After a while you stop telling the police. Their attitude is, 'Hey, that's part of your job.' Probably a lot of women believe that, too. Though I've had less of that attitude from women than men—the attitude that a prostitute is putting herself out there and that she deserves what she gets, whether it's rape or getting beaten up" (Debra and Carole 1998, 95ff).

Debra's experience has been that many men, and many police, believe that prostitutes cannot be raped. She also has encountered the attitude that being hurt is part of the job of being a prostitute. The belief that sexual intercourse with a prostitute cannot count as rape in turn opens several conceptual possibilities. One is that prostitutes are never forced to have sex. Another possibility is that prostitutes would not allow themselves to be raped. A third possibility, which seems to be the one being entertained by the police here, is that prostitutes, having made themselves sexually accessible in a certain way, have surrendered permanently their right to withhold consent. The possibilities are logically nonexclusive. This would be analogous to the way that certain jurists have argued that married women have enthralled themselves to a condition of permanent sexual accessibility to their husbands, rendering marital rape an oxymoron.[7]

Even as the rape of prostitutes seems difficult for many police to imagine (or they act or pretend that they do not believe it is possible), many police also seem to think that violence against prostitutes is inevitable, and part and parcel of the "job." Another woman echoes this perception: "I've heard them say many times that you couldn't rape a prostitute. Once my girlfriends were attacked by some guys. They were in Berkeley and called the police. The police just said, 'That's the price you pay, it comes with the trade . . . so why bitch and scream, you're a prostitute.' Which is totally ridiculous" (Barbara and Carole 1998, 171).

The police response, "That's the price you pay, it comes with the trade," has an inner tension. "That's the price you pay" implies that rape is the consequence of prostitution. "It comes with the trade" suggests that violence is one of the conditions of the work, much as a sore back or a calloused hand comes with handling a shovel. Both women understand the responses as revealing a set of perceptions of them and the conditions of their lives that is worlds away from their own perceptions. Nevertheless, they understand those other sets of perceptions (Lugones 2005). At the same time, their alternative perceptions are not easily communicated. The first woman comments, "After a while you stop telling the police." The intersection of contradictory logics—one that defines prostitutes as incapable of being raped, and another that finds that logic ridiculous—makes communication difficult.

The difficulty is not a question of mere miscommunication. These discrepant perceptions stand in a position of power to one another. The police's perceptions are institutionally backed and eclipse other sets of perceptions, in this case the prostitutes'. Taking stock of the subordinate's perceptions requires taking stock of the dominant set of perceptions, since the latter are usually so prominent in the conceptual horizon of subordinate people—the subordinate, as many have remarked, needs to know the dominator, how he thinks. For women who work as prostitutes, even if they find the dominant perception of the connections among violence, space, rape, and their identity to be ridiculous, they have to know that perception, they have to live with it.

Tracy Quan, in speaking of differences in the forms of violence to which prostitutes are at risk, also writes of the difficulties of being heard as she intends. Yet the meanings she intends are quite different from those of Barbara or Debra:

> The darker side of sex is something I accept but try to protect myself against. Rape is always a danger. What prostitute in her right mind believes it can ever be totally eradicated? There are just too many guys who would like to get it for free—and some will go to lengths, brutal lengths. This is obvious to a woman who puts a price on sex. But this is not a desk job devoid of physical risks. The dangers of prostitution— that a hooker might meet up with a murderous kook, that a condom might break and she could contract a disease—are often presented as reasons to get out of prostitution. But a woman who becomes a fire fighter is applauded for taking "non-traditional" risks with her life. She is expected to wear all the right gear and advance into fire. I acknowledge risks and take steps to minimize them, but life is never risk-free. Being brave enough to understand this is integral to self-protection. There is nothing darker than ignorance, or a false sense of security. (1991, 35)

Quan is a former representative of the organization PONY (Prostitutes of New York) that promotes the decriminalization of prostitution. She pointedly distinguishes her job and her identity from those of other women. "This" she says, "is not a desk job devoid of physical risks." The danger is ever-present. Quan concedes the risks of contracting AIDS, of being raped, battered, tortured, or even killed. Nevertheless, she gives a different understanding of what the risks mean from that of Giobbe. Giobbe sees prostitution as a system that terrorizes women as it is structured to oppress them:

> There are thousands of books and classes that provide women with information on self-defense or rape "avoidance" strategies. Some of the basic lessons they teach us are not to walk alone at night on dark deserted streets, not to get into cars with strange men, not to pick up guys in a bar, not to let even the delivery man into your home when you're by yourself. Yet this is what the "job" of prostitution requires; that women put themselves in jeopardy every time they turn a trick. And then we ask "How do you prevent it from leading to danger?" The answer is, you can't. Count the bodies. (Giobbe 1991, 34)

One of the significant debates among women who work as prostitutes is what counts as rape: whether prostitutes can have sex without being raped. Giobbe sees rape as intrinsic to what happens to prostitutes, as an inevitability given what prostitution requires. On the one hand, based on her interviews with women in prostitution, Kathleen Barry suggests that many women in prostitution consider it rape when johns refuse to pay for the sex (1996). The different strands of the argument are important for a deep and textured understanding of what counts as rape.

Quan, on the other hand, describes the work in terms of presenting a challenge to her character and to her courage. Entering those private spaces where there could be a kook is like "advanc[ing] into a fire." She puts herself in situations of risk but tries to prepare for them, knowing that she is subjecting herself to danger. She continues, "When I first started hooking, I didn't know that sex could bring danger with it. One of my first clients asked if he could tie me up, and I readily agreed because I had no understanding of his fantasy's deeper implications. As soon as I was unable to move, I got scared because I didn't know this man at all—and my stupidity became very clear. Although he didn't threaten my life or hurt me, I found the experience terrifying enough not to let it happen again" (1991, 35).

Quan realized that what had begun as play-acting a state of lawlessness could turn into real lawlessness, where he could beat her, take her money, rape her, torture her. Quan glosses the danger as something that can be known, minimized, prepared for, not allowed to happen (cf. Agustín 2007, 32–33). However, Giobbe sees the dangers as something one is forced to endure. The two descriptions of prostitutes are paradigmatically different. One equips oneself to cross-spaces like a firefighter entering a fire. The other survives those spaces the way one survives a concentration camp, prison, or rape.

Both fundamentally contradict the interpretation of prostitution supplied by liberalism (Pateman 1988; Sanchez 1997a, 1997b). In fact, the situations they feel themselves in when they are with johns more closely approximate the state of war of all against all. Quan tacitly supports this construction of the "prostitute" as thrown out of the protections of civil society when she bemoans the vicious perceptions people have and the mendacious and dangerous assumptions that prosecutors hold that are based on an erasure of violence against prostitutes: "Supporters of the young men accused of raping the Central Park jogger accused her of being a prostitute—as though the rape of a prostitute, or an ordeal that left a prostitute nearly dead, should be of less concern to our legal system than any other violent crime. Prostitutes often find this to be the case, of course, since many prosecutors assume that all prostitutes are liars" (Quan 1991, 29).

If the public speech of the prostitute is assumed to be untrustworthy, then to speak in public as a prostitute is to have one's words count as nothing. To have one's speech regarded in this way could only be a violence that also props up other psychic or physical violence one experiences as a prostitute. Others go further. One woman sees the state as deeply implicated in prostitution: "I believe that the state pimps women, for example, when they fine them and criminalize them when they are prostituted. This is pimping . . . You could invent a new terminology for it: secondary pimping, vicarious pimping, whatever—but it's still pimping, plain and simple" (http://www.friends-partners.org/lists/stop-traffic/1998/0187.html; last accessed 2010).

Some organizations of sex workers or prostitutes take a different position on the state and seek amelioration through legal redress. In their charter statement, the International Committee for Prostitutes' Rights (ICPR) demands legal recognition and relief from rape and other forms of sexual harassment:

> Within the context of prostitution, women are sometimes raped or sexually harassed by the police, by their clients, by their managers, and by strangers who know them to be whores. Prostitute women, like non-prostitute women, consider rape to be any sexual act forced upon them. The fact that prostitutes are available for sexual negotiation does not mean that they are available for sexual harassment or rape. The ICPR demands that the prostitute be given the same protection from rape and the same legal recourse and social support following rape that should be the right of any woman or man . . . Battering of prostitutes, like battering of non-prostitutes, reflects the subordination of women to men in personal relationships. Laws against such violence are often discriminately and/or arbitrarily enforced. The ICPR affirms the right of all women to relational choice and to recourse against violence within any personal or work setting. (ICPR 1994:137)[8]

The members of the ICPR think that prostitutes should be treated the same as other women and men should be. They point out a paradox about their public speech and then act within the paradox: As I cited them above, they observe that their public speech is not taken as credible. But here they affirm their legal rights and demand legal protections. Yet as they themselves observe, their position is one in which their words are assumed to be invalid. Are they involved in a performative contradiction?

The strategy the ICPR employs has important implications for a political theory concerned with forging a space where women can testify to violence. Oskar Negt and Alexander Kluge are two theorists concerned with developing public space where the proletariat can articulate experience and voice positions. According to them, the proletariat runs into difficulty if he or she tries to use the public sphere as his or her venue. Though the logic of their argument is different, they echo the ICPR's worry that public speech is perilous for oppressed peoples (here the proletariat instead of the prostitute):

> *The public sphere . . . lies, without a doubt, far outside the proletarian context of living . . .* It is possible for the worker to have new individual experiences here; however, none of the barriers of his [sic] libidinal structure, of language, of socially recognized modes of intercourse are

torn down. He has increasingly distanced himself from the production process, yet neither alone nor with the aid of the organization at his disposal is he able to set in motion to a sufficient degree new production processes, whose object is, for instance, the production of social relationships among people. What is more, after a while he comes to the conclusion that he is dragging around inside himself the proletarian context of living, with which both his experiences and the blocking of this experience are bound. Thus prepared, he encounters a universal fact of the labor movement experience: as soon as the worker participates in the bourgeois public sphere, once he has won elections, taken up union initiatives, he is confronted by a dilemma. He can make only "private" use of a public sphere that has disintegrated into a mere intermediary sphere. *The public sphere operates according to this rule of private use, not according to the rules whereby the experiences and class interests of workers are organized. The interests of workers appear in the bourgeois public sphere as nothing more than a gigantic, cumulative "private interest" not as a collective mode of production for qualitatively new forms of public sphere and public consciousness. To the extent that the interests of the working class are no longer formulated and represented as genuine and autonomous interests vis-à-vis the bourgeois public sphere, betrayal by individual representatives of the labor movement ceases to be an individual problem. It is not a question of an individual's strength of character. In wanting to use the mechanisms of the bourgeois public sphere for their cause, such representatives become, objectively, traitors to the cause they are representing.* (1993 [1972]: 7; emphasis added)

Negt and Kluge argue that the class-bound nature of the public sphere entails disloyalty to the proletariat's own set of experiences or projects, because his or her whole context of living is bracketed as a set of private concerns. Even when the proletariat wins access to the public sphere, he or she still loses. For Fredric Jameson, the originality of Negt and Kluge resides in their analysis of the alienation of "experience" within public speech: "The structure of the 'public sphere' is now seen as what enables experience, or on the other hand limits and cripples it; this structure also determines that fundamental modern pathology whereby 'experience' is itself sundered, its uneven torn halves assigned to stereotypical public expressions on the one hand, and on the other to that zone of the personal and the private" (Jameson 1993).

Different subaltern groups, including women who work as prostitutes and the proletariat, register a self-conscious ambivalence towards the public sphere given its limitations as an avenue for authentic, unalienated speech. The ambivalence is heightened by the knowledge that such speech is rarely given an adequate hearing. For if putting one's experience into words is difficult, a person's speech nevertheless means little if enunciated in spaces where it is marked as illegitimate, unreliable, or self-serving, or where its content is overdetermined as meaningless, concocted, or expressing only private interest. In the case of women who work as prostitutes, ICPR suggests their public speech is marked as a consequence of who they are as speakers. Debi Sundahl, a stripper and founder of the lesbian erotica magazine *On Our Backs* expresses frustration with being ostracized because of her practices. She links education and the ability to communicate as key preconditions for recognition and consideration of sex workers' voices and identities:

> I for one am tired of being the moral guardian of male sexuality and of suffering ostracism and condemnation if I choose to be sexually active or sexually autonomous. Sex education and the ability to communicate about all aspects of sex is essential to fostering social respect for sex workers as well as respect for personal sexual choice and expression. Like many oppressed minorities, we have suffered under the assumption that we must be protected from ourselves. The quasi-illegal and illegal nature of our work robs us of the power to define and control the conditions under which we are employed. We know better than anyone what is healthy and what is not healthy about our work. (Sundahl 1994, 120)

Sundahl writes that the legal conditions under which sex workers operate rob them of the power of self-determination and definition of the conditions of work. Given the difficulties she faces in being heard, part of the challenge for her project to define and control the conditions under which she and others work is *to prepare the communicative situation*. This brings us back to the concern raised by Negt and Kluge. The public sphere is not amenable to the context of living of sex workers, hence voicing in that sphere promotes self-betrayal. Though as several women point out above, the contradictions of public speech for prostitutes are complicated not only by the disjunction between their context of living and the requirements of public speech, but also by their identity.

Nonetheless, if we listen for it, Sundahl provides an account of the contexts that frame her identity that forces a rupture with any simplistic or unitary meanings associated with sex work. She gives a much different version of what spaces are safe or objectionable from that of other women I have cited—of which spaces permit certain perceptions of her that she would object to in other circumstances. Studying how she discerns and differentiates these different spaces prevents abstraction by giving a concrete description of violence faced by women:

> The hardest part of the job was dealing with my feminist principles concerning the objectification of women. Dancing nude is the epitome of woman as sex object. As the weeks passed, I found I liked being a sex object, because the context was appropriate. I resent being treated as a sex object on the street or at the office. But as an erotic dancer, that is my purpose. I perform to turn you on, and if I fail, I feel I've done a poor

job. Women who work in the sex industry are not responsible for, nor do they in anyway perpetuate, the sexual oppression of women. In fact, to any enlightened observer, our very existence provides a distinction and a choice as to when a woman should be treated like a sex object and when she should not be. At the theater, yes; on the street, no. (Sundahl 1994, 118)

Sundahl likes being treated as a sexual object in adult theaters; indeed, she implies that in (sex) theaters, women *should* be treated as sex objects. In a way strangely consonant with liberal beliefs, she sees sex workers as providing the paradigmatic example of choice, since (as I interpret her) they choose in what context they want to be, and therefore whether they want to be treated as a sexual object. Both Quan and Sundahl challenge the idea of an immutable identity independent of context. According to them, not only their identity, but also their sense of boundaries, how they want to be perceived, and their choices shift in different situations.

It ought to be pointed out that in terms of danger and oppression, Quan and Sundahl, having acknowledged the dangers, are at a disadvantage in arguing that they prepare for them or that they otherwise choose to put themselves in those situations. For even if they have not been violently assaulted, raped, or killed, they remain vulnerable to that kind of attack. Given their mitigated positions as sex workers, they themselves remark that they are in little position to do anything about it. They both insist on one issue: prostitutes possess agency. They can perform well or poorly, they can take safety precautions or not; both take their job as something in which they can take pride.

Giobbe dissents. In giving multiple examples of the systematic misinterpretation given to her identity, she countermands the notion that working as a prostitute is something in which a woman has control. For Giobbe, their status *exemplifies* a form of oppression. But Giobbe does not hold them responsible for it. She puts forward her position to underscore the necessity of including prostitutes in the battered women's movement. In a written account taken down apparently from a speech, she testifies:

I'm a survivor of prostitution. Three years ago that term didn't exist. Women who'd been abused like I'd been abused for eleven years of my life were called whores. Women who were abused like I'd been abused were called sex industry workers. Women like myself who escaped prostitution now have named ourselves as survivors. Between the ages of 13, 14, 15, 16, when adult men paid for the right to rape me while I cried, when the family court system finally caught up with me, I wasn't labeled as a survivor and offered support. I was labeled as a delinquent and I was put in jail, while the men who paid for the right to rape this child were free to roam the streets and pay for the right to rape other children when they weren't availing themselves of their own children in their homes. After I was locked up for my own protection in what I like to call "kid hell"—that was the House of Detention in New York for juveniles—I was raped again by staff members.

When I ran away from there for my own safety and ended up back in the streets and in prostitution and turned 18 years old, I was still not called a survivor. Now I was told that I was a career woman, embarked on a glamorous career. What I'd like to say here today is that women who are in prostitution, myself and my sisters with me in WHISPER [Women Hurt In Systems of Prostitution Engaged in Revolt], have been subjected to the same abuse that every battered woman has spoken about in this room, except men paid for the right to do it. It's not a job. We're abused, and we need help in the movement. (Giobbe, quoted in Massachusetts Coalition of Battered Women Service Groups, Inc. 1992, 70)

Giobbe is providing important testimony on the abuse faced by women who work in prostitution. She is also commenting with bitter irony on the abusive character of the institutions that were supposed to help her, provide shelter, protect her (but see note 5). She describes how women like herself are treated in each of those spaces. Each institution, each space, had a different construction of her; meanings were attached to her that had concrete implications for her identity. But she is also—and this must be emphasized—enlisting support of activists to stop violence against women who are marginal in the society, women particularly vulnerable in many ways to abuse, including institutional abuse. In the context in which she is speaking—a space where battered women were naming the violence against them—she claims a space as a battered woman, a survivor of prostitution, someone who needs help in the movement. And in that context, she makes an important transition, making a case for inclusion in a movement against violence composed largely of nonprostitutes.

The fact that she was abused by men who paid would seem to make the violence itself different. What would otherwise appear to be the same thing means different things depending on whether your batterer is your husband and rapes you in your bedroom, or the person is a stranger who has paid your pimp and rapes you in a car—or in the back of a police station. She gives evidence that the resources available, the accounts you can give of the violence, as well as the meanings of the acts themselves, the places where people will validate your account, and the identity of those people are different in each case. Even the misogynist rationales that deny the name of "rape" in each case are subtly different. On the one hand, a prostitute who claims a police officer raped her lacks credibility since she is seen as an unreliable witness, regardless of the validity of her claim. On the other hand, a wife might be denied claim to being raped by her husband because of the law; even when it is legally possible to prosecute a husband for raping his wife, it has been socially and legally difficult to get credence (cf. Benedict 1992; Russell 1990).

So, why is it that Giobbe, even after giving every evidence of the particularities of her own history, nevertheless refers to her experiences as fundamentally the same as those of other battered women? Is it the self-betrayal that Negt and Kluge argue is entailed when subaltern people speak in the public sphere? This question is a painful and complicated one, and I pose it with care. The pain that forms the background to the question has a lot to do with the sometimes delicate ways we constitute our identity with respect to other people. But it seems important to weigh the political consequences of this strategy of identifying with others.

This line of thinking engenders in turn a host of other questions: how expansive or restricted one's identity is, what motivates a person to identify with or claim common cause with another, in what contexts one does. But it also leads us to ask when does one fail to identify with another, and why, and when does one deny commonality or common identity, or even betray an identity one would otherwise claim? And then more fundamentally—who you are when you identify with someone unlike yourself, what it means to "identify" anyway, what is the cognitive operation, and what are the implications for the continuity or discontinuity of one's own sense of self and one's group identity, and for solidarity (Crimp 1993)? Sometimes, for example, identification can be the source of insight, and other times responsible for self-erasure.

Let me pose a set of questions that takes this conundrum in the direction of its resolution:

> Who are you when you speak in public?
> Are you evading your own particularity?
> What identity are you claiming when you claim an identity with other battered women?
> Are there contexts where you can be understood without simplifying your experience? Are there frameworks for communication and political decision making that we should look to?
> Is the concept of a "counterpublic" a useful and helpful one in clarifying the communicative possibilities?

Michael Warner's description of public subjectivity is instructive and follows from Negt and Kluge: "As the subjects of publicity its "hearers," "speakers," "viewers," and "doers" we have a different relation to ourselves, a different affect, from that which we have in other contexts. No matter what the particularities of culture, race, gender, or class we bring to bear on public discourse, the moment of apprehending something as public is one in which we imagine if imperfectly indifference to those particularities, to ourselves" (1993, 234). Warner insists that in speaking as a subject in public, we adopt an attitude of indifference to our own particularity. We speak as abstract subjects. In his account, that is a condition for the possibility of voicing in the public sphere. Speaking as a public subject means bracketing our particularities of race, culture, and gender, as private interests.

Do women in prostitution, then, face a cruel either/or: to speak as a prostitute and experience the icy frost of having one's identity overdetermine one's speech as false, or to speak as another, and to engage in a rhetoric of disincorporation?

Tracy Quan also addresses forthrightly the antinomies of her identity, recognizing the contradictions of public speech even as she valorizes her identity: "I am in favor of decriminalization, yet enjoy the mystique that surrounds outlaw status. I may turn up my nose at women too prissy to turn tricks—but I myself am too chicken to work the streets. I am angry with feminist prostitutes who have come out against the profession itself, but I am not completely 'out' as a Prostitute. Decriminalization has been my pet issue, but illegality helped to form the identity I'm so proud of" (Quan 1991, 35).

She points to the tie between identity and context, the complex way in which her identity has been formed by working illegally. She embraces the ambiguities, the self-conscious contradictions, and the ironies she takes as central not only to her politics but also, one senses, qualities she thinks are intrinsic to her character. She positions herself haughtily vis-à-vis women who are not prostitutes, yet her own sense of boundaries makes her fearful of the streets. She writes articles like the one from which I have just quoted, yet she does not identify publicly as a prostitute. In this last sense, then, she perhaps does not so much confirm or erase her identity as much as evade the issue by not identifying publicly as a prostitute. However, her speech act, "I am not completely 'out' as a Prostitute" gestures towards being a performative contradiction, except insofar as she is referring to other contexts, besides the public nature of coming out in print media, which is certainly a public sphere (cf. Warner 1990; 2005). She is also being ironic, in playing with the obvious contradiction.

On the face of it, Quan stands in contrast to Giobbe in claiming her outlaw status. But she, too, finds herself in a contradictory position, where discourse and identity are in tension. WHISPER, ICPR, PONY—the different voices and different positions—give fabric to the question of difference, difference not only among women, but also among women who work as prostitutes. Each position addresses itself to a different agenda, a different set of values, and a different problematic. Each has a different understanding of the agency it confers upon prostitutes (or finds lacking in prostitution). Each takes stock of the context of violence in which prostitutes operate, but the institutions, mechanisms, and groups from which they hope to wrest support are different. Some address themselves to the movement against violence against women, others to legal advocates and reformers or to public opinion at large.

TWO ACCOUNTS OF "THE COUNTERPUBLIC"

In order to consider whether it provides a viable framework, we first need to designate the communicative contours of "counterpublic." Two versions of counterpublic are already emerging in the discourse of women who work as prostitutes. One fixes a sphere or zone for oppressed people or groups in which they forge solidarity through commonality, whether through common experience of oppression, through identity claims, or through common interest. Giobbe seems to take part in this account of the counterpublic sphere when she makes a claim based on sameness. A second version of the counterpublic would not be predicated on sameness, but rather finds its possibility housed at the liminal moments of insight born of inner tensions, struggle, multiple consciousness, and an openness to new identities founded in discourse and out of incipient forms of solidarity, often marked by irony. I see this latter version present in the discourse of Tracy Quan and in the language and positions taken by the ICPR.

Version I: Counterpublics and Commonality

Rita Felski, in her book *Beyond Feminist Aesthetics*, designated a counterpublic sphere that will be a feminist domain in contrast to the masculinist public sphere of Habermas:

> The women's movement has offered one of the most dynamic examples of a counter-ideology in recent years to have generated an oppositional public arena for the articulation of women's needs in critical opposition to the values of a male-defined society. Like the original bourgeois public sphere, the feminist public sphere constitutes a discursive space which defines itself in terms of a common identity; here it is the shared experience of gender-based oppression which provides the mediating factor intended to unite all participants beyond their specific differences . . . [I]t constitutes a partial or counterpublic sphere; as in the case of other oppositional communities defined in terms of racial or ethnic identity or sexual preference, the experience of discrimination, oppression, and cultural dislocation provides the impetus for the development of a self-consciously oppositional identity. Yet insofar as it is a public sphere, its arguments are also directed outward, toward a dissemination of feminist ideas and values throughout society as a whole. (1989, 165)

Felski is quite explicit in her premises for the counterpublic sphere:

1. It is defined in terms of a common identity.

   1a. In this case, the common identity rests on a shared experience; specifically of:

   1b. Gender based oppression.

2. The arguments generated within this sphere are directed towards the greater society.

Her account of a counterpublic seems to capture the discursive strategy of Giobbe's plea for inclusion with other battered women in the fight against violence against women. I refer to Giobbe saying that prostitutes are subjected to "the same" forms of violence as other battered women. As Felski describes it, the stipulation of a shared experience is a necessary component of a counterpublic. As Felski writes, "Some form of appeal to collective identity and solidarity is a necessary precondition for the emergence and effectiveness of an oppositional movement" (1989, 168). The consequences of this stipulation are important. The aim of political movement, the strategy of its rhetoric, the style of its activism, the assumptions made about the participants in the struggle, what connects them and the importance of the differences among them are all significantly affected when one makes the assumption of (or otherwise insists upon) commonality of a movement's members and their experiences. Differences can be suppressed; people who fall outside of the domain are at risk of having their experiences distorted or excluded. Felski seeks to house difference within a feminist counterpublic when she promises that she does not understand it as a unified interpretive community governed by a single set of norms and values. She wants to account for the plurality of feminist practices as shaped by the conflicting interests of its members (1989, 10–11; also see Young 1990). This account of a feminist counterpublic is consistent with how she thinks all counterpublics differ from Habermas' canonical account of a bourgeois public sphere. She writes of counterpublics that

> their emancipatory project no longer appeals to an idea of universality but is directed toward an affirmation of specificity in relation to gender, race, ethnicity, age, sexual preference, and so on. They seek to define themselves *against* the homogenizing and universalizing logic of the global megaculture of modern mass communication as a debased pseudopublic sphere, and to voice needs and articulate oppositional values which the "culture industry" fails to address. These new sites of oppositionality are multiple and heterogeneous and do not converge to form a single revolutionary movement. (Felski 1989, 166 emphasis in the original)

Nevertheless, Felski herself clearly thinks a necessary starting point is a commitment to commonality and representative experiences of women as the ideal of a counterpublic, even as she contradictorily acknowledges the utopian and repressive dimensions of such a thought. She remarks that this can be constricting, since this step is often attained by a suspension of other forms of difference, "an erasure felt most painfully by those whose unequal status and particular needs are suppressed by the fiction of a unifying identity" (168). Yet she lays down the gauntlet: "[F]eminist theorists who reject any notion of a unifying identity as a repressive fiction in favor of a stress on absolute difference fail to show how such diversity and fragmentation can be reconciled with goal-oriented struggles based upon common interests (169).

Version II: Counterpublics and Contradiction

Is difference always "absolute difference"? Is stressing commonality the only alternative to marking difference? Commonality is not a necessary ground for a counterpublic. Difference need not be irreconcilable or absolute. A counterpublic ought to make room for multiple voicings, even multiple projects within a communicative sphere. What I would like to venture is that a counterpublic that fully countenances difference and that constitutes itself in terms of that recognition is not only possible but preferable to one based upon commonality. Rather than being predicated within a utopian commitment, counterpublics, which do after all actually exist, need to be pliant enough to both countenance the enormous differences among participants and offer a space to theorize subtleties of difference, even while claiming solidarity across those differences.

The actual discursive practices of women in prostitution enact this kind of counterpublic. Many testify to differences in experience, especially between women who work as prostitutes and those who do not. But they also point out the significant differences among different prostitutes and how consequential those differences are. Nell, an African American woman who works as a prostitute, testifies both to the tie between space and identity and to how that tie is given different readings:

> I think there are class-divisions in prostitution. It breaks down around race, but also class background. I am in an elite position because some friends who had worked for years on the street built up a different kind of clientele, businessmen. When they stopped working, they passed their clientele on to me. That's the only reason I got into this position. When I thought about hooking before, I always thought I'd go to go-go places, massage parlors, and street walking. I thought those were the avenues open to me. I identify more with women on the streets, because we share the same background.
>
> When people talk about hookers and whores, they don't mind the women who are on call, you know, the women who have clientele, it's the women on the street they nab on. They're the ones who get so much shit. When they attack them, they're attacking me. I grew up in projects, and when people start talking about black people and women on the streets, it gets into a whole lot of racism, and sexism, and shit they don't

understand. It makes me angry. That's why I defend all whores and all women on the streets. (Nell and Alexander 1998, 53)

Nell draws attention to location. Some hookers and whores are on the street. They are in massage parlors. Elite women with a clientele are not found in those spaces. Within the spatial distinction is an encoded class and racial distinction. The elites have a "different kind of clientele, business men," from streetwalkers.

The distinctions that Nell draws, however, are not uncontested (see, e.g., Rafael and Shapiro 2004). Evelina Giobbe comments: "My experience in prostitution gives the lie to . . . common beliefs about the hierarchy of prostitution, the streets being the worst-case scenario and call service being the best. As for my well-heeled clientele and their fancy hotel suites, all I can say is, whether you turn tricks in a car by the Holland tunnel or in the Plaza Hotel, you still have to take off your clothes, get on your knees or lie on your back, and let this stranger use you in any way he pleases. Then you have to get up, get dressed, and do it again with the next trick, and the next" (Giobbe 1991, 32).

For Nell, in contrast, the differences between whores and hookers on the street and those on call is not merely a question of semantics or a false distinction; the form of life is different, the women are different, the space is different, and the danger is greater as women on the street are singled out, relatively speaking, for attack.[9]

Despite the distance, physical as well as conceptual, Nell claims solidarity across this space while affirming difference and acknowledging the power at play in hierarchies among prostitutes. Exploring this claim of identity with another and what it means in terms of one's own identity, as well as what "solidarity" means, on whose terms, and with what depth it is held are central concerns for working towards solutions against violence against women (see also Crimp 1993).

Yet a call for solidarity that levels one's particularity in favor of a subject that is common to all is, as Warner alerts us, a call to participate in a rhetoric of abstraction (what Warner calls "disincorporation"). This is not to say that calls for solidarity are tantamount to self-betrayal, since solidarity does not necessitate the category of the "public" or public voicing.

So, then, if a speaker denies the differences, as Giobbe seems to, is that speaker engaging in public self-betrayal?

COUNTERPUBLICS AND MULTIPLE CONSCIOUSNESSES AS DISCURSIVE METHOD

Judging Giobbe as engaging in self-betrayal may be overhasty. Though she does identify herself as the same as other battered women and minimizes the importance of differences among prostitutes, it would bespeak wooden theorizing if we did not look deeper for the method in Giobbe's self-positioning. What we need is a more flexible theory of discourse so that we can attend to the rhetorical positions taken by different women who work as prostitutes, including Giobbe, the ICPR, and Quan. The legal theorist Mari Matsuda has adroitly theorized the multiple consciousnesses of women of color and other outsiders to the law and recommended that multiple consciousnesses be viewed as a valuable jurisprudential method (Matsuda 1989). According to her account, what would otherwise seem inconsistent positions taken or voiced by outsiders in fact make perfect sense; indeed, they are characteristic of a valuable jurisprudence. She takes as one example Angela Davis's denouncing the authority of the law courts during her trial in the 1970s even as she made her case to the jury within it:

> There are times to stand outside the courtroom door and say "this procedure is a farce, the legal system is corrupt, justice will never prevail in this land as long as privilege rules in the courtroom." There are times to stand inside the courtroom and say "this is a nation of laws, laws recognizing fundamental values of rights, equality and personhood." Sometimes, as Angela Davis did, there is a need to make both speeches in one day. Is that crazy? Inconsistent? Not to Professor Davis, a Black woman on trial for her life in racist America. It made perfect sense to her, and to the twelve jurors good and true who heard her when she said, your government lies, but *your* law is above such lies. (Matsuda 1989, 8)

Matsuda sees the coherence in practices that may otherwise seem to be contradictory. Cynthia Young has pointed out a similar phenomenon in the discourse of the Black Panthers, who would liken themselves to the Founding Fathers in public speech and then position themselves as quite opposed to the Founding Fathers in other contexts (oral communication).

Correspondingly, Giobbe's bid for inclusion based on sameness or the ICPR's ambivalent attitude towards the law may be interpreted as exemplifying the multiple consciousness they possess. It makes sense, in other words, that the ICPR would declaim publicly its inability to be heard publicly. The contradiction may be part of its situation. Its words may moreover be a rhetorical gesture, a necessary provocation, a conscientious weighing of the discursive options and making an intervention at the risk that they will be misinterpreted or discounted. It may be speaking against silence. According to Matsuda, multiple voicing resulting from multiple consciousness may be not only judicious, but also a necessary survival mechanism. "Professor Davis's decision to use a dualist approach to a repressive legal system may very well have saved her life. Not only did she tap her history and consciousness as a Black, a woman, and a communist, she did so with intent and awareness. Her multiple consciousnesses were not a mystery to her, but a well-defined and acknowledged tool of analysis, one that she was able to share with the jury" (1989, 9).

Taking account of multiple consciousnesses as grounding a sophisticated rhetoric of public speech does not mean we approach such speech or public performance of identity uncritically. People do engage in strategies that can have bad consequences. Giobbe's claim to identity with other battered women has had an influence on the movement to end violence against all women. But her bid for inclusion buttresses homogeneity in the movement. It also contradicts the accounts of other women in prostitution who frame the issues differently.

With attention to the tonalities, shows of resistance, context, and often painful exigencies and contradictions under which oppressed people must organize, we can develop an interpretive framework supple enough to access the communicative complexity involved. A theory of a counterpublic that would be adequate, furthermore, must make ample room and must provide a space critical of normative standards of credibility, acceptability, validity, and logic. Without that, the counterpublic would seem to me either to condemn or to exclude some voices, while interpreting others within canonical understandings of what it means to be and to live as a battered woman.

WITNESS TO COUNTERPUBLICS—WITH A CAVEAT

The voices of women in sex work give an abundance of detail that belies attempts to simplify. The framing of the voices in a way that reveals the differences among them is an antidote to the tendency to see all violence against women as the same and as domestic. It also contradicts the tendency to see sex work as a monolith. I advocate an emphasis on differences rather than diversity because of the way Homi Bhaba, in a different context, distinguishes between cultural difference and cultural diversity. Though the differences we take up here do not seem to be particularly cultural, I do find his way of drawing distinctions quite helpful as we build a politics. As Homi Bhabha glosses it: "Cultural diversity is the recognition of pre-given cultural contents and customs; held in a time frame of relativism it gives rise to liberal notions of multiculturalism, cultural exchange or the culture of humanity" (Bhabha 1994, 34–35).

Difference implies instead a "negation of the certitude in the articulation of new cultural demands, meanings, strategies in the political present" (Bhabha 1994, 34–35). Incorporating voices of women who have faced violence counteracts the tendency to reduce prostitutes or lesbians each to a pregiven common type and focuses instead on the multiple voicings of location and direction and the modalities of self-identification. The voices I have included give ample testimony to the multiplicity of positions, politics, and spatial trajectories, places of fear, and places of safety.

Can one call a "counterpublic" the discursive arena in which women working as prostitutes voice their accounts of violence? I think one can, as long as one acknowledges the contradictory logics that overdetermine prostitutes' public speech as false; as long as one takes stock of the fact that many listeners are likely to begin by assuming that prostitutes cannot be raped, that violence comes with the territory, or that it is deserved. With that discursive context in mind, one can see and appreciate the innovative strategies that activists employ in order to register their voices. Bruce Robbins has even gone so far as to propose that "the public sphere" could replace "culture" as an important category for social analysis: "It serves as a critique of monolithic notions of power . . . Unlike 'hegemony,' the public sphere is less on the side of rule, more open to opposing views. Unlike 'culture' it is more obviously a site of intersections with other classes and cultures . . . [I]t is to stress a site of interaction and continuing self-formation rather than a given or self-sufficient body of ideas and practices distinguishing one from others" (Robbins 1993, xvii).

The benefit of the "counterpublic" is that it designates a discursive scene in which women who work in prostitution can try to make sense of their situations, communicate their interpretations of their situations, and forge solutions to the multiple forms of violence they face.

How do we account for voices that operate outside of counterpublics and the significance of those alternative contexts in the formation of rich, complex identities? María Lugones (2000) points out that sense making, meaning making in liminal spaces, private spaces, in the doorways and side streets needs also hold our attention. Because they do not follow the same rules, these spaces offer possibilities resources for communication and action excluded by the logic of counterpublics. Alternative spaces may follow logics incommensurate with the logic of the public, but that does not make capacities or potential any less rich. From the standpoint of the public, however, these spaces appear only as absence, as remainder.

Counterpublic spheres are significant, but they are obviously not the only sites for the formation of identity and of politics. Oppressed subjects do not achieve self-realization and autonomy merely or entirely through a process of public recognition of their subjectivities (Lugones 2000). In positive terms, they communicate and achieve politically significant autonomy through a range of activities in discursive realms and alternative spaces outside of the public.

I would suggest, in conclusion, that the concept of counterpublics is useful, as long as one takes full stock of the significance of the realm of women's discursive activity beyond it, as a necessary and inevitable counterpoint to the counterpublic, and as an antidote to reading communication within it naively as transparent to meaning, position, identity, and intention. This chapter has focused on the means of hearing and listening to those voices in all their multiplicity.

CHAPTER FOUR

Homophobia, Structural Violence, and Coalition Building

In this chapter, I argue that one of the problems with seeing violence against women as "domestic violence" is its implicitly heterosexual frame of reference. Such a frame obscures institutionalized homophobia. I focus on how to view violence against women while calling that domestic heteronormative frame into question (Knauer 1999, 333). This will require not only attention to institutionalized homophobia (Knauer 1999; Robson 1990; Jablow 2000), but also how institutionalized homophobia affects white women and women of color differently (Richie 2005; Garcia 1999). It will also provide for a framework in which to question heterosexual assumptions at the core of much discourse on violence against women (Eaton 1994).

I am particularly interested in how to form coalitions among women, given the differences in experiences of violence and in the communities they come from. To illustrate some of the difficulties, I take up one case of a woman who brings her lover up on charges of abuse.

Lesbians who have been subjected to violence are in an awkward position with respect to the law (Knauer 1999; Robson 1992; Jablow 2000). They are often rendered nonexistent within the law as well as in other parts of social life (cf. Hoagland 1988; Frye 1983). As of this writing, the legal right of lesbians to marry, or even to form a legally recognized domestic partnership, remains contested in the United States; lacking a marriage contract, lesbians who are battered by lesbians similarly fit uncomfortably within the standard understanding of battering as occurring within the home.[1]

This chapter has two parts. In the first part, I analyze the complicated rhetorical strategy a white lesbian employs in court and in her written account. This strategy catches her in a contradiction: she claims her experience is the same as heterosexual women who have experienced violence even while what she says underscores how different her experience is from those of heterosexual women.

Attention to context is key to perceiving the inner logic of the fluid way she positions herself. Her account of her identity changes from context to context in a way that forestalls easy comparison with straight women. Attention to context includes attention to how she is perceived, including how she portrays herself, betrays herself, dissimulates, tries to conceal, claims solidarity, lays out challenges, or identifies herself. In her work on violence in lesbian relationships, Janice Ristock emphasizes the need to pay attention to specifics: "We need a much more adaptive, context-sensitive analysis to figure out what is going on. This makes life harder for service providers, and challenges some feminist theorizing, but it offers a much better chance of seeing what is there and responding appropriately" (Ristock, 2002, xi).

In the second part of this chapter, I try to take Ristock's caution for adaptive, context-sensitive analysis to heart. I take up the question of coalition against violence given the differences among lesbians who face violence. White lesbians who face violence may identify with other battered women on some occasions, and for some purposes, just as some women in sex work do, as we saw in the previous chapter. But in so doing, they may not perceive how institutional and structural violence (such as homophobia and racism) adversely affect some lesbians more than others. Perhaps because they are harder hit by structural violence, lesbians of color find this strategy of claiming "sameness" much more fraught, and much more costly, to the extent of threatening to rupture (or revealing a rupture in) the movement to stop violence against women. In this second part of the chapter, I briefly review how several lesbian of color theorists have thought of the question of solidarity across race and sexuality in building a coalition to stop violence.

A RURAL WOMAN'S OWN SPACE

In an essay written for lesbians on violence in lesbian relationships, Mary Lou Dietrich discusses bringing her former lover up on charges of assault after she was attacked in her home. She comments on the implications in her community of her decision to press charges against the woman who abused her. "Now, six months after the attack and three months after the trial, I have no regrets about going to court. I am angry and bitter that the local lesbian community doubled my victimization and continues to tolerate my former lover while it shuns me. Naming lesbian violence for what it is seems to be a taboo among us, the great breakers of taboo" (Dietrich 1986, 162). By turning outside of the lesbian community, she was perceived not only as disloyal, but also as threatening the community. "Turning to the straight world for help—and thus admitting that lesbians batter lesbians—is high treason. Lesbian battering threatens to shatter our fondest theories about women, lesbians, ourselves. It shakes the fragile foundations of our communities" (Dietrich 1986, 162). Her lesbian community first criticized and then ostracized her for bringing her exlover to court.

Dietrich writes that members of her community were conscious to a fault of the potential damage that the legal system could inflict upon them. In defense of the community, it could be argued that the treason was not just breaking a taboo. Homophobia in the dominant culture is real, and the consequences of that homophobia for lesbians are, and can be, quite dire. Now, it could be argued that repressing discussion of violence against women in any community is ultimately a short-sighted and damaging tactic. In this sense, the "treason" could be constructed as breaking ranks in a community under siege. Ellyn Kaschak comments, "Should the injured woman choose to speak outside of the privacy of the therapeutic hour, she may be shunned or shamed. Breaking the silence and violating the frequent demands for secrecy imposed by partners, self, or the community can be seen as an act of aggression toward the perpetrator and this perception can be shared by the lesbian community" (Kaschak 2001, 4–5).[2] In fact, Janice Ristock (2002) entitled her book on violence in lesbian relationships *No More Secrets* (also see Cardea 1995). Dietrich, for her part, *also* felt betrayed, but by her community.

Dietrich's situation bears closer examination to understand the specific circumstances of her life, her projects, her places of sanctity, her attachment to her property, her ardor for solitude. For example, Dietrich's house, and consequently the violation of it, holds for her a special significance. "The fear still lingers months after my former lover attacked me. I live alone in an isolated cabin in the Maine woods. This is the land that I love. This is the house I built with my own hands. This is the space that my former lover violated" (154). A rural woman and a lesbian, Dietrich writes of her lover's assault and how the spatial integrity of her house was ruptured. She feels an attachment to the house she built and the land. Living secluded in the woods, she suggests an elemental connection between herself and the space she has created and inhabits. This space was violated with lingering consequences.

After they break off their relationship by phone, her lover comes over and threatens to break her windows. This threat is particularly worrisome to Dietrich, since she hauled special glass from far away in her truck and installed the windows herself. They struggle. "I tried to push her out of the cabin. She pushed in. We fell to the floor. She straddled me and threatened to rape me. I was raped fifteen years ago in Cambridge, Mass., by two men, strangers. She knew the story, and she opened that old wound. I couldn't get her off me. I screamed 'Get out of my space.' Like a robot responding to a programmed command, she stood, turned around and walked out of the door. I followed her and ordered her off my property. That just infuriated her, and she began to throw me around outside" (156). She refers to the space as "my space." In this case, she not only lives alone; she built the house herself. In fact, in the middle of the fight, her lover accuses her of having stolen the land from the Indians—mocking Dietrich's sense of entitlement to the property by alluding to the fact that *all* the land in the United States was colonized by white people. For this charge of theft to make sense, her lover must presuppose that the land is in her possession; that is, her lover tacitly acknowledges Dietrich's sovereignty by attacking its legitimacy.[3] Indeed, attacking Dietrich's ownership of the land is part of attacking Dietrich—Dietrich's identity, autonomy, and integrity are connected to her land, her space, her hand-built house.

The sense of sovereignty over her space may be tied to her autonomy from men and from other patriarchal arrangements. But she may also benefit from racial privilege and white ascension. Needless to say, not all lesbians have dominion over their space. Another lesbian, a young black woman, says: "But staying home didn't help either in some cases. The boys at home are not better. It's bad when you have to watch your back when you bathe, sleep, cook, or sit down to watch TV. Being gay, they will run a train on you in a minute. But especially the other ones who can't seem to keep their hands to themselves" (Keisha, age 14; cited in Richie 2005). Instead of establishing a space of their own as lesbians, some women face the violence of not having *any* space that is *not* sexually predatory. As lesbians, they name that violence as part of the violence of compulsory heterosexuality. "To me, it was better just to hook up with a younger brother even if you are gay. He won't know as much about how to rein you in. But they get smart really fast, and once you do it, they think they own you. And then they start treating you like you are a punching bag" (Angel, age 16; Richie 2005, 74). So, while it is important to note that Dietrich does have an autonomous space linked to living as a lesbian, it is equally important not to generalize over the experiences of other lesbians, especially across lines of class and race.[4]

Finally, having pacified the woman and convinced her to leave, Dietrich surveys the damage. Beyond a hurt hand and the emotional and physical assault she had received, Dietrich is particularly pained by the damage done to her home. "I freaked out. The house was a wreck. Outside, the door had been kicked apart. Inside, books lay strewn on the floor where they had fallen when we crashed into the bookcase. Tools were scattered where we had struggled on the floor. The place stank of her. At least the windows were not broken" (157). In tabulating the destruction, her attention is drawn to the damage done to her place. This makes sense if we understand her sense of self to extend in some sense to her possession of a home.

Her first impulse is to call a friend. Unfortunately, she cannot reach anyone. She decides to get an order of protection and then press charges against her assailant. She calls the police, surprised that the sheriff seems receptive and not outwardly homophobic. She goes into the courthouse, but is not allowed to file for an order of protection. "[The clerk] told me I was not eligible for an order because my former lover and I had not lived together."[5] She suggests instead that Dietrich talk to the district attorney. Dietrich maintained her own home apart from her lover. Her definition of the "domestic" exceeds the conceptual understanding in the courthouse. Thus, the violence cannot be as easily conceptualized as intimate violence by the court. The lack of a conceptual framework is dangerous for lesbians. As Martha Minow has pointed out in a related realm, societal failure to respond is part of the violence. "These failures to respond to domestic violence are public, not private actions" (Minow 1990).[6]

Since the appropriate deputy is not at work, it takes a week for Dietrich to file a charge of assault. Meanwhile, she goes to a local shelter where she joins a women's support group for survivors of violence. Although all of the other women are heterosexual, Dietrich writes that she shares the feelings and the responses of the other women. "The feelings *are* the same, I've realized. Those of us in the group share a sense of guilt (I must have deserved what I got), shame (how could I have got involved with the batterer in the first place?), shaky self-esteem (maybe I pick batterers to relate to; maybe my judgement is askew), humiliation (how can I face friends, family, the community after this?), helplessness (how am I going to rebuild my life now?), tenaciousness (if I can live through that, I can deal with the police, court, the welfare department, being alone), and rage" (159). But only paragraphs later, she underscores how significantly different her situation is from those of the other women. She makes the point clearly throughout her piece of her need for recognition by her lesbian community of the violation of her space and her person. "I needed the community to acknowledge that my former lover broke the law . . . I wanted other lesbians to recognize that my basic right to privacy and safety in my own home were violated" (160). Dietrich's needs and her anger, her hopes, and her sense of betrayal are not oriented towards the straight world, her family, or her place of work, but rather towards other lesbians, women she knew, whose ethos she was transgressing. This places her in a significantly different position from heterosexual women as she describes them.

Within the lesbian community with few exceptions she finds herself isolated, denied, and ostracized. "These lesbians not only denied my fear, isolation and hurt, but even denied that I had been attacked. The lowest blow came when a friend called me the day before a pre-trial hearing. 'You should drop the charges,' she said. 'We in the lesbian community take care of our own.' 'But what about me?' I asked. 'Who's going to take care of me? Who's going to guarantee my safety and see that my house doesn't get trashed?' She had no response. I need other lesbians to realize that I was a victim of a kind of violence particularly hard to deal with" (160). She is more sanguine about her interaction with the authorities themselves. The sheriff and the district attorney did not evidence any homophobia to her mind. Soon after she filed assault charges, they arrest Dietrich's batterer, to Dietrich's relief—tinged by guilt.

Pivotal is how she is portrayed (and portrays herself) once she gets to court. Neither of the lawyers mentions that they were lovers, the defense lawyer emphasizing that they were "just friends."[7] "Next, the judge asked me what happened. Briefly, I described the attack. I was vague about the threats, and I did not say that we had been lovers . . ." (162). Dietrich's exlover received fifteen days, suspended sentence, and was required to spend a year in counseling.

But let's look a little more at her comportment in court. When she is finally allowed to give courtroom testimony of her experience, she avoids any reference to being a lesbian, nor does she mention her former lover's threats, including threats of sexual violence. She is caught between a community that shuns her for her violation of silence and an institutional setting that perpetuates another kind of silence. She sidesteps the transgressive aspects of the situation and of the relationship so that it looks to the judge like a (literally) straightforward case of assault and battery. Her description to the court is consistent with an understanding of what counts as a violation in the civic realm, a violation of the bodily integrity and private property of one citizen by another.

Actually, several contradictory constructions of her are in simultaneous operation. She is betrayed, and she feels she also betrays herself as she passes from her own house and land to the courthouse, to the spaces of lesbian friends, to the shelter, to the courtroom. She is variously supported, criticized, accepted, and rejected as she is seen as a battered woman ("the same" as any other), a complainant, a traitor, a friend, an assault victim. She aligns herself in different ways, from challenging her lesbian community to identifying gladly with battered heterosexual women, to suppressing elements of her identity, her relationship, and her sense of spatial autonomy when she is in court. She finds herself in different situations, each with its own, distinct expectations for her behavior.

The ways she pilots through these situations is instructive. Towards other lesbians, her discourse is marked by an appeal to the integrity of her space. In court, she remains quiet about being a lesbian, yet she gets public acknowledgment of her injury, and she insures that her batterer keeps her distance. She succeeds in manipulating the idiom of citizenship, rights, privacy, property, and protection by the law in her description. It would be a mistake to conclude that her selective appropriation of this vocabulary is wholly conscious; moreover, as she is at pains to point out, she is hardly in control of the situation.

The delicacy of her situation is only heightened by her own fragility and vulnerability as she decides where to speak and how to frame what she says. Through an irony born of passing through spaces of conflicting ethics, she is accused of exposing her community by going to the courts, even while she does not "come out" when she is in court.

If any more proof were needed that her situation is not the same as any other, one need only turn to the venue in which this account of violence is voiced. This is an article written for a volume on abuse in lesbian relationships for lesbians and for activists against violence against women (Lobel 1986). Significantly, her expected audience would include lesbians. Her piece may even be an address to lesbians in particular. This colors the words; it does not change her indictment, but it changes the character of it. "After the attack, I needed other lesbians to recognize how terrorized I was and how unsafe I felt, I need other lesbians to realize that I was a victim of a kind of violence particularly hard to deal with" (160). In this passage, the change in tense is significant. At the time of the attack, she "needed" other lesbians to recognize how terrorized she was. Now, at the time of writing, she "needs" other lesbians to realize she was a victim of a kind of violence that is particularly hard to deal with. The sentence begins as a description of past events, of the failure of community. Midstream, artfully, she changes the tense and ends the sentence with a plea and a challenge to her audience. Her expression of gratitude to the police for their receptiveness could be read as advice to other lesbians, her description of rejection as warning to other battered lesbians. Thus her article needs to be read as an insider's document, for use and distribution among lesbians. I do not think it is intended to embolden the reader to cynicism about the lesbian community. And despite her claims, she does not make a completely convincing case that violence against lesbians *is* the same, even though she describes her experience as the same.[8]

ANALYSIS: HOMOPHOBIA, STRUCTURAL VIOLENCE, AND
COALITION BUILDING

Homophobia and Structural Violence

"As a lawyer," writes Sandra Lundy, "I know from experience that litigating openly queer cases in civil court is never easy. You can be sure that somehow, somewhere, when you least expect it, homophobia will rear its ugly head in the courtroom, derailing your arguments, upsetting your client, making it impossible to be heard" (1999, 43). "Given how difficult it is for out queer people to be treated well in the civil justice system, particularly when they seek relief from abusive partners, I understand why some in our community urge queer people to bypass the court system entirely and instead bring issues of abuse to friends, private mediators, and counselors" (Lundy 1999, 44–45). Nevertheless, Lundy concludes that on balance the court's protections and ability to enforce the law are important. She urges lesbians who face abuse to take their cases to court.

Dietrich does not dwell on public homophobia, though she must have perceived the space of the court as homophobic if she decided not to come out in court. We must read between the lines to see how institutions and the public construction of violence work to make violence against lesbians invisible. Perhaps if she had spent more time describing the array of structural forces she faced, the community she was in, the risks she and her lover and her community perceived, it would have been more difficult for her to say the violence she faced is the same as that faced by straight women. One might argue that it is only in severing the links between intimate violence and questions of community, resources, and institutions, that violence—or a woman facing violence—can be perceived (or perceive herself) as "the same."

Additionally, it might be that the structural forces at work, such as racism, disappear more easily from the perception of a middle-class, white woman. It is when they disappear that it becomes easier for her to say that the problems are just the same. Other women might be less inclined to see their situation as the same as all others.

In her thoughtful and discerning book on violence in lesbian relationships, Canadian researcher Janice Ristock has observed,

> The difference in conceptualization leads to different responses. When same-sex partner abuse becomes the focus, we see work that emphasizes the need for new services, new programs, and interventions that can address sexual identities as a primary focus. When lesbian abuse remains within feminist gender-based analysis, we see writings that focus on women's shared experiences of victimization and a reassertion (with minor adjustments) of the tools, categories, and constructs we have in place to respond to gender-based intimate violence. Neither approach is wrong. (Ristock 2002, 18)

Another way of framing her situation is in terms of a vicious either/or. Women who face forms of violence that fall outside the conventions of domestic heterosexual relationships often face the either/or of being considered essentially the same or fundamentally different from other women. If they are the same, then they fit the solutions that the courts come up with or that the shelters offer. They fit the psychological models and the warning signs of abuse. However, if their lives do not conform to the imagined model, then they are outside of the ambit of shelters, the courts, or other places of refuge or redress for (some) heterosexual women. Sometimes they can go to those places, but there they face a set of presuppositions that simplify them and their identity, the spaces they must traverse, the people to whom they matter or who matter to them, and those spaces regard them as conforming to an abstract sameness with any other—all other—battered woman.

They face the either/or when structural or state violence is taken out of the equation. When violence is structural or institutional, then women either look the same as other battered women, or they are unrecognizable *as* battered. Homophobia is a form of structural violence. State violence is in evidence when that homophobia is institutionalized in such a way that to identify as a lesbian is to run risks. In this case, lesbians (and gay men) fit awkwardly in the traditional schema of partner battering (see Lundy 1993).

Inside the marriage contract, tools exist, such as orders of protection, to reorganize the relationship. The lack of a marriage contract has historically marked an absence of a technique for thinking conceptually. Certain kinds of violence are harder to conceive for the popular imagination. And this is a way in which structural violence works indirectly: in the maintenance of silences, in the evasion of unthinkable identities, in the suppression of unthinkable activities.

As Dietrich's account makes clear, there was no easy way in which her situation could be adjudicated. She was comfortable at the battered women's shelter to the extent to which she found her experience to conform to the same paradigm as those of straight women. However, her particular experience, in her own occupation of space, in terms of her relationship with a woman who lived apart from her, firmly ensconced in a lesbian community, is necessary to take into account in order to develop an account of what the violence meant, what was violated.

The either/or of passing as the same or being excluded/erased is not merely institutional but implicates how women identify and act. It can govern how women position themselves.

Some women feel they need to identify as *the same* as other battered women or risk being excluded from those institutions that provide support or assistance for battered women. This either/or is not a *choice*; that is, women are excluded and/or erased as what they are, and it is not always up to them.

I have shown how this contradiction is lived, maneuvered, and handled. In other words, I do not introduce the story of Mary Lou Dietrich as a stand-in for a type: rural, white, middle-class, homeowner, lesbian, property owner. My methodology is to approach multiplicity in its particularity rather than as an aggregate of stereotypes. Comparisons and connections between and among different lesbians are useful and illuminating, as long as the presupposition or conclusion of sameness is avoided.

COALITION BUILDING

The question of identifying is important. Can we launch a project not predicated on commonality of identity? It does not seem necessary to claim commonality in order to be included in a coalition. Certainly, coalition can be grounded on many different claims or foundations. In fact, "coalition" implies heterogeneity of membership (otherwise it would not be a coalition).

After I showed a draft of this chapter to my students, one student, who identified as a lesbian, wrote back to me, "The idea of sameness does not make sense to me. However, the idea of a shared experience does. People in any situation need to know they are not alone, and there are other people out there that share a similar situation. I think that is why there are so many support groups for all kinds of situations. Having similar situations does not mean everyone is the same." Dietrich writes of how she looked for company and for recognition. She sought out recognition, remedy, and women with experiences of violence with whom she could share and analyze. In this sense, she exercised herself as a social agent, self-reliant, even at the risk of ostracism from her community.

Her steady search and meditation on company and commonality get to a key aspect of the problem—how to form coalitions among both people who have similar experiences and people whose experiences have little or nothing in common. While it may be easier to articulate the reasons why people who are similar would come together, the question of solidarity amidst difference is equally important, if more vexed. When we think of solutions, we ought to discern the similar without reducing what is different, because otherwise, the tendency to frame coalition in the terms of commonality will predominate. Can one adopt an attitude that seeks company not based on commonality, sameness, or a simplistic understanding of coalition? How can the coalition be deep as it sustains an understanding of the differences? But then, how can I be a faithful advocate for someone who may have little in common with me? How can I realize the stake I have in their liberation when it is not apparent that I do have a stake? What if I benefit from the oppression? And what if any apparent similarities belie deep differences? How does one persevere in developing a coalition?

In an article critical of how "sameness" and "commonality" have guided the battered women's movement, Latina lesbian Martha Lucía García, a long time activist, comments,

> The battered women's movement continues to be dominated by the idea that to create unity we must focus on our commonalities and that the experience of being abused and being a woman is enough to create bonds. The underlying message is that we must be the "same" if we are to be united—the same in our perspective and philosophy, the same in our ideas about how to work with women. We are expected to share the belief that our focus is solely on the violence the women experience and that our function is solely to assist women with the issues of violence in their lives. (1999, 166)

García questions the perceived need to base a movement to end violence on commonality. Instead, she seeks to frame violence within a larger array of social forces that women face. These larger social forces have engendered different social histories depending on the social group. Without a sense of these larger forces, the violence cannot always be seen. Luanna Ross, for example, has tied the conquest of the West to the criminalization of Native women. Without the history of conquest, she believes her ethnographic account of Native women would be deplete, absent of meaning, including a deep sense of where Native women face violence (for example, in prison), as well as the meaning of the violence they face. An incarcerated woman she interviewed tells Ross that her identity as a lesbian made the prison authorities interpret otherwise innocuous gestures as sexual transgressions and therefore as an infraction: "They considered [touching another prisoner's leg] sexual misconduct. To me, sexual misconduct is having sex—not touching somebody on the leg. But come on, if I touched somebody—beating the hell out of them, or doing something like that—I can see going to a max cell. But just because I touch somebody's leg I cannot see sitting in this cell. That is wrong" (cited in Ross 1998, 147). Only with an expanded notion of violence against lesbians—one that includes institutional homophobia and institutional violence—can we see this as violence against lesbians. Since the incarceration rate of native women is geometrically greater than that of white women, the marginalization of violence against incarcerated lesbians is also a marginalization of racist violence.

In this way, we have returned to Beth Richie's recommended strategy of putting the most marginal at the center. This strategy is a corrective to narrow views of gendered violence that erase or exclude racism, heterosexism, and other forms of oppression. Earlier in this chapter, I referred to Richie's study of the violence faced by young black lesbians serving time in detention (2005). In focusing on them, she notices how the mainstream queer movement and the antiprison movement each tends to overlook or ignore young black, queer women who are engaged in illegal activity. She argues that it is through putting the marginal at the center that a movement to end violence against all women would be made that much stronger: not by focusing on commonalities, but by paying attention to differences. She is also in this way reminding us that it would be a mistake to homogenize *lesbians* as a group of women. Luana Ross cites one woman, "They put me in a max cell where I can't see nobody; can't talk to nobody but the guards. Come on—what are they trying to do? Destroy me? And that's what's going to happen. You know, if they're trying to kill what I have going for me and people think that being gay is wrong, and a lot of people don't agree with it but it's just the way I feel. And, I don't push it on anybody, so they shouldn't push back. It's not like I'm pushing to hurt anybody, yeah, this place reminds me of [the drug treatment center] where they take you and tear you apart and build you back up. Only this place don't build you back up—they just tear you down" (cited in Ross 1998, 149). Compulsory heterosexuality is a crucial force in the lives of all women, but it may manifest itself differently for poor women and women of color. Psychological manipulation, isolation, punishment cells, and sensory deprivation are forms of violence. These are manifestations of structural violence as they affect lesbians.

If white, middle-class lesbians encounter a split as property-holding members of the dominant class in a caste-bound society, lesbians of color face marginalization at the dangerous conjunction of race, class, and sexuality. In conclusion, let me expand this thought a bit in a way that will bridge this chapter and chapter 2, which focused on Latina women.

In an essay at once melancholic, sharply analytical, and ultimately hopeful, Maria Lugones (2003b) argues that the "geographical memory of Latina homoerotic subjects is sharply discontinuous." She sees the Latina homoerotic subject—the *tortillera*, the *pata*, the *cachapera*—as split. Their lives "out" as *tortilleras* are often confined to the spaces of Latina lesbian bars inside the geographic limits of Latino/a communities. Outside the bars but within Latino communities, according to Lugones, many Latina lesbians live closeted lives, given the heterosexist cast of the nationalism of Latino communities under siege by the dominant, colonizing white/*anglo* culture. On the other hand, Lugones is aware of the perils of a lesbian movement that marginalizes Latina homoerotic subjects. She worries that the dominant (white) lesbian movement only preserves the split for *tortilleras* when that movement does not take up crucial questions of colonization and racism. She sees only a limited self-affirmation within a lesbian movement, "in white landscapes, locales, geography . . . Movement that lacks a taste for conversations inside the locales and ways that risk complicity with colonization, with our cultural and material erasure. Movement that does not take our integrity seriously because it affirms the confines of its own territoriality" (175). At this conjunction of Latino/a communities and lesbian movement, the Latina lesbian is constituted by a spatial split that mirrors a dangerous split in her identity. "Latina/Lesbian is an oxymoron, an absence of relation. Latina/Lesbian lacks a hyphen. The territoriality of the movement erases the hyphen. Latina/Lesbian necessarily speaks with a bifid tongue . . . the Latina/Lesbian moves within a movement that lacks a sense of its geography and becomes aware of territoriality only when it stops outside the nations" (175). Lugones' challenge is dual: to the nationalism of dominant Latino/a communities in fighting structural racism and to a Lesbian movement that does not take up the split of *patas, cachaperas,* Latina homoerotic subjects harmed by the split.

The claim of sameness made by white lesbians such as Dietrich are not as easily made by Latina lesbians under siege, split by nationalist and lesbian feminist movements. This is why Lugones' essay is entitled The Discontinuous Passing of the Cachapera/Tortillera." The violence is in the erasure, it is in the forced splintering and fragmentation of her life.

White lesbians sometimes perceive themselves to share experiences and problems with other women. They have formed connections based on what they see as comparable or parallel, as well as observed similarities. They may see a tactical reason for claiming sameness (Schneider 2000). Though I do not dismiss their claims to commonality, the claim of commonality may come at a cost. In the case discussed earlier, a lesbian's emphasis on private violence, on interpersonal assault, leads to claiming sameness. Disregarding institutional and structural violence leads her to misperceive the muting affects of institutional homophobia and to affirm the disjunction between the lives of white property holders and those at the racial and class margins, women in Latino/a, African-American, and native communities who face the withering forces of colonization and racism. The claim to sameness may work as a barrier to coalition with lesbians of color. The purpose of this chapter has not been so much to analyze battering per se as to focus on the need to take on and take into account institutional and structural forms of violence in order to have a proper analysis of the way in which interpersonal violence works. Otherwise, sustained coalition may not only be unlikely, but it may be at some women's expense—where expense is marginalization. The sustained focus on one woman's voice, which I have tried to situate among other lesbians' voices, has been the vehicle to underscore the urgency of focusing on those larger social forces that affect the very structure and meaning of violence.

CHAPTER FIVE

Spaces of Judgment and Judgments of Space

Competing Logics of Violence in Court

In the previous three chapters, I examined the experiences of women who face violence but are marginalized by mainstream discourse and institutions that respond to violence. In this chapter, I will examine how state power is directly implicated in hiding, flattening, and homogenizing difference in experiences of violence. In order to do so, I focus on the daily, unremarkable practices of the law courts; in particular, I look at how women's accounts of violence are steam rolled in the courtroom.

BACKGROUND: FEMINIST LEGAL REFORM AND AMBIVALENCE ON STATE INVOLVEMENT

The extent to which the criminal justice system has acknowledged or been responsive to gendered violence is due in large part to the pressure of feminist activists (see Wittner 1997). Nonetheless, as I argued in the introduction to this book, the feminist movement has been ambivalent about the role of the state and its agents in its response to violence. On the one hand, many activists have sought solutions from the government: "In the past 20 years, activists in the U.S. battered women's movement have argued successfully that the state has an obligation to intervene in personal relationships to protect women from their abusive partners, that it can and should remove violent husbands from their private homes to protect women in their private homes, that the police should arrest husbands for assault, and that the state should prosecute them" (Shepard and Pence 1999, 5).

On the other hand, many strands of feminism have treated the government, the courts, the social service sector, and the police with far more distrust (Mills 1999). Even Shepard and Pence comment that "as women seeking refuge in the shelters turned to the state for financial resources or legal protection, the state's role in reproducing relations of dominance and subordination was repeatedly demonstrated" (1999, 8). They see the courts and state agents failing to act:

"Lawmakers, police officers, judges, prosecutors, probation officers, and social workers consistently failed to use their institutional powers to protect women from further abuse or to sanction men for their violence" (1999, 8; also see Minow 1990). Other feminists (e.g., Bhattacharjee 2002a; Bhavnani and Davis 2000; Smith 2005; Ogden 2005; also see Bumiller 2008) see the state as a direct source of harm to women, especially poor women, immigrant women, and women of color. In an influential article, Linda Mills (1999) comments that the state's regulation of domestic violence in the United States is "tinged with emotional violence" in a myriad of ways: "[S]uch policies as mandatory arrest, prosecution, and reporting, which have become standard legal fare in the fight against domestic violence and which categorically ignore the battered woman's perspective, can themselves be forms of abuse. Indeed, I argue that, ironically, the very state interventions designed to eradicate the intimate abuse in battered women's lives all too often reproduce the emotional abuse of the battering relationship" (554–55). An advocate from the Duluth Project bridges the concerns of the last chapters and this one by discussing how assumptions about domestic violence lead the courts to miss the crucial concrete aspects of women's lives. (I quote her at length): "We had convinced the judges always to order a pre-sentence investigation before sentencing a person convicted of assaulting a partner or former partner . . . The first pre-sentence investigation I attended really opened my eyes to how little the court system knew about battering. The probation officer asked Carol, the woman I was with, 'How many times has your husband hit you, kicked you or in some manner physically harmed you in the past three years?'"

She responded, "four or five times."

The probation officer kept probing for information to determine if her abuser had committed criminal acts of abuse.

> The interview lasted twenty minutes. The probation officer ascertained that Carol's husband physically abused her about once a year, was a weekend drinker and had never been to any kind of counseling . . . He did not understand that Carol's husband kept her a virtual prisoner in their home with no phone, no transportation, no visitation with friends and no outside activities. He did not discover that Carol's husband demanded that she have sex with him every day, constantly threatened to take the children away and to kill her if she even looked at another man. Carol was not allowed to wear jeans, sleeveless blouses, long hair or make up. He called her a whore and a slut daily in the presence of their three children. He gave her sixty dollars a week for groceries, clothing for the children and household items, and he made her account for every cent with receipts. (Cited in Pence, et al. 1987)

The plan of this chapter is to listen to the accounts of women in court in order to assess the possible limits of family courts and domestic violence courts in apprehending gendered violence. The previous chapters reviewed how some of the most marginalized women are excluded from domestic violence courts, or if they are included, it is in a distorting and sometimes demeaning, even violent, way. Holding the previous chapters in mind, I look at the way the courts themselves, as instruments of governance, constrain women, punish women, and collude with the violence the women already face.

The accounts are drawn from my field work looking at the everyday practice of law in domestic violence courts in Chicago and family courts in New York. I spent several years conducting participant observation in the courts; this data was supplemented with a body of interviews I conducted in New York and Chicago with advocates, judges, shelter workers, activists, and formerly battered women.[1]

I focus on three cases here in order to illustrate a larger claim about the disparities between a woman's lived experience of violence and the kinds of arguments that the court can address. Three cases do not and are not intended to offer a proof that courts universally do not and cannot understand a woman's testimony. Judges, like any group, hold a diversity of understandings of violence. Nevertheless, the examples capture how the courts tend to impose an abstract understanding of "domestic violence." The cases I describe are unexceptional in many ways: they capture the routine of our criminal justice system. In that respect, they show a patterned miscommunication common in courts. Some have argued that given the nature of courtroom interaction, the miscommunication is nearly insurmountable (Conley and O'Barr 1990); narrative theorists of the law (e.g., Delgado 1996) argue that courts systematically disrupt the stories of witnesses and defendants.

As one can see from the lengthy citation from the Duluth advocate above, law courts and the criminal justice system often insist on quantifying violence. In fact, petitioners for orders of protection in Chicago are routinely asked, as a matter of course, "How many times has he hit you and over what period of time?" This emphasis on quantifying violence has several important consequences. Violence is reduced to one person acting physically against another. Discrete acts (punching, biting, kicking) tend to be emphasized, rather than, say, emotional abuse or intimidation.

"Violence" cannot be easily quantified without losing something important.[2] The Duluth Project was right in seeing violence tied to context. However, quantifying violence often requires abstracting it from the situation in which it occurs and thereby missing much of the ineffable features—hostility, dread, menace—that color violence and support it. In fact, quantifying violence is a product of modern forms of knowing, of converting knowledge into statistical form (Davis 2003; Porter 1996).

A paradigm that depends on quantifying physical abuse does not admit the full texture of women's experiences of violence. Studying violence against women requires more than tallying incidents of abuse. Understanding violence requires an exploration of the terror, of the anxiety and apprehension that suffuse an atmosphere. What is called for is an inquiry into women's own descriptions and analyses of the spaces of violence (see, for example, Agtuca 1994).

Using the text of courtroom interaction and analyzing how the courts tend to view the spaces of violence against women is my way of explaining that gap between the courts' views and understandings of violence and those of women in the grips of violence. The analysis also explains the courts' common failure to countenance the point of view of the women who come to court. The women's narratives of the spaces of violence are not recognized *as* alternative logics of space.

Regardless of the women's testimony, the courts tend to frame the violence as confined to the space of the home. When discrete, countable acts in the home are the frame of analysis, then other structural forces in women's lives tend to disappear from view. This narrowing of violence to the private sphere is itself violent.

In privatizing violence, the courts and other agencies mask the role of state power itself, the role played by health and welfare agencies, and not least the courts themselves, in colluding with violence or in creating violent situations for women. These institutions are all left aside by law courts that focus on individuals who are perpetrators of harm.[3] Structural and institutional forms of violence go unseen and unnoticed. The intersection of gendered violence with other forms of oppression, like racism, xenophobia, and ablism, go unaddressed or ignored. This makes it impossible to view histories—histories of bodies, of communities, of resources—since the abstraction makes violence all domestic and interpersonal, not structural, and each case separate from and unrelated to every other case.

Though their motives and intentions vary, many women nevertheless turn to domestic violence court or family court (see Wittner 1997; Fischer and Rose 1995; Merry 1995a; 1995b; Ptacek 1999; Schneider 2000; Trinch 2003). These women often come to plead for a specific protection, often in the form of an order of protection against a specific individual, or they come to redress a certain situation of ongoing harm. For them, courts offer some promise of rectification, whether in the form of a protection order, criminal prosecution of a batterer, or privileged access to certain spaces (the home, the place of employment, the children's school) (see Yngvesson 1993). Not all women go to court when they face violence. In the first half of the book, I took up the situations of women who rarely come into court to seek redress for violence, or who come to the court in significant tension with normative expectations, for example, women who identify as lesbians, who are undocumented, or who are otherwise marginal or marginalized. In this chapter, I will show how the courts foreshorten the accounts of the women who do come to the law courts.

One of the dangers of seeing "violence" as *only* interpersonal (that is, only as partner battering or stranger rape) and not institutionalized is that state agencies are let off the hook when they reproduce relations of dominance and subordination. Despite the occasional willingness and even dedication of some agents in the legal and criminal justice system to stop violence against women, the courts and the police may have limits as institutions. Unfortunately, when the criminal justice system takes over, other ways of stopping violence fade from view in favor of criminal justice solutions.

THE LOGIC OF ABSTRACT SPACE

The courts usually uphold a version of "home" where "home" is the space of the family. The home is private property. The version of space, and how it is imposed, conforms to what I will call, following Henri Lefebvre's usage, "abstract space" (1991). Abstract space is the dominant regime of space in modern liberal societies. It has three components. First, social relationships rule out aggression among citizens. Each individual is guaranteed in civil society what could be considered a cone of propriety that is legally and socially inviolable. Second, space is ordered according to the logic of private property. Spaces are owned, either temporarily (I put my hat down on my seat while I go to get the newspaper from the rack) or permanently (I have legal title to this land) (cf. Goffman 1971). Holding property is a fundamental right—what makes one human and free. Third, violence is implicit in this understanding of space. Violence is implicit in two ways. On the one hand, according to traditional social contract thought, the social pact of nonaggression is what protects the citizen from the war of all against all. The State is the guarantor of protection from spontaneous violence by my neighbor, in exchange for which I offer allegiance to the State, which holds a monopoly on violence as the enforcer of the contract. On the other hand, the public condemnation of violence exists alongside hidden and invisible forms of violence, such as the violence of class exploitation, racism, and sexism, not to mention violence in the private space of the home.

Why is a theory of "abstract space" relevant in a study of how courts judge cases of violence against women? Abstract space is the logic of space held by and imposed by the courts. It often contradicts women's testimony to violence. It is an unequal conflict, however. The court's version of space always trumps, at least officially. Judging from the language of the court advocates, district attorneys, defense lawyers, and judges, when women testify in court to the violence they face, it is not clear that anyone listens to or hears their accounts or incorporates them into the decisions. The courts do not countenance or even recognize alternative perceptions, inhabitations, or experiences of space. The abstract space is not a description but a project to make space homogeneous. "Abstract space *is not* homogeneous; it simply has homogeneity as its goal, its orientation, its 'lens.' And, indeed, it renders homogeneous . . . Thus to look upon abstract space as homogeneous is to embrace a representation that takes the effect for the cause, and the goal for the reason why that goal is pursued" (Lefebvre 1991, 287).

Abstract space appears at first as a description, a commonsense truism about the nature of reality, which hides its tendency to try to bring reality in accordance with it. Abstract space is not only misdescription; it also engenders a prescriptive claim—a goal to make space homogeneous. Abstract space reflects the results sought.

In this case, the abstraction is to a prototype, a simplified, simplistic concept of "home," "violence," and "woman." The imposition of this abstract version of "domestic violence" is itself a violent process.

In the body of this chapter, I will draw on courtroom evidence that supports the claim that jurisprudence under abstract space dismisses other accounts of space.

"OVER FIVE HUNDRED TIMES"

Domestic violence court, Chicago

I arrived early in court this morning, around nine thirty, and the court was not yet in session. The scene in domestic violence court was like a production I once saw of Thorton Wilder's *Our Town*. The players slowly file in, take up their places, chatty. Spectators are already in the gallery. I take a seat in the third row, in the corner. In the front of the courtroom, lawyers greet each other with a comfort and heartiness that is slightly exaggerated and histrionic on a stage otherwise so freighted with expectation. But they are waiting, too. The court reporter walks in and sets up the stenography machine. Then the bailiff strides in and in a loud booming voice calls out, "Here ye, here ye," and ushers in the judge, who then pronounces a cant. "This counts as a Class A misdemeanor . . . You have the right to an attorney . . . This is a serious matter." And then the players take their places. It begins.

The complaining witness before us is a Latina, Ms. Ramirez,[4] who appears to be in her mid-thirties. Through a translator, she testifies that her husband has beaten her "over five hundred times" during the course of their ten-year marriage, a declaration uncontested by the defense. She left three weeks before, she testifies, after he had told her he was going to kill her and had punched her in the breasts. Since then, she has been staying in women's shelters, her sisters' homes, sleeping on floors. He has been following her, appearing at the children's school and threatening to kill her within hearing of other parents. On her behalf, the State was petitioning the court so that she could have exclusive rights to live in the house, a petition the defense counsel challenged. During the cross-examination, the public defender brought out that Mr. Ramirez is HIV positive, and Ms. Ramirez testified under questioning that indeed one significant source of her fear is that the husband spits on her and the children and threatens to infect them.

A great deal of the court discussion of the case was the fact that she and her children were economically dependent on him since his disability payments were twice hers, even though she fed the children.

The judge found that there was, in fact, an instance of abuse, and he "prohibited" the man from "breaking the home," observing that it is "her home, too." But by the same token, the judge continued, "it is his home, too." Although the "balance of hardships" weighs in her favor (she testified that she received less disability benefits than he, while she was the primary caretaker for their three children), the husband is "entitled to access" to the basement at least.

The case concluded with an extended discussion of the kind of barrier that would be erected between the basement and the rest of the house to prevent the batterer's access. The lawyers and judge decided that it should be a strong, steel-reinforced door paid for by the batterer as a condition of his occupancy, and he would have to put it up in a reasonably timely way.

* * *

Solomonic in his wisdom, the judge split the difference. If, the logic ran, it is her home, but "his home, too," then dividing the home into separate but equal shares would be a sound judgment. Both retain access to the land; both continue to have housing. In this age of rampant homelessness, one concern seemed to be dispossessing people, particularly people who are HIV positive.

In trying to establish a mutual nonaggression pact in the home, the judge's imagination becomes very concrete: a portal will be constructed that will remain closed, separating the "rest of the house" from the batterer's own domain.

It is as if he did not quite see the violence either within the home or how the batterer persists in threatening her across different spaces. His ruling is consistent with not perceiving "violence" as anything more than, say, mutual dislike. His solution is to propose the kind of spatial division that two unrelated families might produce to preserve the integrity of each were they forced to live under the same roof. In particular, the experience of terror—even the possibility of it—is not taken up at all.

The judge's assertion of the defendant's "right to his home" was a recurrent motif in this case and in many others. It is an interesting linguistic innovation. The right to property is a constitutionally given right. The right to "his home" is not. "It is his property, too" might sound bloodless, but it is more accurate. The vocabulary of home invokes a series of affective and ideological associations relating to domestic life.

Lefebvre alerts us to the tension between the appearance of security and the constant threat of violence. Since Mr. Ramirez stalked her (to take one form of abuse to which she testified), the spatial arrangement the judge proposed would hardly reassure the battered woman and her children of their safety. The decision excludes any consideration of the man's abuse in its spatial dimension. It is a *line*, a door. In the judge's sense of geometry, space can be bisected into discrete units. But this view of space does not understand the fear engendered by having a batterer living on the other side of the wall, the creepiness of a stalker that permeates beyond the mathematical division of space in which separate spaces are imagined as safe, private, and sacrosanct, divided from others through a judge's decision. Nevertheless, the public defender, prosecutor, and judge reached a consensus about how all the particulars would work.

They also reinforce a patriarchal idea of the home and the family. Mr. Ramirez received more relief money than Ms. Ramirez. One more reason to allow him to stay was so he could provide for them. But it is the State that confers more solvency on the man than the woman because of his disability. In receiving more money, he looks to the judge like a provider for his family, even against the wishes of his wife, who is the one who feeds the children, even against her testimony that he threatens to infect them with AIDS. Thus one can see an implicit collusion between government, batterer, and judge. This collusion does not require congruent imaginations of space. It is quite compatible that the court ruled in a way favorable to the defendant while not recognizing his inhabitation or conceptualization of space at all.

It might be asked why Ms. Ramirez petitioned to have exclusive access to the house. Having exclusive access does not seem to fit the violence to which she was subject. After all, he stalked her, and he threatened her at the children's school yard. One rationale is that a supportive court ruling can position her more advantageously to call the police and have him ejected, arrested for trespassing, and so on. She is not so much protected from him as made a little less vulnerable. In a broader sense, her bid for an order of protection can be understood as her trying to use the court, even if her own ends only approximate what the court was prepared to bestow. In a display of nonpassivity, she presents herself as a battered woman and petitions for a space of her own. While her account of space was not countenanced by the court, she was able to portray herself and her circumstances in such a way that she was granted something that she did not have before, even if it is not sufficient to alleviate her circumstance nor quite meet her in her specificity.

The judgment in this case exemplifies at least some of the problems of using the courts as an avenue for social amelioration. But even cursory review of the space of violence for the Latina and her children would show that the violence would not be prevented merely by erecting a secure door.

The man and his lawyer used race, class, gender, and HIV status strategically. The complications of the situation are hard to handle, hard to assimilate into a straightforward picture of tranquil domesticity disrupted through male violence. Both the man and the woman stood in a compromised and particularly vulnerable position—each in danger of homelessness, each dependent upon financial support from the government. The discourse of disease and infection suffused the debate and the judgment.

THE "HYSTERICAL WOMAN"

Chicago: The Trial of David Rebat

David Rebat is on trial. The complainant is his former wife, Sylvia Rebat. Mr. Rebat went to her home to talk to her because she had told her daughter's school to stop allowing Mr. Rebat to pick up their daughter. He is alleged to have pushed

Ms. Rebat and threatened to kill her with her own guns. He waives his right to a jury trial.[5]

The first prosecution witness is Sylvia. She appears to be Caucasian, dressed in pressed, chestnut-colored slacks and high heels. She is in her midforties.

Prosecutor: How long have you known David?

Sylvia: 15 years. We have a six year old daughter.

P: Now, on the tenth of March you were by yourself?

S: I was with my daughter. I let the dog in, as I always do, when I get home from work.

P: What happened?

S: I opened the side door and I saw my husband inches from me.

P: How far?

S: In the entrance way.

P: What did you say?

S: I say "Get away."

P: Then what?

S: He pushed me back into the house.

P: How far is the wall, opposite?

S: About two feet.

P: What part of his body did he push you with?

S: His hands.

P: Then what?

S: I screamed for him to get out, get out, get out . . .

P: . . . then what?

S: I screamed for a couple of minutes and he said he just wanted to talk.

P: What was he doing?

S: He held me on my shoulders with his hands, held me down against the wall.

P: For how long?

S: Two minutes.

P: Did you resist?

S: Yes, but he is a big man.

P: Then what?

S: My daughter was there.

P: Did she say anything?

S: She said, "Daddy, stop."

[Objection: Hearsay]

P: [I'm] trying to see if this had an effect on the daughter.

[Overruled]

S: He said, "Get the hell out of here!"

[Objection: Hearsay: Overruled]

P: Then what . . .

S: [He] said I'm going to shoot you with your own gun.

P: What did you do?

S: I got my guns out of my house.

P: What do you do?

S: I am a police officer.

P: How long?

S: Nineteen years.

P: Carry weapons?

S: No, I never wear them in house.

Ms. Rebat, through the prosecutor, led a tour of the space of violence. The particular details relevant to the violence are positioned in relation to her body. Her account highlights the intimate terror of the event through details not just of actions, but of objects, proximities, sounds.

As she is cross-examined by the defense, her account of violence is not so much contested as side-stepped. In the following, the Defense does not challenge or review but rather insinuates the weaknesses of her subjective account by making an appeal to the bureaucracy of domestic violence—doctor's reports, police reports, the legal indicators, and documentation of battery (cf. McElhinny 1995).

D: You didn't file an assault complaint until a month after?

S: No.

D: You didn't receive medical injuries?

S: Yes, I did.

D: You didn't receive medical treatment.

S: No, I didn't. I have a six year old at home . . .

D: . . . Ma'am, you've answered my question . . . You have signed this misdemeanor charge. Does it say anything about the battery?

S: No.

D: You had a chance . . .

S: Yes.

D: You have filed numerous reports as an officer for nineteen years?

S: Yes. That's correct.

D: You knew what a police report was?

S: Yes. What did you want me to do? I couldn't put him under arrest when he was holding me down.

D: You have guns? What kinds?

S: A Smith and Wesson.

D: You don't like David very much do you?

S: No. I don't like him. He free-loaded off of me for years . . .

D: You didn't talk for a whole month [Ms. Rebat filed a complaint on April 12. The events described are alleged to have happened on March 10] . . .

S: Yes.

D: Didn't go to a doctor?

S: No.

D: Why the delay?

S: I have a life to lead, a life to lead with my daughter. This has happened so often before . . . he broke three locks.

D: Why the delay?

S: 'Cause I knew not a damn thing would be done. He broke three locks.[6]

D: No further questions.

P: The State rests.

One of the impressive aspects of this exchange was how the defense lawyer used the woman's status as a police officer and her experience as a nineteen-year veteran in order to cast aspersions on her account. She should have known, the implication is, that filing a police report a month after the alleged incident and failing to get medical documentation of injuries would weaken her case. "Why the delay? . . . Why the delay?" The lawyer asks her. Although he asks her with reference to her status as a police officer, she tries to answer first as a working mother, "I have a life to lead, a life to lead with my daughter," and then as a woman who knows how the system will treat her, "'Cause I knew not a damn thing would be done." In the end, he presses her on why she, as a seasoned officer, elected to delay, to fail to document the battery, to file necessary papers.

The reversal that the lawyer managed was remarkable. It is a cliché of courtroom wisdom that police are given more credibility than other people. In this case, however, any possible fault lines in her account are exploited as falsehoods because she was a police officer. So, because she was armed and trained in the use of handguns, she should have been able to defend herself had there been any threat. Because she knew the importance of medical records and police reports, she would have made them if there was the basis for a criminal complaint. The defense lawyer strategically invoked her profession, her gender, and her location as homeowner. The machinations of power are such that each of those identities can be turned to her advantage or used as grounds for dismissing her credibility: How could an armed police officer be so easily assaulted and overpowered? Why didn't she call a hospital or the police? This line of questioning cut off examination of her representation of space.[7]

Time is further manipulated when the lawyer makes a transition and asks her: "Do you have guns?"; "You don't like David very much?" The questions speak to aspects of their relationship in a timeless present: enduring qualities rather than the procession of events. The effect is to distract and detract from temporal flow. The lawyer evokes and manipulates time to mystify and clothe the space of violence. His questions steer her clear of that space, even when she veers towards it:

D: You knew what a police report was?

S: Yes. What did you want me to do? I couldn't put him under arrest when he was holding me down.

D: You have guns? What kinds?

He orients his questions towards the enduring and the general, decentering the details of spatiality and events of the encounter. The aura that she describes is intrinsically linked to time. Fear is a state of mind that depends upon time for its meaning. Anxiety, apprehension, and anticipation require a temporal flow, since they are forward-looking emotions.

More generally, he underscores the lack of official corroboration of her account of violence to imply that no violence occurred. Thus,

D: You didn't receive medical injuries?

S: Yes, I did.

D: You didn't receive medical treatment.

S: No, I didn't. I have a six year old at home . . .

D: . . . Ma'am, you've answered my question . . . You have signed this misdemeanor charge. Does it say anything about the battery?

S: No.

D: You had a chance . . .

S: Yes.

He provocatively implies that not receiving medical treatment signifies that she received no injuries; the misdemeanor charge says nothing of battery. How then could his client be said to have battered her? For her account to be true, it needs official registry, a record in the relevant institutions. The truth, the existence, the actuality of the claims she makes cannot be evaluated without them; more precisely, they can be doubted to have occurred without that documentation.

David Rebat takes the stand. He is an unemployed construction worker. Blond and strapping, he wears a clean, sky-blue work shirt rolled to the elbows, exposing stout forearms. He testifies that he has had a good relationship with his daughter and has been allowed to see her as often as he likes. When he was not allowed by the school to pick up the girl, he began calling Sylvia. He testifies that he called three or four times each day for about a week, a total of about twenty-five times. He then went to her house.

DR: I wanted to talk with Sylvia. I was upset.

D: Then what?

DR: She became hysterical[8] and she started screaming.

D: Where were you?

DR: I was in the alley.

D: Then what?

DR: I stayed. I said I wanted an answer.

D: And your daughter?

DR: She had sent her into the house. I told her I wanted an answer.

D: Did you grab or push her in any way?

DR: No.

D: How long were you there?

DR: The whole thing took about two minutes. I left after two minutes. She wouldn't let me in the house. I was frustrated . . . She kept screaming, becoming hysterical, turning into another person.

Mr. Rebat's testimony gives some background on the environment created. All he wanted, he says, was a response. "I stayed. I said I wanted an answer." He testified that he had called her as many as twenty-five times in the preceding days and that after he showed up he had refused to leave.

I want to linger a little longer on the tenor of the space implied by his testimony.[9] Quite apart from any further physical gesture such as throwing her down, he called her persistently for days, and he appeared at her door and refused to leave. As he testifies himself, the consummate effect was to put Ms. Rebat to screams when he showed up at her door. Although this is not an admission of guilt of domestic battery, it is a public avowal of harassing and terrorizing behavior—actions whose effects are disavowed. Although they provide an aura that has everything to do with violence—that *is* violent—the combined testimony to his comportment does not indicate the crime of domestic battery. Rather, her screams are evidence that "she became another person."

Sylvia Rebat's description of the violence, however, was not addressed at all. She reconstructed a picture of how dangerous and acute a situation it had become for her, with his relentless phone calls and his nonnegotiable presence in her doorway the day of the alleged battery. Her testimony gives evidence of this, regardless of whether she was actually assaulted. It counts as evidence, however, only if one acknowledges a phenomenological experience of space. As I have mentioned, this also requires that tempo, frequency, and interval all be admissible categories of experience that in this case ground her account of intimidation.[10] I am not presupposing that she was "telling the truth." What I am interested in is how she portrayed the space of terror and whether this was acknowledged by the court.

The court did not enter her perspective on space. Her subjective account of space is inadmissible. This failure was buttressed by both counsels. Both defense and prosecution emphasized Mr. Rebat's interpretation of space. He framed his conduct in terms of his role and rights as father. He confronted Ms. Rebat out of indignation at the violation of his privileged relationship with his daughter. "She stopped me from picking up my daughter from school. [I] went to see why. I practically had a carte blanche to see her . . . I stayed. I said I wanted an answer. I told her I wanted an answer . . . She wouldn't let me in the house. I was frustrated."

The prosecutor's cross-examination stressed the resentment that Mr. Rebat felt in having been so suddenly cut out of his daughter's life.

P: Any attempts to talk with her?

R: I called her.

P: How often?

R: Several.

P: How many times?

R: As much as four per day.

P: So as many as twenty times between the third to the tenth?

R: Possibly. Possibly three a day.

P: I'm talking probable?

R: Well . . .

P: You may have called her as many as thirty times?

Judge: How do you get thirty? He testified that some times as much as three to four, and some days not at all.

P: Out of all of those times, did you talk to her?

R: No.

P: How did that make you feel?

R: I felt like it left me outside.

P: Did it make you angry . . . [H]ow did it make you feel?

R: It made me feel left out . . . It made me frustrated. I see my daughter every day. She is seven years old.

After a pause, the judge ruled, "I have observed the demeanor of the witnesses to determine their credibility. There is no dispute that they have an encounter." There is a dispute about what occurred. The judge is required to rule "in cases with charges brought in the vacuum of the courtroom." He observes the witnesses and considers the evidence. In this case, "the denial is just as forthright as complainant. This does raise a reasonable doubt especially if it is an officer. I just haven't the evidence."

**

The judge fashions the courtroom as a "vacuum." *Tabula rasa*, the participants enter without a history. Bodies, responsibilities, trustworthiness have to be determined anew, from scratch, without prejudice. The judge is presented with two equal and contradictory claims. Inevitably, the situation turned into a "he-says/she-says." Since the evidence must show "beyond a reasonable doubt" that the man was guilty of the battery with which he was charged, the judge is acting in accord with principle in finding him not guilty.[11]

What happened? The two spaces, the space of the courtroom and the space of violence, are radically decontextualized. The participants contend for making sense—for having their sense be *the* sense, the authoritative sense of space. Explaining his position, the judge suggests he is required to assume nothing. Ostensibly, he excludes history, including the local history of the actors, and he excludes any connection this case has with anything else he has seen or heard or understood about violence.

Although he says he assumes nothing of the space, of course he assumes it is a domestic space. He assumes it is linked to no other structural or institutional consideration. It is necessary for him to assume that if he is to argue that he can know nothing about it a priori, no matter how many cases of domestic battery accumulate, no matter the structural positioning of the actors. Through this process, each case of violence is made unrelated to any other. The connection of this case with any other, which might lend it meaning, is steadfastly denied by the judge.

The history of the actors is also excluded from evidence. What is being determined is whether a certain discrete act, "The Push," was performed. The act is almost made into a fetish. One must establish its reality through evidence. That is what the case, finally, comes to rest on. Ms. Rebat's account of abuse would only make sense if history is taken into account. She did make several bids: "He broke three locks"; "He freeloaded off me for years." But these attempts were quashed immediately, and her testimony in this regard was excluded. More significantly, her logic of space, which required an attention to her own subjective sense of the space she was in, was rejected. In the antiseptic "vacuum of the court" a different criterion for evidence was being used. As if nothing else could be known, this logic *creates* a vacuum in space. Jurisprudentially, the reduction to "he-says/she-says" ultimately renders her account of space not just different from Mr. Rebat's, but subordinate. Since he is presumed to be not guilty, her account is negated by his denial of the specific act of pushing her down.

Her account of space can be resuscitated, brought back from oblivion, if only to expose the difficulty the court has to grasp it. According to her, the scene of the encounter was already marked as a space of violation, of his intimidation and her dismay, of his aggression and her screams in response (which signal what? Surprise? Fear?).

On reflection, one can see that Ms. Rebat's account of violence was actually largely *corroborated* by Mr. Rebat in significant respects. He did call an enormous amount of times. He did appear at an open door and refuse to leave. This is testimony to what was for her an ambiance of horror and anticipation. He admits many of the violent essentials.

Some women's reluctance to follow through with a criminal complaint is often erroneously chalked up to their women's psychological or emotional instability, their irrationality, or in some cases, to their suffering from battered women's syndrome (see Benedict 1992). Prosecutors and police often term it "victim non-cooperation."[12] These facile readings of women's responses do not take seriously their justifiable skepticism and hesitancy. Pence (1999) remarks:

> "Why should a woman cooperate with a process where there is very little in it for her?" The Domestic Abuse Intervention Project tried to argue from the standpoint of the woman: She does not want to testify at a trial that is taking place months after she was beaten; she knows the court will focus on one blow and not all of the abuse she is experiencing; she has nightmares of a courtroom scene in which a defense attorney will subject her to a sophisticated and legalistic version of her abuser's attacks on her, during which she will not be free to argue back; she sees that her abuser has an attorney but she does not; and she knows that none of the results is particularly helpful to her, whether it is a fine, a jail sentence, or an order telling him not to break the law again. (32)

"YOU DON'T HAVE TO DEFEND YOURSELF"

Family court, New York

A small room. Legally it's a private affair, so I am the only disengaged observer, having been approved as a guest by the judge. The others in the room are the judge, clerk, court reporter, and lawyers. Before the parties in the next case enter, the clerk looks at their file and comments to the judge and the court reporter that given their address, they must be wealthy. She reports that he is a cardiologist. They enter. As the lawyers make their respective cases, it comes out that they are in the midst of a divorce.[13] Her lawyer argues that the cardiologist comes into her room and asks for sexual favors. She testifies that he comes in uninvited and that she screams at him to get out. Denial of sexual favors is one of the grounds for the divorce. The women's lawyer is requesting an order of protection. Each accuses the other of "poisoning the kids" against the other.

> Judge (to lawyers) [the couple had been asked to leave the room]: I will make an order, but not an order of protection.[14] I will make it very clear that they are not to molest the other. I will give them a hell-raising lecture, too. The order is that neither party enters room of the other.

[The couple reenters.]

Judge: I don't want to micro-manage the house. I don't put kids out, I put parents out. Both sides are in danger. I expect them to be grown up. I'm sure it wasn't 100% him or 100% you. I know it wasn't the kids, but the kids are going to suffer. You know, you're orphaning them, or half orphaning them . . . You don't have to defend yourself. You don't have to. It's for the *children*. I will see which parent has bent over backwards to make the house good for the child.

She has testified that he comes into her room unsolicited and asks for "sexual favors." She responds by screaming. To see his actions as *encroachment* on her space assumes that the expression "her space" is a meaningful one in the context of marriage, family life, domesticity, home life. Her screams are a defense against his encroachment, as is her petition to prevent him from entering her bedroom.

The judicial response presupposes a particular construction of events. In attributing responsibility, the judge levels the asymmetry. What were specific nonreciprocal positions and experiences, he makes gender-neutral and mutual. "I will make it very clear that they are not to molest the other." Although it was only the woman who was asking for protection, the judge returns, "The order is that neither party enters room of the other." Finally, he assesses responsibility, "I'm sure it wasn't 100% him or 100% you. I know it wasn't the kids . . ." He seems to impose on the space a presupposed version of blame and also what would be best. What is best is what he imagines to be the best for the children, and what he imagines to be the best is to have both parents present. For example, he finds that divorce, or "half-orphaning" the children, will hold negative consequences for the children, in fact "make them suffer."

Perhaps most significant, however, was what held the judge's *attention*. Although the woman testified that she screamed when her husband came into her space, the judge dismisses her travails in favor of "the children": "You don't have to defend yourself. You don't have to. It's for the *children*. I will see which parent has bent over backwards to make the house good for the child."[15] Having your husband enter your room and make uninvited sexual overtures is not perceived as something against which you need to defend oneself.

Early in this book, I recalled Marilyn Frye's observation that "attention has everything to do with knowledge" (Frye 1983, 121). The judge's reasoning had everything to do with attention. He could only rule the way he did *if he did not pay attention to the woman's occupation of the space.* He had a preconceived idea of the children's well-being and what it would take to insure it.

The judge's decision did not so much ignore space as render a particular version of it. The analysis of space in this example helps to unveil violence in the form of male domination of space and sexual harassment that is ignored by the court. The decision to make the order mutual reveals the impulse towards homogeneity. In this case, it sidesteps the man's sexual harassment.

CONCLUSION

In this chapter, I have presented several cases with the intention of disclosing a central tension in each. The tension is between each woman's account of violence and the official court judgment of the case before it. The court flattens the multiplicity of women's spaces and supplants it with its own version of space, one that joins home and property.

In the cases I examined, each woman was very differently placed from the others. Each came from a distinct set of circumstances, with her own experience of violence. I have taken up the accounts of violence that each presented by focusing on the spatial description of the violence. This has allowed me to see some of the unique complications of the violence that each faced, the details that made it irreducible to the others. Using courtroom testimony, I have suggested that a range of logics animates the women's descriptions of lived spaces. Each gave evidence to indicate the psychological terror that suffused her home and often extended beyond it.

The clear relationship between the women ends there, however. I have culled court cases where very different women testified to disparate forms of abuse, harassment, or battering. This I did purposefully to refute any claim of internal homogeneity. Commonality between them can be argued only at the risk of simplifying, confusing the link of violence with sameness of circumstance. This implies a consequence of analyzing space as a way to uncover and interrogate violence against women.

As one looks at institutional response to violence against women while attending to the multiplicity of spatial constructions, one sees that institutions dealing with violence tend to homogenize it: all battering is turned into and constructed as the same, requiring a sameness of solutions. Attention to women's experiences and accounts of violence disrupts the homogenization of space by showing the multiple ways space is constructed and maintained by different women.

Compelling similarities are found less in the circumstances of the women themselves than in the judgments made in each case. In particular, the courts did not address themselves to the accounts that the women were voicing. I suggested that this had to do with an inherent conflict between the logic of abstract, geometric space and the subjective accounts of violence voiced by the women. In arguing this, I am not claiming that the testimonies of battered women—these or any others—are incontrovertible. Rather, I am noting that abstract space eclipses competing understandings of space with its own.

Several judges mentioned the right of a batterer to his "home." They interpreted it their duty to aid in preserving it: indeed, several decisions collapsed the right to property and the right to home. The space of "home" mixed with the space of private property trumped and superseded the voices of women in their own account of space and its relation to violence.

The case of the Rebats illuminates another element of this flattening of space. As we saw, the court decision rested on a reduction of context to "he says/she says," which was then not sufficient to convict Mr. Rebat. Because the testimony was given in the "vacuum of the court," the court claimed it was unable to see the witnesses in any way other than as two individuals who made conflicting claims about past events.[16] No structural or sociohistorical evidence, no understanding of gendered violence, was admissible. Thus, though the court had heard that morning a veritable parade of cases of violence against women, the case of the Rebats was considered wholly apart from all of them. This reduction to a pair of disputants, evacuated of history and larger social patterns, was typical of the other cases as well.

Women and their situations *are* related to one another, and solutions must come, in part, through seeing the ways in which people and their situations are tied. But to see the way in which people are connected does not mean one needs to see them as identical. It is an ethical and political imperative to recognize how our individual and collective fate is intertwined without flattening our experiences or our histories.

CHAPTER SIX

"Why Doesn't She Just Leave?"

In the previous chapters, drawing on interviews with activists, the insights of women of color and women involved the criminal justice system, I argued that violence against women is not and should not be treated as a monolithic phenomenon: different women face different forms of violence. The violence is not necessarily domestic violence. Violence is often backed up, implicitly or explicitly, by structural violence and the state. Indeed, sometimes the state is the primary instrument of abuse. Some communities have a history of being subject to subordination or abuse by the larger society, and this abuse often includes, or takes the form of, the abuse of women. But these different experiences of violence are cloaked under a discourse of sameness.

In this chapter, I will flesh out these claims by thinking through the many spaces women face violence.

WHY DOESN'T SHE JUST LEAVE?

. . . looms large over many women's lives. It is the question asked of any and all women who are in the grips of violence. "Why doesn't she just leave?" is asked without end, without history, without any view to social context. It presupposes that women are battered in a *place* (the home) and that they can leave. It presumes that women are safe once they leave.[1]

WHY DOESN'T SHE JUST LEAVE?

The question is sly. It blames the victim. Voiced in a certain way, it is a way of already taking sides, rendering a judgment. In an interview I conducted with an African American woman from New York City, she commented on the use of this "question": "The other day, some of the men were saying, 'Why do women stay with men who abuse them?' By saying that, they are *condoning* what the man is doing. Men need to learn not to participate in the disrespect of women." The question they were posing was not innocent. The men, according to this woman, were not even "asking" at all. Consequently, the operative verb, that they are "saying," is not infelicitous. She takes it that posing the question "Why do women stay with the men who abuse them?" is already to take sides, to render an opinion, to condone violence.[2] She sees men who ask this as participating in disrespect of women *in the very act of saying*. So, Why doesn't she just leave? might not always be a *question*. Although of course it can be. Depending on how it is asked, of whom, and who is doing the asking.

Why doesn't she just leave? is often posed abstractly, about any and all women who face violence. In the course of doing research and writing on violence against women, I am asked over and over why women don't just leave. In the present chapter I will visit and revisit its possible senses, the layers of meaning added to it, in considering specific women and their specific accounts of violence. This "question" will be taken up with attention to the violence particular women face, in order to show how the question is *in*attentive to the spaces women are in. Through this encounter with many different ways of occupying, passing through, resisting, speaking about, and living within spaces of violence, I will reveal that the presumption that all women can "just leave" really assumes a very narrow view of what violence against women is, where it happens, and how it can be stopped.

Women of color have testified to how structural violence (poverty, racism, the history of colonization) and institutional violence (sterilization campaigns in communities of color, skyrocketing incarceration rates) are vivid and central forms of violence in their lives. Facing these forms of violence, "leaving" does not apply. Given public or state support for or participation in violence, "leaving" does not always make sense even when the violence is rooted in the private.

Claire Joyce Tempongko was twenty-eight. The police were summoned to her apartment for the first time on April 2, 1999. Her lover, Tari Ramirez, had shown up drunk and on cocaine. He had smashed the bedroom window with his fist, according to the police report, and when he had finally gained entrance to the apartment, grabbed Tempongko by the hair and dragged her down the hallway. He slammed her to the ground, then picked her up, kissed her, and left. The police found him later and arrested him. Tempongko "did things right." She reported him. Subsequently, he was arrested several times for abuse, including violating an order of protection. "Don't leave me here with him," Tempongko had said to police.

Ramirez left notes for her, notes Tempongko took to the police. She secured more orders of protection. Ramirez was convicted of spousal abuse and sentenced to a program for batterers. At a women's gathering in the summer of 2000, Tempongko said, "This program doesn't work. Either he will kill me, or I will kill him." Ramirez continued to attend the program for batterers, although he was picked up several more times for battering. In October of 2000, he allegedly killed Tempongko in the presence of her children.

Claire Joyce Tempongko. We ask the question urgently, insistently, "Why didn't she leave?" But now it means something completely different. To leave does not just mean to move to a new address. It would mean to be forced to disappear as Claire Joyce Tempongko and to be reborn as someone completely different somewhere else. Taking up her situation, one might rather ask, "Who was she?" What was her life like? Were the police, the courts, prepared to help her? How did they abet her killer? In this case, even though she had several orders of protection, the authorities tacitly supported him in his abuse. They did not heed her pleas and released him. It was she who faced having to make herself disappear. From *inside* that space, one is led to ask about the details of her life, the institutions she encountered, the spaces through which she moved, her ingenuity, her frustration.

By attending to the particular circumstances faced by Claire Joyce Tempongko, one can begin to uncover the web of dangers, senses of safety, likely and unlikely places of refuge and resources that make up her situation. Her inability to find—or a collective failure to afford her—some recourse, some solution that was attentive to her circumstances, can be addressed in the context of the particularities of the situation she faced. For example, Tempongko was killed *after* she separated from Ramírez, (Mahoney 1991; see note 1 in this chapter on "separation assault").

Context is crucial (Ristock 2002). Different women face different forms of violence, maneuver, respond, and survive in different ways. What counts as violence shifts. Different women see violence emanating from different sources. A woman who works as a prostitute describes the violence she faces:

Q: What kind of violent experiences have taken place in your work?

A: Well, I don't know if this is violent or not. To me, it was. It was the first time I was arrested in San Francisco. I was with a girl. I didn't know her. She had two guys with her. She said they wanted to date her, so we walked around to the place that we were supposed to date at, and we find out that the guys were policemen. So the police said, "You're under arrest," and he said, "Bitch, if you make a move, I'll knock you down in the streets right now. Do you hear me?" I said, "I'm not going to do anything," and he said, "Did you hear me, bitch?" You know, he screamed and hollered at me. (Cited in Delacoste and Alexander 1998, 166)

For this woman the violence was the verbal harassment and threats by police officers. In order to understand it as violence, to think of the dangers of the situation, to understand police as the most obvious sources of (rather than, say, the protectors from) harm, requires an attention to her situation, her work, the dangers she faced and from whom. She implies that her understanding of what counts as violence may not be shared, since she leads into her description by wondering whether what she experienced counts as violence—or more accurately, whether it will count as violence *for the interviewer*, since "To me, it was [violent]."

The first time, I took this trick to the trick pad. It was evening time, probably 10:00 or 11:00. He was a young guy. It was really busy at the trick pad. He didn't want to wait. I didn't know you don't ride back with a trick who hasn't dated. So, I'm driving back and I'm looking out the window and the guy put a knife to my throat. He took me off for three, four hours in the hills of Albany. I tried every move I knew. I mean I cried, I pretended I liked it. I finally talked him into getting a room so that we'd spend the night together. Finally! So, we rode back to Berkeley and I jumped out of the car and I told him that he better get the fuck out of there and he drove away with his door flapping. He'd raped me numerous times.

Q: Wasn't it hard to get into a car again after that?

A: No, I knew that I'd done it wrong. It's a dangerous business and you have to protect yourself. (Delacoste and Alexander 1998)

Understanding her experience of space clarifies the conditions of her work, the decisions she makes, the actions she takes, and her experience of violence. Gaining insight into these questions is a precondition to fashioning solutions that meet her and her own occupation of those spaces. "Wasn't it hard to get into a car again after that?" her interviewer asks. This question can be interpreted two ways. It could be voiced from the outside, as a visceral unbelief that someone could get into strangers' cars again after such horror. But that would be to underestimate the conditions of a woman's life, what impels her or compels her to work in prostitution, what choice is, or is not, involved, in getting into another car after being raped.

The question does suggest another reading, however. It could reflect a little more insight into the spaces and perceptions of women who work in prostitution. Survivors of rape sometimes have trouble sleeping with *anyone* afterwards, including loved ones they do not fear (see MacKinnon 1987). In that spirit, the interviewer could be asking if the prostitute had trouble getting into cars with tricks who did not particularly telegraph danger, such as tricks who *had* dated. The difference in the interpretations is whether the question is asked from the inside or outside the prostitute's occupation of space.

The prostitute's response can itself be read two ways. "I knew that I'd done it wrong," might sound like self-blame. Alternatively, it could be a cagey response of a woman in a dangerous business that has nothing to do with blame: an astute calculation.

Spending time on those shades of meaning throws into relief the oddness of the question, "Why didn't she just leave?" as it is asked of any and all women. In the case of women who work in prostitution, when we ask anew, "Why didn't she leave?" the question sounds different. More than that, it sounds inappropriate. The impropriety lies in presupposing a narrow view of the spaces violence occurs.

Where could she leave from? From the street to a home? Into a car? From the car into the street? Where would she go? Who are the people that would offer support? The police? Other prostitutes? Her pimp? A shelter? Could she continue to go to work if she stayed in a shelter? (see Koyama 2006).

By asking these questions, one can notice the assumptions people make about women, violence, identity, location, and relationships (Soja 1996) and how different they are from the presuppositions of the question when it is asked of a woman who shares a home with her assailant. Indeed, for all women who live in the street who are subject to violence, the question cannot be raised easily, or if it is, it would have a different sense. Why didn't she just leave? is not the kind of question one asks of women in gangs, homeless women (Zorza 1991), squatters, women who work as prostitutes.

The prospect of refuge with the police, in a battered woman's shelter, in the court system: each poses systematic complications for her. Noticing the complications does not in and of itself provide the solution to violence, but it is a necessary preliminary to fashioning solutions.

Leaving is predicated on freedom of movement. In the case of many women who live in insane asylums, old people's homes, and prisons, they have somewhere to leave from, but they may have nowhere to go, and they are surely not free to leave. Each of these spaces is significantly different from the others. Living in and being unable to leave an old folks home is quite different from living in and being unable to leave a prison. The finality of a woman who lives in an old person's home having nowhere else to go is remarkably different from a woman who lives in an insane asylum having nowhere else to go.

Freedom of movement is particularly restricted for women with a criminal record. I have interviewed at least half a dozen women who are on parole or who are in a relationship with or related to someone on parole. I conducted these interviews as part of our ongoing community-based research on challenges people face once they get out of prison (see the introduction). Many women we interviewed complained about the actions of parole officers. One woman told us that her husband's parole officer constantly follows her in his car, shows up at her work and their home unannounced, searches them, searches their things, goes over the call history in her cell phone, frisks her. Other women have told me their parole officers comment on their appearance, and threaten to send them or their spouses back to prison. Some parole officers seem to have a peculiar intolerance of interracial couples and try to taunt them with sexual banter. How does a person "leave" if her parole officer is stalking her under the guise of monitoring her? If she "leaves," then she would become an absconder from the law, a fugitive. Can she go to a shelter? What if she is not on parole but stays because she feels protective of her son, daughter, or lover on parole? What mechanisms exist to protect her?

Many of the women we interviewed have been convicted of crimes. They have acted in ways that challenge the distinction between innocent victim and perpetrator. Who will protect them? Who will listen to them? Who will stand with them? If a woman has been convicted of committing a crime, especially a violent crime, or if she has associations with people who have committed crimes, she is offered even less protection.

What if she is not threatened by an intimate but by a group? A woman I know was receiving death threats from a gang. The threats were extremely graphic. She called a shelter, but she was told that the shelter was for women threatened by their partners, former partners, or family members, so they couldn't take her. They recommended that she call the police. But she has a criminal record and does not know if the police will protect her. She was in a tight situation, with few resources. Where can she go? Who will help her?

VICTIM NONCOOPERATION

Women who *do* call the police on an abuser are sometimes reluctant to follow through with pressing charges. They are often labeled "noncooperative" victims. The "problem" of "victim noncooperation" continues to vex prosecutors, police, and some advocates (see, e.g., McLeod 1983; Dawson and Dinovitzer 2001). Many paint noncooperative women as weak, even fickle, as disloyal to themselves and to those who try to assist them.

In order to combat this phenomenon, and in order to force police to be more responsive, some advocates for women started pushing in the mideighties for "mandatory arrest" policies when police answer domestic violence calls. These policies were followed by other, parallel, experimental measures, such as prosecutorial "no-drop" policies, where district attorneys could use "excited utterances" (e.g., 911 tapes of women calling for help) to pursue prosecution even in the face of a woman who recanted earlier testimony.

Academics and policy makers continue to debate the best use of "mandatory policies" as Donna Coker (2001) has termed them. Different policy recommendations are put forward on how to combat noncooperation, often backed by qualitative or quantitative studies (e.g., Beloof and Shapiro 2002; Holder and Mayo 2003; Robinson and Cook 2006). But as several commentators have pointed out (Coker 2001; Ford 2003), framing women who do not follow through as noncooperating victims is a narrow, and prejudicial, way to characterize them. David Ford (2003) suggests noncooperation favors a prosecutor's way of looking at things.

Indeed, despite its quasilegal and clinical sound, victim noncooperation, is tinged with official condescension and even exasperation. Much like the question, "Why doesn't she leave?" calling women who face violence "noncooperative" is to see them as curiously recalcitrant, as if no barriers exist to cooperating with police, as if the women are addicted to abuse. One *could* explore with seriousness and discretion why a woman does not collaborate with the police or prosecutors; instead, noncooperation is framed as itself part of the problem and as something to be overcome. Usually the suggestion is that the victim is engaged in self-destructive behavior.

But what of women who do not conform to the portrait of the innocent victim—those women who face mocking or indifferent police or stony, unresponsive prosecutors? What of women (or men) who do not want to "come out" as LGBT in court and thus refuse to press charges (cf. Lundy 1993)? In the last chapter, one woman, a veteran police officer, delayed filing a report because, she said, "I knew not a damn thing would be done." She was not wrong: she lost her case. When we pose victim noncooperation as a problem to be overcome through "victim" cooperation, we may be gainsaying the seasoned judgment of women who know that the courts, the police, and so on may not ultimately stop the violence they face.

SPACE AND COMMUNITY

In some communities that perceive themselves as (and may in fact be) under siege, it may be unacceptable to turn outside the community by calling the police. Within some South Asian communities in the United States, Anannya Bhattacharjee notes, the domestic space is constructed by the immigrant Indian bourgeoisie as the center of identity amidst a hostile, dominant Anglo culture. The domestic space is fashioned as a rampart against the forces of white racism and assimilation. In that context of public social conflict, complaints or criticism of the domestic sphere in an embattled community can look like disloyalty to one's culture. "Confronting accusations of having betrayed one's national cultural heritage is not an uncommon experience for members of Sakhi, a women's organization that deals with domestic violence in South Asian communities in New York City" (Bhattacharjee 1992, 19). Bhattacharjee sees the accusation as rooted in the kind of identities some immigrant communities assume.

> [W]e need to examine the private spaces constructed by the Indian immigrant community. It is in this space that the immigrant bourgeoisie guards what it perceives to be the nation's cultural essence against contamination by dominant Western values. It is here that the immigrant bourgeoisie steadies itself in the face of changes in a foreign country. This private space appears to be defined at two different levels: the domestic sphere of the family, and the extended "family of Indians" which is separate and distinct from other communities. (Bhattacharjee 1992, 38)

The space of the home protects "the cultural essence" from dominant Western values (see also Lynch 1994). Bhattacharjee and Sakhi refuse to let Indian immigrant bourgeoisie appropriate what it means to be an "Indian." "Indianness is not a natural excretion of a genealogical tree, but a continual struggle along multiple modes through a negotiation of the inescapable tension between secure definitions and a consciousness of the oppressions that such definitions rest upon. The struggle in the shifting grounds of immigrant experience hold numerous possibilities for liberation and for the invention of new social arrangements" (1992, 41). Since the space of the home is a staging ground for the preservation of the Indian community, the women of Sakhi are accused of jeopardizing that bulwark against Western values in a time of communal changes necessitated by immigration. So, in working against violence against women, one must acknowledge the perceptions, and the reality, of domination by the dominant culture, as well as, in this case, an Indian bourgeois nationalism. That does not mean ceding or conceding the grounding of "culture" as fixed. But it does mean acknowledging the stakes of what and who one is working for—and against.

Albert Memmi long ago identified the fixing or ossification of a living culture as posing an obstacle in many colonial (or postcolonial) communities (Memmi 1965, 87–79; also see Rosaldo 1989). As a culture becomes ossified, some community members develop an obstinate attitude to any threatened change. In a context of racism and xenophobia, where a community is struggling to maintain itself amid the real threats from the outside, some colonial or former colonial subjects may fear that any change will be a change towards assimilation—that is, a change towards the dominator's culture and values. Bhattacharjee encounters among the Indian immigrant bourgeoisie a need for their culture to be untouched. This itself is a clue that the culture is ossified or in the process of ossification.

Cleaving to cultural essence disallows deep critique of cultural practices. In this case, the grip has a sexist cast. The stance that the space of the home is the bulwark against the West implies that changes, even if they are good for women, are changes towards Western culture away from Indian culture. To put it differently, control over identity implies a struggle for control over women's lives.

Immigration, colonization of culture, fixed notions of masculine and feminine linked to an essence of national culture for the Indian bourgeoisie: these elements conjoin and partly define domestic space. The material alternatives to staying— facing homelessness, deportation—and the ideological and cultural stakes of leaving—being perceived as betraying one's nation or community, losing one's cultural identity—make leaving complicated, more taxing, even when physically possible.

But physical movement is not always possible. Attention to space draws one's attention to the social relations that make inhabitation and movement safe or dangerous, possible or impossible, meaningful or unmeaningful. Attention to space, for example, shows how one's identity can be cast into doubt as one responds to violence in one's community. In an immigrant community that is trying to construct an identity, a place, and a history for itself, to transgress a prevalent version of domesticity and home is to trespass: it is to indict some of its members' sense of nation and community. The consequences of violating these norms can be particularly severe, as Bhattacharjee notes. An immigrant woman's legal status is often dependent on her husband's sponsorship, which makes her even more vulnerable to exploitation (I explored this in an earlier chapter). Bhattacharjee notes vividly the gap in the dominant models to understanding the tight situation of immigrant women. "If she arrives in the United States through a decision that she did not participate in or agree to, then her classification as an immigrant which implies agency and free will is at best inadequate. When a woman abandons her abusive spouse in order to save her life, she may be out on the street overnight with no legal status, no home, no money, and, more often than not, no community" (Bhattacharjee 1992, 36–37). If she was forced to emigrate in the first place, lacking immigration papers, money, family, or community, "leaving" may be synonymous with "losing everything," "becoming homeless," or even, "no longer of the Indian community." One risks one's identity if it is tied to one's community. On a more basic level, in the context of forced immigration, it is presumptuous to assume that leaving is always physically possible. Some women, in the words of one lawyer, are spousal hostages.

Immigration policy changed significantly after 9/11. In an environment increasingly chilly even to legal migrants, Immigration and Customs Enforcement has detained ever greater numbers of immigrant men and women. This has raised the stakes for immigrant women as they try to maneuver. They can be subject to all sorts of abuse and extortion. This has led at least one shelter for South Asian battered women to recategorize destroying immigration papers or passports as a form of violence against women.

Elsewhere, Bhattacharjee has looked at cases of the police, immigration officials, or other government agents who invade the homes of immigrants (Bhattacharjee 2002b). She considers these assaults on women of color. She makes the radical move of proposing that raids by Immigration and Customs Enforcement are forms of 'violence in the home' (2002b). She poses this as a challenge to the movement to end violence against women.

Bhattacharjee also describes how nannies, cleaning ladies, domestics, and domestic cooks are subject to unfair and exploitative working conditions and to sexual harassment by employers, often without the (admittedly scant) resources that exist for women working in other sectors of the labor market (Bhattacharjee 1997). They work in isolation, often without a contract or fixed hours, and without many of the other formal and informal protections that other workers sometimes have. She concludes, "In my experience with immigrants in the South Asian community, I have found that 'home,' commonly accepted as the primary site of domestic violence, represents multiple concepts for people whose consciousnesses are shaped by migration" (1997, 308). Having these women in mind, she asks what it would be to place the *immigrant domestic servant* at the center of the analysis of domestic violence? To do so would be to tie the movement against sexual harassment at work to labor organizing efforts, to the immigrant rights movement and the movement against domestic violence and the antirape movement. This would be to think in coalitional terms but it would also mean challenging perceptions of violence against women and the "home."

Bhattacharjee introduces a dynamic way of thinking about culture in responding to violence against women in a context marked by cultural imperialism, class exploitation, and racism. The struggle is less one of individual redress (such as "leaving") than of collective engagement and redefinition (such as "the invention of new social arrangements"). She advocates a reconceptualization of culture; she rejects the appropriation of Indian culture by Indian nationalist bourgeoisie. Analysis of the spatial construction of Indian immigrant identity reveals a link between struggle for control over identity and its implications for the lives Indian women lead, the strictures under which they can define themselves against the grain, and the ways in which they can organize against violence.

These forces are not just external to women's lives. Certain areas of a city may be intrinsically tied up with who a woman is, how she is accustomed to acting, the language she uses, the set of understandings that are central to her form of life. She may go from place to place, but that would change radically who she is, how she is seen. Each part of her life is not irrelevant to who she is in those other spaces; however, each of those identities and the spaces that they are tied to need to be taken seriously.

***

The context of immigrant South Asians can be usefully compared with the tie between identity and social ties in other communities. For example, a group of activists from Massachusetts collectively authored a book that draws heavily on women's testimony to violence: "After my grandfather put a gun to my grandmother's head, she went to her rabbi. He sent her home to 'make peace.' Over the years her rabbi continued sending her home to keep shalom bayit [a peaceful home], even at the cost of her own life. When she divorced him in her seventies, she lived for ten more years, free of the abuse, but shunned by the community" (cited in Massachusetts Coalition of Battered Women Service Groups, Inc. 1992). In recalling the story of her grandmother, this woman reveals how the complications her grandmother faced in freeing herself of violence in a Jewish community significantly complicate the context of violence. Her response to the violence, going to the rabbi, is culturally specified as a meaningful recourse. The rabbi in turn invoked an abstraction: "shalom bayit," conjuring up a generalized and idealized conceptualization of domesticity (Horsburgh 1995). Nevertheless, it is a culturally specific one: a Jewish vision of domesticity, even if that vision is simplified, restricted, imagined, or patriarchal (Prell 1997). Shalom bayit is a Jewish institution that the grandmother is supposed to keep, even, as the granddaughter points out laconically, at the cost of her own life. The granddaughter's shift to the Hebrew term is another way it marks its distinctiveness from the Gentile mainstream.

The specific (though not unique) nature of her situation is marked in other ways. At the conclusion, the grandmother is said to have lived the last ten years of her life "free of the abuse, but shunned by the community." The parallelism constructed,

> free of the abuse
> shunned by the community

draws into relief the balance—and the tension—of the resolution.

Jewish women, Mimi Scarf points out, "have often been taught, sometimes in very subtle ways, to believe . . . a Jewish family is sacrosanct, and that the Jewish home is a bulwark against the 'outside' world." "Rabbis and other Jews in the helping professions, in their zeal to promote the Jewish home and family, frequently prevent themselves from recognizing that problems that afflict other cultural, ethnic, or religious groups exist in their own. Thus a situation has been created which contradicts reality; this in turn leads to a cognitive dissonance, for those involved deny what is happening to them by clinging to what they believe ought to be the reality" (Scarf 1983, 52; also see Price 2002). Jewish women who live in a tight community may find themselves in a dilemma similar to some South Asian women in at least this respect: if they complain about abuse or try to flee it, they face ostracism from a community invested in a self-protective discourse on the sanctity of home that is supposed to afford protection against the larger depredations of the dominant culture.

***

What is required is a cartography of violence against women that reveals the connections to other cartographies of oppression and domination. "Leaving" for some women brings no relief. Captivity is not always four walls. Once one hears many different accounts of violence, one begins to see that women do almost every conceivable combination of things to be free of violence. "Leaving" is too often collapsed into physical movement, into getting away. We have to reconsider inside and outside, passage through space, through time. Situations are turned into nightmares, unbounded situations, where there is no escape, no succor, no solace, even beyond the four walls . . .

> Your neighbors hear you screaming. They do nothing. The next day they look right through you. If you scream for years they will look right through you for years. Your neighbors, friends, and family see the bruises and injuries and they do nothing. They will not intercede. They send you back. They say it's your fault or that you like it or they deny that it is happening at all. Your family believes you belong with your husband.
>
> If you scream and no one helps and no one acknowledges it and people look right through you, you begin to feel that you don't exist. If

you existed and you screamed, someone would help you. If you existed and you were visibly injured, someone would help you. If you existed and you asked for help in escaping, someone would help you.

When you go to the doctor or to the hospital because you are badly injured and they won't listen or help you or they give you tranquilizers or threaten to commit you because they say you are disoriented, paranoid, fantasizing, you begin to believe that he can hurt you as much as he wants and no one will help you. When the police refuse to help you, you begin to believe that he can hurt or kill you and it will not matter because you do not exist.

You become unable to use language because it stops meaning anything. If you use regular words and say you have been hurt and by whom and you point to visible injuries and you are treated as if you made it up or as if it doesn't matter or as if it is your fault or as if you are stupid and worthless, you become afraid to try to say anything. You cannot talk to anyone because they will not help you and if you talk to them, the man who is battering you will hurt you more. Once you lose language, your isolation is absolute. (Dworkin 1989, 331–32)

Andrea Dworkin vividly represents a situation of facing violence in its sociality. Neighbors, friends, family, look right through you, send you back, pretend it is not happening. Doctors threaten to medicate; police are unsupportive. Dworkin reveals the social relations that allow and maintain the space as violent. The social and institutional failure to acknowledge her abuse reinforces her isolation as language ceases to mean anything. The desolate isolation that she experienced in her home, sent back by family, made invisible by neighbors, is emphasized by how peopled her life was. In fact, her web of relations is connected to her isolation. Rather than offer solace and succor or even merely recognition, in their willed inattention to her situation and to her attempts to communicate, they grounded her isolation: "Once you lose language, your isolation is absolute."

Dworkin's account discloses with intensity and apparent clarity how violence against women often works within a net of people larger than a couple. Working one's way into the situation that supports violence is a condition for seeing how other people do not necessarily alleviate her isolation. When one asks here about "leaving," one is forced to confront the lack of even superficial discourse around violence—how Dworkin was left to languish in an aura of culpability and failure by the willful ignorance of others. Her account communicates a claustrophobia that shades into a metaphysic: the lack of substantiation of her "regular words," and her "visible injuries," makes her begin to doubt that she exists, makes her doubt the efficacy of language, makes her despair of the possibility of communication.

Her experience is nevertheless narrower than it may seem to be. Although it is a powerful insider's description of violence, it is of a *particular* insider. She uses "you." The direct address is arresting, challenging, solicitous. Maybe it is a way of saying, "I know what it is like." This might be accompanying for some women.

But "you" is not an adequate placeholder for all women (Spelman 1988). While the experience she describes is not unique, it is not a universal experience of abuse. Even if the "isolation" she speaks of were a universal experience (which it is not), the *meaning* of the isolation is heterogeneous. For different women isolation has a different meaning; the difference counts since for some it includes isolation from one's homeland, from one's barrio, from straight people or from other lesbians, from one's family and friends, or from any human contact at all. Being trapped in a house as an undocumented Polish or Irish au paire *means* something different, the danger, the apprehension, the isolation itself, from being shunned by the rural Chicano community where your family has lived for three hundred years. Both are fundamentally different from the isolation that is faced by Dworkin's "you." All are profound forms of aloneness, but in each the character of the isolation, the degree and the way in which one is contained in space, the tie one has to the space in which one experiences violence, the spaces one can think might be less violent: each is different. Can you go to the neighbors? What could you tell them? Do they speak your language? Do you and your neighbors speak the same language as those outside of the community? What do you risk by going to a different space? What if the space you are in offers you refuge from other forms of violence? The claim to universality fails not only because the experience of "isolation" is not a universal one, but also because "isolation" itself is variable through space and identity. Who is turning their back on you? Why? What does it mean to you? What depends on their company? Your survival? Your comfort? Your ability to remain where you are? Your ability to remain who you are? "I found that straight people didn't want to hear what I had to say, and I found that my lesbian sisters didn't want to hear what I had to say. I was alone in dealing and getting out of the relationship" (cited in Massachusetts Coalition of Battered Women Service Groups, Inc. 1992). Straight people may not want to hear about any kind of domestic violence, as Dworkin's account depicts. Their inattention to violence between same-sex couples may be colored by homophobia, since straight people generally do not like to hear too much about gays and lesbians, anyway (cf. Warner 1993). As we saw in an earlier chapter, a lesbian's lesbian friends may have trouble admitting that a woman could be abusive. They also may worry about admitting to instances of lesbian battering in a fiercely homophobic culture.

The Native American poet Chrystos draws out some of the damaging implications of assumption of heterosexuality in her poem "'What Did He Hit You With?' the Doctor Said" (Chrystos 1986). Her poem begins,

Shame. Silence.
Not he.
She.

Chrystos identifies the assumption of heterosexuality. It shames the lesbian, leads her to keep her "silence." The institutional assumption of heterosexuality makes it harder for her to give an account of the violence she faces, preserving her in her isolation.

One is led to examine afresh Dworkin's vivid description of violence and ask what silences are buttressed by her evocative "you." Dworkin has her eye on family, friends, doctors, and neighbors. She wants desperately to disrupt the silence surrounding the space of domestic violence. Chrystos, identifying as a lesbian for a collection of essays on lesbian battering (1986), is writing to see the silencing of violence in the context of lesbian relationships. She is silenced by what may well have been an inadvertent gesture by a well-meaning doctor.

Returning to the question Why didn't she just leave? again and again forces a confrontation. We can see the insidious work that posing the question does— whether it works to condone men's abuse, to pose simplistic solutions, to blame women, to skirt structural violence, or to defer attention from abusers' own domination of space beyond the domestic sphere.

SPACE AND TIME UNBOUNDED: SEPARATION VIOLENCE

Crystal Brame first filed for divorce in 1998, alleging that her husband had threatened her, pointed a gun at her, and tried to choke her multiple times. David Brame was the chief of police for the City of Tacoma. He showed up at the divorce attorney's office with several police officers outside.

Intimidated, she did not press again for divorce until 2003. He continued to show up at divorce proceedings with other officers. "She felt she had to go up against the entire Police Department." City officials had also failed to follow recommendations from human resources that he have his badge and gun taken away. "She'd say, 'Who is the court going to believe? Someone who's been home for years or the police chief?'" Crystal Brame's skepticism was well-founded: a later investigation discovered that David Brame had suppressed an internal investigation years earlier that he had raped a co-worker in the police force. On April 26, 2003, after she had filed for divorce papers, David Brame pulled up next to his former wife in a parking lot and shot her with his service revolver within sight of their two children. He then committed suicide.

In this case, the policeman's domination of a woman's space is supported by the police force and by complicit state agencies charged with regulating the police. Subsequent investigation by the *Seattle Post-Intelligencer* pointed to widespread departmental and prosecutorial collusion with abusive officers throughout the region (Teichroeb and Davidow 2003) The example may illustrate some of the pitfalls of seeing criminal justice solutions as the road to stopping violence against women. It also illustrates the shortcomings of thinking women can always just leave. Crystal Brame had already left (see Mahoney 1991); as with many women, the danger from her abuser became even greater after she had separated. Another woman comments: "He has told me repeatedly that neither my children nor myself would ever be free from him and that he would stop at nothing to destroy us" (cited in Schechter 1982).

Some abusers see themselves not just as king of the home. They count themselves the king of infinite space. It is within their purview to follow a woman with a gun, to hunt her down years after separation. Counting oneself the king of infinite space cannot be maintained alone. An abuser must be implicitly or explicitly maintained in his or her position by a network of friends, family, coworkers, neighbors, the police, judges, and prosecutors. These networks and institutions collude in dominating women's spaces. The construction of spaces is a social process, implying social relations. David Brame acted with impunity because he was within an elaborate and powerful web of social relations, of people, offices, and organizations.

In an interview with me, an activist talked about her own experience of abuse. I had known her for some years and knew that she had been battered. I made a practice of talking with her about my research. In this particular conversation, we had been talking about violence against women for some time and had begun to discuss how the spaces of violence are a useful way to interpret the form violence took. "I recall," she began,

> I recall, and it has forever marked my inhabitation of spaces, that I would be outside controlled, I would be so far away from my batterer and nevertheless it was like I was absolutely visible to him. So that, all of my movements were . . . it is as if there was an omnipresence, so that all the spaces were spaces . . . under his definition. There was a sense in me that the space where I lived with him, where he beat me up, and it was never a public space, that that space a special, a special horror. I entered that space, and I had a physiological sense of a complete reunderstanding of myself that I can't go into. It was a very significant reconstruction in entering that space. A mixture of I think deep depression. I used to call it the "House of Sadness," that I'm entering the House of Sadness. The thought as I was traversing space, I would always think, I'm going to the House of Sadness. But at the same time, there was a distinction between that space and the street and all the spaces I would be in. But nevertheless, his reach was very much internalized by me. So that this construction of *all space* that I was traversing as having a meaning that was different from the meaning that other people would have, that if I had gone to court, the court would have. But at the same time, I would, like, escape, you know? I remember one time I met a woman who was in my class, and she asked me to go to her place. And I knew it wasn't right. I knew it was a violation of his construction of space that I go to her house. But nevertheless I went. And I had a sense of lack of volition in going, you know? That there was a submissiveness both in my

going and in not going. It was an enormous high-rise; it was a people's project, a poor people's project? I remember going, and it had a sense of fantasy about it, like I was entering a forbidden space. So how I constructed it was outside his reach but at the same time overdetermined by his reach. And as I was in there, I remember vacillating in and out of his construction and the construction of these people. And it was kind of liberating to be in a space that was so removed I think from his imagination at the same that some of the time it was reconstructed by his imagination. And I couldn't tell him that I had gone there. Because it was like a confirmation of absolutely every justification he had for beating me up. Except that I hadn't slept with anybody. But that . . . it wasn't possible in his definition that I hadn't slept with anybody. I had done already everything necessary to betray him—to betray his control over me. (Field notes)

As Trinidad theorizes it, she passes back and forth between different, contradictory constructions of the spaces through which she moves. In her account she draws into relation the multiple, contesting perspectives that construct her spaces. Since his "reach was very much internalized by me," she could feel herself "vacillating in and out of his construction and the construction of these people." Although this account is very much about space and about battering, she focuses primarily on the "construction" of space, and how it is intersubjectively imagined, lived, resisted. One of the implications of this focus is that it challenges and reroutes attention from the literal map of her movement, as in, "There she was! Outside of her batterer's grasp at last! Run!"—to an attention to her inhabitation and articulation of that inhabitation. Having to respond to his "omnipresence," she gives an elaborate description of the phenomenological experience of arriving at and then crossing the horizon of spaces that were under his "definition."

With this acute account of the experience of living under a construction of space, of *all* space as being defined by one's abuser, I return to our question Why didn't she leave? Writ on the world as he is in a way that she has simultaneously internalized and is actively resisting, the question is rendered overly literal, caught in an overly abstract logic of space that appears as overly concrete: since she passed in and out of the House of Sadness ostensibly on her own locomotion, the logic runs, she need not have returned. But abstract maps, with their deceptive and generalized logic of space do not meet this narrative on its own terms, as the subjective experience of the space. She apparently acknowledges this gap in understanding of space, even attributing to that gap the difficulties in finding recourse or refuge: "this construction of *all space* that I was traversing as having a meaning that was different from the meaning that other people would have, that if I had gone to court, the court would have." Not only is the space she was in a violent space, and one that defined "all space," but it was also an understanding that was not shared—a meaning, as she says, "that was different from the meaning other people would have and that . . . the court would have." However, she was able to go back and forth "vacillating in and out of his construction and the construction of these people." Trinidad had to negotiate her way through this multiplicity of meanings of space. She had to move among them without company, at great risk.

CONCLUSION

"Why didn't *you* leave?" The question is shocking, arresting. "Why didn't you leave?" when asked with frequency of women who face violence is not usually a good faith question open to their accounts of space. But "Why didn't you leave?" if it is asked from within an understanding of the space of the woman is a question about possibility, about whether a woman can change her situation, and if she does, at what cost?

Asking about movement, space, and violence within the framework of meaning of a woman who has faced violence can be an attempt to understand a person in her own account of space, the lived experience, the way that she perceived violence, the way in which particular spaces made certain things violent, opened certain possibilities and foreclosed others. But it is usually not asked from inside a woman's construction of space.

In recalling her circumstances when she was battered, Trinidad remarked to me, "From within that situation I had a sense that to leave and do well I would have to be or make myself into a different person. That loss: the risk of metamorphosis was part of the risk you are taking" (field notes). Understanding the experience of violence means taking up the possibility that to "leave" means a fundamental reconfiguration of the self vis-à-vis others—taking the risk of metamorphosis.

Many responses have been made to why women do not "leave." The assumption is that the violence is domestic, however, and make few distinctions between men and women in different circumstances, such as between Jewish lesbians in a small town, a Latina woman who works in prostitution in Minneapolis with a white pimp, women who are in prison or who have been in insane asylums, people with physical disabilities, Native Americans living on a reservation. We need to pay attention to people whose accounts are often excluded. This includes older women, women who don't speak English, lesbians, rural women, women who are HIV positive, undocumented women, homeless women, women who live with a cop, women who batter their own children. A student of mine writes to me:

As I was reading your manuscript, the question "Why doesn't she just leave" really stood out for me. I began reflecting on the times I heard that question in my own life. As a teenager, I can remember my mother being asked that question, and her response was "And go where?" . . . I remember getting into our new apartment and being afraid that he would find us. We were so scared we slept with a loaded gun in the living room . . . I was also asked the same question. My answer was not the same as my mother's. I said, "He won't leave." It was my house, my car, and basically it was all mine, and he took over like I was nothing. In looking back now I think the real answer was fear. It was simple. I was afraid to die.

In this chapter I have tried to challenge the homogenization and normalization of violence by focusing on the multiplicity of lived spaces that women occupy, construct, and traverse. By paying attention to space one can uncover not just details of a relationship and its structural positioning. Taking up Jewish women, lesbians, women of color, and colonized women in their understanding of space is a technique to begin to reconsider violence against women and organizations and institutions that respond to that violence, from law courts to battered women's shelters. What solutions make sense? Whose "sense" do they make? Particular dialogue on violence that is open to multiple constructions of spaces and violence is an essential precursor to offering solutions.

CHAPTER SEVEN

Tentative Conclusions and Small-Scale Solutions

An immigrant to the United States told me she awoke one night to the sounds of someone trying to gain entry to her apartment through the back door. She was scared and alone, so she called several friends. "The next day," she remarked to me a bit sardonically, "I learned I was supposed to call 911." Part of becoming acculturated, it would seem, involves learning to rely on the police. I was struck by how, even in this moment of urgency and potential emergency—catching an intruder trying to gain entrance to her apartment in the middle of the night— she had no impulse to call the police. It is not that she considered calling the police and decided not to; she did not even contemplate it. She relied instead on friends. A common rationale in the United States for calling the police, even for people generally skeptical or suspicious of the police, is for crisis intervention—for example, when someone is breaking into your house or when you are in imminent threat of bodily injury. It did not even occur to this woman.

I take this story, and my own initial surprise, as signaling something important of U.S. culture with respect to the law. It suggests the strong, almost instinctual turn many have to criminal law and law enforcement as the response to violence against women. The turn to the law is taken for granted in many cases. For many, especially for many born outside of the United States, this is not always self-evident, necessary, or natural. Such a posture is instructive.

People in the United States are often ambivalent about law enforcement (cf. Coker 2001). In communities of color, the police are often treated with suspicion, as a source of harm, or even, as James Baldwin remarked of the police in Harlem, as an occupying army. In some communities, a person may face repercussions from neighbors, such as being shunned, if he or she calls the police (I discussed an example of this in an earlier chapter).

While some directions in radical feminism have always maintained a critical distance from the state, these days many projects to stop violence against women are involved with the state, either because state or federal monies fund the projects or because they were created, regulated, and/or limited by state and federal legislation (see Gottshalk 2006 for extensive analysis; also Bumiller 2008). Nevertheless, feminist critics have made trenchant criticisms of state participation in the antiviolence movement. Susan Schechter's landmark (1982) book, *Women and Male Violence*, and the more recent work of legal scholars like Elizabeth Schneider (2000), Ann Romkens (2002), and psychologists Michelle Fine and Lois Weis (2000), chart how the government has imposed outside controls on shelters and hotlines, requiring credentialing of workers and advocates, and subjecting feminist projects to the caprices of government cut-backs.

A deeper, or more radical, critique sees the state as responsible in many ways for the violence perpetrated on women (see, e.g. Mills 1999, Bhavnani and Davis 2000; Ritchie 2006). "Over the past couple of decades, the public has become more familiar with the reality of domestic violence, but too often people see the government and law enforcement as the answer to this pervasive problem. But can a government/state which is based on violence, which wages continual war against other nations, and here at home imposes the violence of poverty, miseducation and policy brutality on communities of color—can this government be expected to genuinely oppose domestic violence?" (*Fire Inside* 2004). Sue Osthoff of the National Clearinghouse for the Defense of Battered Women echoes this critique of depredations by the state, particularly in communities of color:

> Unintended consequences are surfacing from over-reliance on the criminal legal system. Twenty-five years ago, women of color were saying that we should not turn to the criminal legal system. But we put all our eggs in one basket without seeking other creative ways of community intervention. The battered women's movement has contributed to the increase in the police state and the increase of men in prisons. We are telling battered women to turn to a system that is classist, sexist, homophobic, arbitrary, and not unlike the batterer. (Cited in Bhattacharjee 2002a, 15)

Prominent legislation such as the federal Violence against Women Act tends to fund law enforcement solutions—buying equipment for police or other measures in favor of prosecuting offenders—more than funding educational projects. The victims' rights movement also promotes criminal justice solutions. In this dominant frame, it is self-evident that "violence against women" is basically an issue of domestic violence and that the solution is to criminalize it. Prominent advocates such as Evan Stark still promote criminal justice solutions, despite years of critique from immigrant rights groups and many women of color (see Stark 2007; 2009).

By putting the voices of women at the margins at the center (Richie 1996; 2000), as I have tried to do in this book, one notices some of the problems with criminal justice solutions. Because of racism in the criminal justice system, men and women of color bear the brunt of these policies, as well as some poor white women (Ritchie 2006, 138ff). As many commentators have pointed out, the incarceration rate for both men and women of color is skyrocketing—higher than it has ever been. The organizations Incite! and Critical Resistance argue that criminal justice solutions tend to take away women's agency and undermine women's grassroots struggles. It is not even clear that criminal justice solutions have led to any decline in the number of women who are abused or are killed, for example (Incite! 2006, 223–26).

The enduring paradox is that most people in the United States tend to see violence against women as domestic and the solution with the state. These two faulty (in my view) perceptions are linked. When we see all violence against women as *domestic* violence then it becomes possible to see the state as providing solutions. Rather than presuppose the "home" as the site of violence and the government as the solution, the starting point for this book has been with what the most marginalized women claim as violent.

For example, in the last chapter, an interviewer asks a sex worker what violent experiences she has had. She describes verbal harassment from the police. "I don't know if this is violent or not," she starts, implying she does not know if her criteria are shared, but she concludes, "To me, it was." Her criticism of the police is echoed by many other sex workers. Indeed, I cited one woman who held that the government "pimps women" when it fines and criminalizes prostitutes. "You could invent a new terminology for it: secondary pimping, vicarious pimping, whatever—but it's still pimping, plain and simple."

In chapter 3, the woman I profiled, Mary Lou Dietrich, paid a heavy consequence for reporting her former lover to the police after her lover assaulted her. For having broken the taboo against speaking publicly of violence in lesbian relationships—and for having turned another lesbian over to the authorities, Dietrich wrote that her lesbian community "doubled my victimization and continues to tolerate my former lover while it shuns me." Ironically, having paid the price of ostracism by reporting the abuse to the police, she did not "come out" in court, which I attributed to the muting effects of institutionalized homophobia, so she was silenced on all sides.

Dietrich found company with other battered women, including heterosexual women, and she wrote approvingly of police and prosecutorial response. At the end of that chapter, I suggested that her relatively easy identification with other battered women might have been more complicated if she had kept in mind the experiences of lesbians of color, especially those at the margins of the law.

In that same chapter I compared Dietrich's situation to young African American lesbians studied by Beth Richie. They provided examples of being forced to prostitute, of risking gang rape, and of being battered by young men they felt forced to pair with. The incarcerated native women Luana Ross interviewed told how their jailors' homophobia meant they were punished harshly—medicated, kept in isolation, verbally harassed—for any gesture of affection they showed towards other incarcerated women. These examples add important dimensions to what could be a new cartography of gendered violence.

Because the mainstream LGBT movement has not done enough work to fight racism and colonization, argued Beth Richie and María Lugones, many gays and lesbians of color are left on their own and not supported. At the same time, they charge that many antiracist groups, and often communities of color in general, though they may fight racism, colonization, and xenophobia, have not done enough to support gays and lesbians of color. As a result, many LGBT people of color live closeted lives or keep a low profile in the neighborhoods they are from. This makes them particularly vulnerable when they face intimate violence, since only a few larger cities have organizational resources for gays and lesbians in communities of color or in immigrant groups. This was well illustrated by the interview I conducted with Juana Liliana. Despite the vital work it does for Latinas, like many other community-based organizations that respond to abuse, her organization continues to operate around a normative model of heterosexual monogamy, which makes it a less hospitable option for women who fall outside of this relatively narrow mold.

The structure of vulnerability in which lesbians of color must live has been made more menacing by the policy of stepped-up immigration detention and deportation under Bush and Obama. Of course, these policies hold consequences for all immigrants. But as I argued in chapter 2, following Syd Lindsley, the war on immigrants disparately affects women. Juana Liliana remarked that many women she knows and counsels prefer to suffer through battering because, "they fear the authorities more than the fists of her batterer."

If we attend to examples like these, we could draw a new set of maps of safety and danger, multiple maps where the same space can be a place of liberation and a place of fear, confusion, or risk. The key methodological device has been to follow women in their descriptions of spaces of violence as a way to uncover difference. This focus on space leaves a great deal of theoretical room for formulation of what "violence" is, how it is enacted, and the psychological component of ambiances that are infused with fear or a sense of danger. From these descriptions of space, I have tried to make a countermap of violence against women that emerges from an attempt to listen and record what counts as violence in a given situation, who does it, where, and under what conditions. This countermap reveals what is sometimes hidden from the dominant angle.

Listening to their voices alone does little, however, without a shift in cognition. I have tried to accompany the listening with a methodological openness and a cognitive attitude of ginger uncertainty in taking up outsiders' accounts. This would include countenancing many realities. If to simplify is to mute, then to approach things in their complexity is to listen while distrusting that one understands everything one is hearing. By the same token, the accounts in the preceding chapters include both firm and hesitant narratives, convoluted forms of address as well as direct, clear, harsh, unambiguous testimonies.

By focusing on women at the margins, I have tried to decenter the home. The voices of the women lead us to focus not only on battering per se, but also on the women's relation to the complex set of institutions they move through—they are often forced to move through—with greater or lesser ease, with greater or lesser vulnerability.

One theme that has emerged has been how many women engage in complex rhetorical maneuvers: at times they identify with other battered women, including women from the dominant class. Much of my analysis has been trying to follow how they see themselves in relation to other women both like and unlike themselves and the reasons they may claim sameness even as they mark their difference. Echoing the work of Martha Lucía García, María Lugones, Beth Richie, Kimberlé Crenshaw, and others, I have noted that the claims to "unity" may be sometimes at cross-purposes with focusing on problems in their particularity. This is especially true if unity is about claiming sameness or commonalities instead of attending to difference.

In the first chapter, I showed how the Power and Control Wheel has come to redescribe violence as *domestic* violence, where the solutions are from outside institutions; in other words, it has come to separate interpersonal intimate violence from the structures and institutions that support it. The Cycle of Violence also does this. Seeing violence against women as not just interpersonal (battering, rape) but also structural (denial of resources to live and flourish) allows us to be more ambitious and far-reaching in the aim having a society in which women (and men) live violence-free lives.

In the second part of the book, holding in mind the analyses by women at the margins, and my own account of structural violence, I reviewed institutional accounts of violence that privatize violence and separate interpersonal violence from the institutions and structures that support it.

"Interpersonal" violence and "structural" violence are not dichotomous. They exist on a continuum and are related in many ways. The very structure of poverty or of immigration law is violent to women. And though these are forms of structural violence, they are not entirely impersonal forces; I do not want to let the decisions of agents of policies off the hook, because the treatment— the mistreatment—is ministered by *someone*. Social service providers, police, or prosecutors are sometimes helpful to women in individual cases. But as we have seen in the previous chapters, they can act in abusive ways towards immigrants, women in prostitution, and other women at the margins. And when they do, they generally act with impunity. Here, then, is a link between state and interpersonal violence, where the state is personified in its agents. The analysis of and fight to stop violence against women must be accompanied by an equal effort to analyze and stop the prevalent socially embedded forms of structural violence against women.

The analysis of social structures cannot be limited to an ahistorical glance at the present. This is because often what people understand as violent has a history behind it. I have looked at how some Jewish women, South Asian women, and others who live or have lived as members of oppressed groups suffer because those groups sometimes construct the home as a place of refuge against the dominant, historically hostile, culture. This makes exposing violence in the intimate sphere particularly difficult. Historical genealogies have a profound impact on the meaning of gendered violence, on its stakes, on the solutions that make sense, on who is a potential ally, on who one identifies with, on who is the subject of suspicion, to what one is loyal, what one is prepared to betray, or what one may inadvertently end up betraying. I can learn those genealogies, and in this way I experience the movement as heterogeneous and heterodox.

Histories, of slavery, of native genocide, of medical control of reproduction, will resonate deeply with some, while others must learn these legacies, especially if the commonsense notion in the dominant white culture is that the United States has largely liberated itself from the racism of the past. We live in a social reality peopled by a contradictory heritage and many widely divergent conceptions of oppression. The histories inflect the meaning of acts of violence, from small gestures to the character, methods, and strategies of political movements.

Part of providing solutions means dwelling on all of the problems and their histories in their complexity. Lingering on the questions without answering them too quickly might also open up possible solutions. For example, arguing for a shift in how sexual and domestic violence is conventionally understood, Native American activist Andrea Smith writes that if sexual violence "is also a tool of colonialism and racism, then entire communities of color are the victims of sexual violence" (2005, 9)." She writes, "The struggle for [Native] sovereignty and the struggle against sexual violence cannot be separated" (137). Applying this frame, she analyzes a range of activities not usually associated with violence against women. She includes environmental racism, spiritual appropriation, sterilization campaigns against Native Americans and others, and the notorious but underreported abuses at Native boarding schools as all parts of the colonial practices that have meant suffering, alienation, expropriation, death, disease, the occupation of native lands, and the genocide of many Native peoples. She rereads all these experiences in terms of how they are all practices of sexual violence against Native women, where they are the more prominent target in an ongoing war against Native peoples.

Women of color have pointed out that doctors who sterilize poor and minority women without their knowledge or consent or encourage them to take unsafe contraceptives like Depo-Provera are also guilty of violence against women (Roberts 1998). Dorothy Roberts provides an important way of contextualizing our research at the county jail which reveals a wider and different understanding of violence against women. She argues that overprescribing dangerous birth control medication like Depo-Provera to African American and Third World women is linked to the sterilization campaigns of the twentieth century (Roberts 1998).

I think of Dorothy Roberts' analysis when Noelle Paley, a student, comes to talk to me. Noelle is involved in our project to document health care abuse at the county jail (see Paley and Price 2010). She tells me that she is concerned for the safety of a young pregnant woman she interviewed at the jail. Both Noelle and the prisoner herself are concerned about her pregnancy because she had started getting injections for Depo-Provera but became pregnant anyway and is worried the Depo will affect the fetus. She is not getting prenatal care, and she cannot get her questions answered.

The sterilization campaigns Roberts describes were systematic, self-consciously and explicitly organized by medical, governmental, and nongovernmental organizations to sterilize groups of women, including poor white women, those classed as "feeble-minded" and women of color. The pressure to have the medical procedure done was coercive and manipulative.

Is the woman at the jail, suffering side-effects of Depo, unable to get prenatal care and worried about her health and the health of her fetus, living the consequences of these earlier sterilization campaigns? Is she subject to a form of gendered "violence"?

Such questions could be greeted with puzzlement if we take the mainstream view that "violence" is only a one-on-one act of intentional bodily harm and do not look at institutional and racial history. She is indeed subject to institutional violence for here are clear examples of practices that limit a woman's potential, and that of her offspring, which is the test for structural violence (Galtung 1969).

If this is so, then this brings us far beyond the conventional terms for framing "violence against women." This necessitates that we understand other wars, other forms of domination, beyond (but including) gender oppression: the history of colonization is important to understand the meaning, purpose, and systematic nature of the sterilization campaigns. The struggle for reproductive justice comes together with struggle for adequate health care, the fight against poverty, against incarceration, and against racism.[1] This framing encourages us anew to go beyond the state for solutions to the problems associated with violence against women.

In that spirit, let's return to the initial vignette in this chapter of an immigrant calling her friends. What are solutions to violence against women that do not involve the law or legal reform? Forging solutions takes creativity and imagination. It also takes more attention to the ways women, here and abroad, *already* respond to violence without necessarily privileging state agencies, including the police.[2] Cultivating alternatives would take thought and care: I do not suggest this lightly or in a utopian way.

Many inspired projects have emerged in recent years. Figueira-McDonough and Sarri (2002) review a large number of organizations, associations, coalitions, and other grassroots projects that challenge interpersonal and institutional forms of violence against women, especially against women located at the margins. Though Natalie Sokoloff's collection *Domestic Violence at the Margins* is (as the name suggests) largely focused on domestic violence, many of the contributors frame interpersonal violence within larger social structures and forms of oppression (Sokoloff 2005). Lisa Sun-Hee Park, for example, shows how an organization that ran a hotline for Korean and Korean-American women was invited to join, and joined, a coalition to fight for immigrant rights (2005). Websdale and Johnson describe how a domestic violence intervention project in Kentucky was useful because it countenanced how abuse was linked to other forms of structural inequality, especially economic disadvantages in a poor community. They show how the project addressed the structural inequality through supporting housing and "job readiness" training (Websdale and Johnson 2005). Two anthologies published by the collective Incite! *Women of Color against Violence* (2006; 2007) feature reflective, thoughtful self-descriptions of antiviolence projects. Many of the essays explain concrete methods, tactics, and review experiences. They do not ignore contradictions sometimes engendered by working against violence against women in the shadow of the legacies of racism, colonization, homophobia, and the dangers of institutional co-optation. These projects, and the essays that treat them so subtly, are constructive, practical, and inspiring.

Restorative justice approaches are often put forward as an alternative to criminalizing violence. Restorative justice emphasizes individual and community accountability and in some cases restitution and conciliation, instead of punishment and retribution. Some attempts at restorative justice propose solutions that do not involve the police or the courts. But as Andrea Smith (2005) acknowledges, "restorative justice" is a broad term and includes an array of practices, including some that act hand-in-glove with the criminal justice system. As she and other commentators have pointed out, moreover, restorative justice approaches must be used discerningly, because often they are used in ways that implicitly or explicitly suggest that an abused woman continue to put up with abuse.

Similarly, alternative dispute resolution is sometimes recommended as an alternative to the courts. A concern raised by many feminists is that alternative dispute resolution overlooks the differences in power between people—especially between abuser and abused. The assumption that they are socially equal is a dangerous conceit artificially maintained in the moment of mediation.

Alternative dispute resolution also tends to individualize the protagonists in a scene of violence. Instead, this book has tried to paint a picture of violence that includes structural violence. Since the abuse is not just personal but also backed by institutions and social structures, responses to violence ought to engage these larger structures. (In this case, Brenda Smith has recommended a "truth commission" as a technique [2005]).

Contemplating some of these thorough and thoughtful grassroots projects and the essays they inspired, I cannot avoid a certain pessimism: the solutions seem so provisional, and either so ambitious as to be unlikely or so small in scale as to leave relatively unchecked the massive amounts of violence. In rolling up my sleeves, I consider the enormous financial support for other kinds of "solutions" such as prisons or other forms of surveillance and monitoring which has grown at a tremendous rate in recent years. Pharmaceutical companies are successful and profitable in cynically marketing dangerous contraceptive devices to women of color. Violence seems to saturate the society, seems to constitute our history.

My pessimism is certainly no criticism of their perceptive selection of hopeful examples. Activists have fought successfully against the sexual abuse of incarcerated women in Australia (George 1993); Puerto Ricans have organized against doctors who have waged sterilization campaigns. These are attempts to solve pressing problems without looking for a silver bullet, a fixed model, or a set technique. There is no silver bullet, no one model or solution.

On that note, I would like to temper the pessimism: perhaps solutions must be small in scale and careful. It is a cliché that all politics is local. However, given such a multifaceted phenomenon as violence against women (Das 2008), as we continue to learn and discern the plight of specific women, groups of women, and particular communities, we must remain pliant enough to adjust our responses, rethink our tactics, reapply our energies, and reconsider our paradigms and assumptions of the world around us. This is even more the case when we stop to consider that it has often been the most marginal who have been excluded, overlooked, or fit into preexisting ways of working against violence.

This would not so much produce a single model or solution as generate an ethic of reflective and critical vigilance on one's engagement. In a similar vein, Janice Ristock has commented that "all monolithic understandings of abuse are flawed" (2002, xi). "'Mutual abuse' is wrong, 'power and control' is wrong, 'effects of patriarchy' is wrong when indiscriminately applied." She concludes by arguing that "we need different ways of responding that attend to the complexities of these differing power dynamics" (2002, xi).

I do not mean to propose reflection *outside* of practice so much as *in* practice.

A Chicana activist I know worked in a shelter in the border region of Southern Arizona where most of the employees were white women, and most of the women who had come seeking shelter were Latina. One night, when a group of women was going out, the shelter workers laughingly gave them all condoms and warned them to be careful, much to the chagrin of my friend. She and I discussed the gesture at length. Was it a laudable feminist gesture to give women control over their bodies? Or was this was a way of taunting Chicana women by inappropriately suggesting that they are sexually loose? Was it a way of urging them not to get pregnant? Was there some undertone of control? Or was it simply a liberatory gesture, with no racial overtones, of providing prophylactics to women? The act is ambiguous and open to interpretation.

In prisons and jails, women have to put up with invasive strip and cavity searches, often coerced. Amanda George (1993), Angela Davis (2003) and others have put strip searches on the map as a form of routinized violence. Why aren't strip searches of women prisoners a more visible object of the fight to end sexual harassment and sexual assault? If they occurred anywhere outside the prison, they would be (George 1993). As George observes, while a cavity search is invasive for anyone, if a person has been sexually molested, then it can be retraumatizing. The strip search is a violent practice, even if it is legal and routine. Identifying it as "violence against women" requires focusing on women's experiences and perceptions of where violence comes from, what it amounts to, and who does it.

We interview an older, disabled woman in her home, who relives being forced to strip and shower at the jail after her arrest, ringed by laughing male and female guards who refused to touch her, who said they were repelled by her smell.

I see an entanglement between sexual violence, institutional violence, a war on the poor, a war on women, neglect and mistreatment of the afflicted. Scrutinizing their lives, trying to accompany them in their struggles, overcoming obstacles, facing down terrors, we can rethink the map of violence against women. We can take the personal, individual accounts of particular women and frame them within larger structures and histories that limit the lives of women, crush them and their potential. I tell this woman that the health care at the jail has been privatized (much to the detriment of the inmates) and invite her to join us in interviewing others. That she joins us is a sign we are on the right track.

The women and men we interview at the jail tell us that it is important for the administration to know that people are checking up on them, that they are not alone. The incarcerated people are always invited to join us; they also give us tips and pointers. We make connections with people once they get out; we work together on the nest of other problems we encounter—problems with parole officers, with childcare workers, and with health care delivery. In this way we try to overcome the social fragmentation in our town and in our society.

***

Taken in its entirety, this work points to coming up with many solutions. Not just one. The spirit of this book is ultimately hopeful. The goal of this research is to examine with great care and attention women's depictions of violence and its circumstances in order to contribute to fashioning solutions that change those circumstances and thus end violence. The critical aspect of this work derives from a commitment to construct analyses and solutions that end violence that are not based on false beliefs regarding the experiences that women voice, who the women are, how individual women's identities change and evolve, and how this affects their conception of the violence they face.

I began with an older woman bruised, beaten, and neglected, in the same jail her sister died due to negligence twenty years before. The history is a special kind of history, because it is not a history of change, nor is it a history of progress or of advance. It's more of a spiral history, a history of return, a history inhabited by ghosts, where people still invoke slavery as a way to understand our social relationships, living out its consequences today, where people still live a present and a future haunted by the past, hunted, caged, and enchained. In some ways, it's a history of stasis.

Let me end with another story that I place alongside the one with which I opened. A grandfather whom we interview about his experiences in the jail calls to encourage me to interview his granddaughter at the jail, who is pregnant and not receiving proper medical care. The granddaughter has not been found guilty of anything. She is just awaiting a trial. We spend several months, my students and I, checking in on the woman each week. She is glad for the visits, but it is not clear to me that they have any salubrious effect on how she is treated by the jail. Quite the contrary, sometimes she has to deal with the sarcasm and suspicion of guards who ask about our visits. Yet she asks us to continue to come. She is scared about her health, but she is punished for asking too often to see a doctor. I send her a copy of *Killing the Black Body*, a book about reproductive justice and African American women. She tells me of others who have been on Depo-Provera and the terrible side effects.

After several months in jail, still incarcerated, she gives birth to a baby boy. A week later, the district attorney drops all charges. When she was arrested, she lived with her son, had a job with the government, and lived in a fully furnished house forty-five minutes outside of Binghamton. When she is released, she has lost her job, all her furniture has been stolen, her lease has been taken away, and her boy's father, who lives in California, has gained custody of her son. Moreover, her baby is born in chains, if you will, in the place of unfreedom, the modern carceral, to a mother who is in chains, shackled, and who is the descendent of people who came to this country in chains.

I continue to meet with her, and I see how she reconstructs her life, with the support of others, including one of my students who is also a mother. I see how the boy slowly grows, healthy and happy.

I am not a hopeful man, and I see this as an ambiguous and ambivalent story, right beside the story of the woman who is in jail still, with the memories of her brutalized dead sister to accompany her. I see these issues as at the center of our lives: the shame, the mortification, the violence that complicates the distinction between victim and perpetrator, helper and helped, protector and violator. I submit this story as hopeful and also as saturated with pain and the gray of institutional walls. The work of fighting violence needs to name and expose the private, the hidden, and the invisible. This is true of domestic violence, but it is also true of institutional violence. If we see the connections, then we can imagine and work towards new links and coalitions.

Notes

INTRODUCTION

1. I have assigned pseudonyms and changed identifying details in order to preserve people's privacy and confidentiality.

2. On violence against women in prisons, see Amanda George (1993), Luana Ross (1998), Paula Johnson (2004); on violence against women who work in prostitution, see Giobbe (1994), Sanchez (1997a; 1997b); on violence by border agents against migrant women, see Bhattacharjee (2002a), Saucedo (2006).

3. I would like to thank Lubna Chaudhry for discussions and analysis of structural violence. See Johan Galtung: "Violence is present when human beings are being influenced so that their actual somatic and mental realizations are below their potential realizations" (Galtung 1969, 168).

4. I draw here and in the following on text I develop more fully in Lugones and Price (1995).

5. I discuss this further later in the book. The following are a few representative examples:

"The huge pile of data about battered women which the victim blamers have amassed reveals one critical fact: one battered woman is as different from the next as night from day. Taken all in all, the studies show that all battered women have only one significant characteristic in common—they are all female.

"Some battered women were abused as children; others were not. Some battered women never got past grade school; others hold advanced degrees. Some battered women have never held a job; others have worked all their lives. Some battered women were married very young, others in middle age, others not at all. Many battered women are very poor; many are well-to-do. Many battered women have "too many" children, others none at all. Many battered women are passive introverts; others are active extroverts. Some battered women drink too much or use drugs; others never touch the stuff. Many battered women are black; many others are white, yellow, red, brown. Many battered women are Catholic; many others are Protestant, Jewish, Hindu, Muslim, agnostic, atheist, Buddhist, Mormon. In short, there is not [a] typical battered woman. Or to put it another way, any girl or woman might be battered" (Jones 1994, 85).

"Battered women come from all types of economic, cultural, religious, and racial backgrounds. They are millionaires, and they are women on welfare; they are uneducated women, and they are practicing professionals with J.D.s and Ph.D.s; they are mothers and they are childless; they are religious and they are atheists; they live in rural areas, and in cities, and in small towns all over this country and all over the world. They are women like you. Like me. Like those whom you know and love" (Walker 1989, 101).

"The ones that are on there I think are core tactics that almost all abusers use" (*Power and Control* 2010, in reference to the Power and Control Wheel. Also see Crenshaw 1991, for a similar analysis).

6. See Sudbury (2005); Richie (1996); Roberts (1998); Bhattacharjee and Silliman (2002); Andrea Smith (2005).

7. Ultimately, racial differences that encode hierarchy may have emerged from colonialism itself (see, e.g., Quijano 2000). If that is true, then it is not useful to presuppose racial difference and then use "race" as an explanatory device.

8. Though I will not explore here the paradoxes of the construction of home, I have discussed elsewhere how the "home" is ideologically constructed as a place of safety and refuge that cloaks violence against women (Price 2002): "Homes figure centrally in most Americans' perception of an ideal: of peace, succor, tranquility, achievement, intimacy, even moral rectitude; homes have accrued even a sense of sacredness for some. The desire for a home, moreover, the solace it seems to promise, makes it even more difficult [to perceive violence], especially if one becomes invested in that desire. It might seem initially intolerable, it might signal a deep sort of failure or a collapse, to countenance violence, even if violence is at the core of the construction of the home. 'Home' connotes a normative ideal that excludes the possibility of violence against women at the level of the meaning of 'home.' That notion of home needs to be shaken off in order to see that violence against women is abetted, enabled, by that normative ideal." In that essay, just as in this book, I take up the voices of battered women to disrupt that dominant construction of the space of the home. Even as violence is erased at the level of the conventional meaning of home, battering and abuse are presupposed to occur *only* (or primarily) in the home.

9. For a fascinating ethnographic study on the way in which statistics on violence against women are "produced," see Kevin Haggerty's *Making Crime Count* (2001). Crenshaw gives an example of how the incidence and range of violence against women of color are generally undercounted (Crenshaw 1991, 1258).

CHAPTER ONE. THE POWER AND CONTROL WHEEL: FROM CRITICAL PEDAGOGY TO HOMOGENIZING MODEL

1. See *The Revolution Will Not Be Funded: Beyond the Non-Profit Industrial Complex* (2007) for an extensive analysis of the way in which nonprofits can be assimilated into projects of state domination. Kristin Bumiller (2008) has also traced this history in state co-optation of the struggle to end sexual and domestic violence.

2. A proper genealogy of the method would include accounting for the influence structural linguistics, theories, and methods of popular education developed and practiced by Antonio Gramsci and the *comunidades de base* of the Liberation Church in Latin American. However, full explication of these progenitors and the implications of such a genealogy on the pedagogical methods used are beyond the scope of the present book.

3. I thank María Lugones for this observation.

4. Their focus on oppression rather than possibility has consequences for the direct actions that the women plan. Thus, in analyzing misogynist advertising, for example, after analyzing it from personal, cultural, and institutional standpoints, a group of battered women confines its response to writing a letter to the offending sponsor of the advertisement. Their response is to the *oppression*. It does not come from any attempt to nurture or stoke a previous show of resistance. It is itself the resistance.

5. If it is consistent to apply models for white heterosexuals to nonwhite nonheterosexuals, the consistency is a result of hegemony: the ideology of the dominant group is exported and imposed on nondominant groups.

6. I thank Karen Wenzel for discussion of this point. Earlier we saw that Pence has acknowledged this problem of distinguishing intention from consequence and desire from a sense of entitlement. Also see Franz Fanon's famous formulation of psychosis under colonialism in *The Wretched of the Earth* (1965). Fanon talks briefly of domestic violence in Algerian homes during the process of colonization by the French. He sees violence by Algerian men against Algerian women as displaced rage by one colonized person onto another. Nevertheless, it is significant to point out that he sees no distinction among the oppressed. He has no theory of the complications and interconnections of different oppressions. Interestingly, neither the method of the Duluth Project nor the philosophy of Paulo Freire, one of its theoretical progenitors, has a theory of multiple and interconnected oppressions.

7. The Cycle of Violence theory was authored by Lenore Walker, a psychologist. The Cycle of Violence describes a three-stage cycle of tension build-up, violence, and a "honeymoon" period in which the abuser begs for forgiveness, acts decently, and so on. Together, the cycle induces a state of "learned helplessness." It is enormously influential. It has been the subject of criticism for evacuating battering of analysis of power. Ellen Pence remarked in a 2010 documentary: "This was the one that I remember really got to me, this woman said 'If you live with a batterer, it is not cyclical, it isn't something that comes and goes you live with a batterer every day. Even when he's being nice to you, it's a part of the violence. Because if he's raping you and telling you you're no good and you're ugly here and then three days later he's telling you 'You're beautiful' and 'I need you and I want you it's all part of the same thing and don't think it's cyclical.' I went . . . well I never thought that'" (*Power and Control* 2010).

I provide a fuller analysis of the incompatibility between the Cycle of Violence and the Power and Control Wheel in the next chapter. Also see Ptacek (1999) and Schneider (2000) for other criticisms of the Cycle of Violence.

CHAPTER TWO. DIFFICULT MANEUVERS: STOPPING VIOLENCE AGAINST LATINA IMMIGRANTS IN THE UNITED STATES

1. A pseudonym.

2. This xenophobia and presumed white hegemony have taken the form of perceiving or assuming that all Latinos and all Asians/Asian Americans are immigrants, or recent immigrants; Ronald Takaki writes of being asked by where he is from even though his family has lived in the United States for four generations (Takaki 1998). Some Latinos/Chicanos are descendent from families who have lived in what is now the Southwest United States before it was incorporated into the United States.

3. For example, one of our team interviewed at the jail a man who had been arrested for harassing his girlfriend. He had come to this country as a small child. Now he was

facing deportation to a country he had never known. His plight raises a thorny question for advocacy: how do we advocate for the rights of immigrants, but in a way that promotes safety for women? Eternal banishment from the only country he has ever known seems a severe punishment. However, do we advocate to let this man stay, putting at risk the woman he may have harmed?

4. The marked rise in immigration detention could be attributed not only to xenophobia but also in part to the profit motive, as private companies take over detention facilities in lucrative government contracts. Many local communities have also tried to profit by building immigrant detention facilities on speculation or by agreeing to hold immigrant detainees in local jails in return for per diem pay from Immigration and Customs Enforcement.

5. The "honeymoon stage" is the colloquial term in the battered women's movement to describe the third "tranquil" stage of the Cycle of Violence.

CHAPTER THREE. SPEECH AT THE MARGINS: WOMEN IN PROSTITUTION AND THE COUNTERPUBLIC SPHERE

1. On discussion of the vocabulary of "sex work" versus "prostitution," trafficked women," etc. see, for example, Rosen and Venkatesh (2008) and Agustín (2007). I will generally refer to "women who work in prostitution," or "women in sex work," and occasionally to "prostitutes."

2. In larger stroke, American society exerts a powerful influence on its citizens and on other people living here to claim a common identity with people so evidently different from themselves; it is part of Americans' founding mythology. There also may be a humanistic impulse: "We are all just people underneath." Although they may have little to gain from these ideologies that level their experience as survivors of violence and hence are responsible for the distortion of those experiences, some women may voice these ideologies nonetheless. Attributing this to "ideology" begs the question of where this comes from and defers important questions of what this has meant for the movement to stop violence. In a more specific sense, as we shall see, one motivation for claiming straightforward commonality may be tactical; women who fear exclusion based on difference may claim commonality to try to leverage inclusion: "We are the same as you, we face the same violence you face, and we need help, just as you do."

3. The historian Joan Landes (1988) sees a counterpublic in the salons in France, in which women participated, prior to its delegitimation during the French Revolution. Negt and Kluge (1993) thematize a proletariat counterpublic in which the proletariat's experience is unsundered. They also intimate the intriguing character of a children's counterpublic. The anthropologist Bruce Robbins (1993) sees the notion of a counterpublic as a useful substitute for the culture concept. Culture critic José Esteban Muñoz (1998) draws a portrait of Pedro Zamora, the Latino AIDS activist, as cleverly exploiting the counterpublic potentialities of MTV. As a sympathetic but revisionist reader of Habermas, Nancy Fraser (1993) promotes the utility of the category of counterpublic, emphasizing its public policy possibilities for disenfranchised groups. She draws on the work of the literary critic Rita Felski (1989), who charts out the contours of a feminist counterpublic. Also see Marcia Stephenson (2000), Asen and Brouwer (2001), and Michael Warner (2005).

4. Elsa Barkley Brown (1988), following Bettina Aptheker, recommends instead of decentering one's experience, "pivoting the center": "I believe that all people can learn to center in another experience, validate it, and judge it by its own standards without need for comparison or need to adopt that framework as their own. Thus, one has no need to 'decenter' anyone in order to center someone else; one has only to constantly, appropriately, 'pivot the center.'"

5. It seems relevant to note that Giobbe has faced several charges of sexually harassing former prostitutes she worked with in the 1990s (see City Pages Staff, 1997). Ironically, she was accused of coercing former prostitutes to say self-demeaning and sexually humiliating things. It is beyond our purposes to investigate whether these claims are true. I do not mention the charges to invalidate what she argues. But if the accusations are true, they raise significant questions about Giobbe's public and private politics and personae.

6. This reading benefits from Nahum Chandler's reading of Tera Hunter's book *To 'Joy My Freedom*. He suggested this reading at the Dialogue on the Politics of Resistance at SUNY-Binghamton, April 1999.

7. The exemption for rape in marriage has a long history in English common law. Legal precedent for the marital exemption is attributed to the seventeenth-century English jurist Lord Hale. "[T]he husband cannot be guilty of a rape committed by himself upon his lawful wife for by their mutual matrimonial consent and contract the wife hath given up herself in this kind unto her husband, which she cannot retract" (Hale 2004, 1:629). Although many aspects of the marital exemption have been overturned, important elements are still in place. Legal scholar Jill Elaine Hasday has recently pointed out that at least twenty four states retain some element of marital rape exemption (2009, 1464). For example, many states impose additional procedural barriers for prosecution and impose less serious criminal sanctions in cases of rape in marriage. Thus, she concludes that the marriage exemption has been abridged, but not entirely overturned (Hasday 2000; 2009). Emily Sack observes that successful prosecution of rape in marriage is difficult in practice even when possible in theory (Sack 2009, 51–52).

Looked at from a certain standpoint, it is a small step from the exemption of rape within marriage to the general exemption for rape of a prostitute, a general exemption still de facto in effect in many cases. As Hasday puts it in her review of the history of the marital exemption, this parallel has long troubled (patriarchal) legal theorists, "Structuring the legality of sex so that it turned exclusively on whether a woman was married to her sexual partner was crucially important because it obscured how the marital rape exemption made a wife's position resemble that of a prostitute" (2009).

8. As I suggested in the introduction to this chapter, the issue of legalization is an important subtext here. Some prostitutes believe that a remedy to the dangers would be equal protection under the laws, which are at present either unequally enforced or as written unfair to prostitutes. At the same time, many prostitutes argue that the legal system itself is oppressive; some of these women advocate education and reform, while others see the system as antithetical to their well-being, bankrupt, and incapable of being reformed. A full exploration of the issue of legalization is beyond the scope of this chapter. (But see, e.g., Nagle 1997; Delacoste and Alexander, 1998.)

9. She is making a claim about the popular perception of prostitutes and the dangers street walkers face. She does not address the question of whether call girls are treated any better by johns than street walkers are.

CHAPTER FOUR. HOMOPHOBIA, STRUCTURAL VIOLENCE, AND COALITION BUILDING

1. Although the law is evolving, as I write, at least three states still explicitly exclude gay and lesbian relationships from their domestic violence statutes (see La. Rev. Stat. Ann. 6:2121.1, 46:2132; West 1999). But see La. Rev. Stat. Ann 46:2151 (2009); Mont. Code Ann. 45-5-206 (1999); S.C. Code Ann. 20-4-20, 20-4-40(a) (Law. Co-op 1985 and Supp. 1997) (2009). See a recent (2008) study by the American Bar Association http://www. abanet.org/domviol/pdfs/CPO_Protections_for_LGBT_Victims_7-08.pdf   (accessed August, 2010). Nancy Knauer (1999) has even gone so far as to argue, "A domestic or private sphere is something that same-sex couples have never enjoyed" (327). Although this seems to me to be clearly an exaggeration, Knauer does a neat analysis of the tie between domesticity and heterosexuality. Also see Eaton (1994).

2. Dietrich's response was potentially injurious to the batterer, who would be vulnerable to a homophobic culture, could lose her children, could be thrown in jail, and could face public scorn, none of which might serve Dietrich or the community particularly well.

3. Although Dietrich's batterer's perception of Dietrich is problematic, it also says something about how she saw Dietrich in terms of *race* (i.e., as a white woman), which she then tied to a sense of entitlement to land.

4. In their introduction to *Same-Sex Domestic Violence: Strategies for Change*, Leventhal and Lundy write, "The queer communities have been treated as a monolith, and when the issue of queer domestic violence has been addressed at all, it has generally been in "one size fits all" terms that ignore and disrespect our diversity" (Leventhal and Lundy 1999, ix–x).

5. States vary on whether domestic violence laws apply to current or prior dating relationships when the couple has not lived together; currently, in several states, domestic violence law does not apply. See the American Bar Association Commission on Domestic Violence (http://www.abanet.org/domviol/pdfs/dv_cpo_chart.pdf; accessed August, 2010).

6. The problem of institutionalized heterosexuality not only is explicit homophobia. It is also manifest in the lack of a structure to take up and respond to women whose sexuality does not fall within the norm. Cabral and Coffey comment, "The criminal courtroom can still be an unsafe place for the same-sex victim not only because of whatever blatant homophobia may exist but also because many law enforcement personnel lack the background and skills to deal with the cases effectively" (Cabral and Coffey 1999, 57). Also see Lundy (1993, 291).

7. An advocate for battered women writes of a case she observed where a woman had not "come out" in court (she had described her lover as a "roommate"), until she was forced to by the judge's prying, possibly voyeuristic questions. Eventually, the judge granted the order of protection. The advocate is left wondering if answering the judge's borderline lurid questions was the price of the order of protection. "Paula could protect herself from her abuser but not from the system to which she entrusted her safety" (Cabral and Coffey 1999, 60).

8. One element in this shift may be the process of self-abstraction in counterpublic spheres. I explored the perils of self-betrayal in speaking in counterpublics in the previous chapter. Michael Warner pointed out both the seductive promise of self-abstraction and its political cost: "[T]he rhetorical strategy of personal abstraction is both the utopian

moment of the public sphere and a major source of domination" (Warner 1993, 239). Self-abstraction is seductive because, with it, one can imagine oneself participating in a utopian public of unity and commonality of purpose, while it is simultaneously a yielding to domination, since one abstracts from one's particularity, one's history, including one's history of embodiment, in favor of a homogeneity in which that history is subordinate, extraneous, caricatured, unnecessary, superficial, superfluous, misunderstood, unseen, or unacknowledged.

CHAPTER FIVE. SPACES OF JUDGMENT AND JUDGMENTS OF SPACE: COMPETING LOGICS OF VIOLENCE IN COURT

1. It is important to distinguish between "domestic violence court" and "family court." While their relationship varies state to state, in New York, they often share concurrent jurisdiction. Central to the function of family court is the preservation of the family unit and child welfare. Correspondingly, on the one hand, family court operates in private. Domestic violence court, on the other hand, operates in public. It has specially trained advocates and resource coordinators and offers judicial education on domestic violence issues. It hears cases that would typically fall under the domain of family court as well. One of the most significant differences is obvious in the way the court is conducted. Family court has the putative interest of "the children" much more in mind than domestic violence court does. Such a distinction is of fundamental ideological concern, yet it is impalpable because one can see it in evidence only in the character of the questions the judges ask and the reasoning of their decisions. The wording of the statutes usually insinuates this ideological difference.

Domestic violence court is a relatively recent judicial innovation, but now specialized domestic violence courts can be found throughout the country. Chicago, where I did research through the mid-1990s, is distinguished by having one of the oldest domestic violence courts in the United States (but see Quinn 2008, who claims a forerunner to the modern courts as far back as 1946; also see Wittner 1997). Until the mid-1990s, most cases of domestic violence went to "family court." New York, where I conducted supplemental research for this chapter, in the wake of a series of well-publicized cases of women murdered by their batterers in 1996, joined a nationwide trend and instituted a felony part domestic violence court in Kings County (Brooklyn). As of 2010, according to the New York Division of Criminal Justice Services, domestic violence courts operate in Binghamton, Manhattan, Brooklyn, Albany, Troy, Glens Falls, Saratoga Springs, Syracuse, Auburn, Buffalo, Clarkstown, Spring Valley, Westchester, Queens, Bronx, and Erie, Nassau, and Suffolk Counties. Since 1996, when the first modern-era domestic violence courts were established, these courts have tried more than one hundred thousand cases in New York State.

2. Legions of mainstream studies on violence against women quantify acts of violence as a way of demonstrating frequency. I refer, for example, to the influential and important annual surveys carried out as part of the federal Violence against Women Act, or the Bureau of Justice Statistics, or the FBI's own data. According to a certain dominant logic, counting incidents and prevalence shows how widespread a phenomenon is. If one cannot count incidences, the logic seems to go, then the knowledge is impoverished and hopelessly subjective. If knowledge is not quantified, then it is not useful; it is anecdotal and unreliable. As I argued in the introduction, this methodological disposition in the social sciences

and criminology towards *counting* can foreshorten a deeper, better sense of the contours of violence. On the problems of quantification of violence against women, see Haggerty (2001) and, generally, Erickson and Haggerty (1997); on quantification of violence against women of color in particular, see Carraway (1991), Crenshaw (1991), and Wang (1996).

3. Similarly, most studies of violence against women, especially sociological surveys, leave aside the force of the state. In this chapter I examine the state's role in privatizing violence through law courts.

4. I have used pseudonyms throughout this chapter.

5. Unlike the other cases I examine in this chapter, this one was a criminal case. Due process was required. In many other sorts of cases, such as petitions for orders of protection, quite different rules apply; for example, the judge may grant an ex parte order of protection based solely on a battered woman's testimony to battery and her fear of the batterer.

6. In the next chapter, I discuss in greater depth the issue of so-called "victim non-cooperation." On assault after a woman has separated, see Mahoney (1991).

7. Perhaps Frohmann's account provides an understanding of the realtime unfolding of negotiated identity in court: "Judgments are made through challenge and negotiation over whether descriptions 'fit' 'normative requirements of categorical incumbency'. For example, do this woman's actions leading up to an assault give her the moral authority (i.e., her behavior corresponds with typical features of the cautious woman) to call herself a 'victim'?" (Frohmann citing Matoesian in Frohmann 1997, 532).

8. No one asked him to explain this characterization. The prosecutor went so far as to concede that even if she were hysterical, this would not justify his assaulting her.

9. As a caveat, I relieve myself of the responsibility to attend to the legal standards of evidence, proof, relevance, that govern court procedures. Besides, as Patricia Williams points out, "the boundary between the legal and the illegitimate is just a metaphysical scripting of negotiated power" (Williams 169, 1992). Thus, my conceptualization of violence does not follow the same criteria of legitimacy as the court's. The analysis is motivated by an acknowledgment that space is produced in multiple ways, and not all of those ways have legitimacy conferred upon them. This writing, however, does focus on illegitimate, unheard, and unseen accounts of violence from the standpoint of the production of space.

10. See Bourdieu (1977) for an analysis of how understanding tempo is crucial for an understanding of the nuances of gift giving.

11. The presumption of innocence would thus systematically work in favor of the abuser when there are two accounts that directly contradict each other.

12. I provide a brief critique of the concept of "victim non-cooperation" in the chapter "Why Doesn't She Just Leave?"

13. Divorces themselves are not handled in family court.

14. Many judges in family court and in domestic violence court are loathe to issue orders of protection for couples undergoing divorce proceedings. A popular belief in court is that such petitioners for orders of protection will use such orders for favorable rulings in their divorce proceedings.

15. This is an instance in which the orientation of family court is markedly different from that of domestic violence court. It is also worth noting that in this district family court judges are elected; in the elections for family court judge, "family values" featured prominently in campaign discourse. "Family values" here implies the importance of the putative family unit, children's well-being, the necessity of having a mother and a father

that live together, and so on. This ideological background is relevant to note given the judge's emphasis on "the children," on how divorce will "half-orphan" them. The judge's insistence on these points and the consequent evasion of the sexual aggression faced by the woman provides some material to demonstrate how the ideology of "family values" is bad for women.

16. Even that is not quite accurate: whatever she testified to was in the final analysis irrelevant. Whatever she *said* would not have pushed his culpability beyond a reasonable doubt. Absent other evidence, his denial was sufficient to earn his release.

CHAPTER SIX. "WHY DOESN'T SHE JUST LEAVE?"

1. Martha Mahoney named "separation assault" the violence of batterers *after* women separate—the violence that seeks to block her from leaving, to retaliate, or to forcibly end the separation (Mahoney 1991). Empirical research over the last two decades confirms that the risk of assault or even homicide remains significant *after* separation and in some cases is heightened (Fleury Sullivan, and Bybee 2000; DeKeseredy, Rogness, and Schwartz 2004; Brownridge 2006).

2. See Ann Jones (1994) on how this question can be a statement or a judgment. Hoff (1990) finds the issue of a woman's "micro-network" crucially overlooked.

CHAPTER SEVEN. TENTATIVE CONCLUSIONS AND SMALL-SCALE SOLUTIONS

1. Roberts (1998) details many cases of medical personnel collaborating with police or prosecutors in arresting women who test positive for drugs, often in violation of confidentiality rules.

2. I have been invited by activists and human rights workers to visit their worksites in shanty towns in Lima, Peru, and to a camp for internally displaced people near Baranquilla, Colombia. In both places, I learned of efforts by women to organize autonomously against gender violence in the absence of state presence. In some cases, this involved groups of women confronting abusers. (Because of the nature of their work in conflict zones, I am withholding the names of the women who took me.)

Bibliography

Agustín, Laura. "The Disappearing of a Migration Category: Migrants Who Sell Sex." *Journal of Ethnic and Migration Studies*, 32.1 (2006): 29–47.

———. *Sex at the Margins: Migration, Labour Markets, and the Rescue Industry.* London: Zed Books, 2007.

Agtuca, Jacqueline R. *A Community Secret.* Seattle: Seal, 1994.

Arnold, Rick, Bev Burke, Carl James, D'Arcy Martin, Barb Thomas. *Educating for a Change.* Toronto: Between the Lines and Doris Marshall Institute for Education and Action, 1991.

Asen, Robert, and Daniel C. Brouwer. *Counterpublics and the State.* Albany: State University of New York Press, 2001.

Barbara and Carole. "Interview with Barbara." In *Sex Work: Writings by Women in the Sex Industry*, ed. Frédérique Delacoste and Priscilla Alexander. Pittsburgh and San Francisco: Cleis, 1998.

Barkley Brown, Elsa. "African-American Women's Quilting: A Framework for Conceptualizing and Teaching African-American Women's History." In *Black Women in America: Social Science Perspectives*, ed. Micheine R. Malson et al. Chicago: University of Chicago Press, 1988.

Barry, Kathleen. *The Prostitution of Slavery.* New York: New York University Press, 1996.

Beloof, Douglas E., and Joel Shapiro. "Let the Truth Be Told: Proposed Hearsay Exceptions to Admit Domestic Violence Victims' Out of Court Statements as Substantive Evidence." *Columbia Journal of Gender and the Law* 11 (2002): 1–37.

Benedict, Helen. *Virgins or Vamps?* New York: Oxford University Press, 1992.

Berlant, Lauren. *The Queen of America Goes to Washington City: Essays on Sex and Citizenship (Series Q).* Durham, NC: Duke University Press, 1997.

Bhabha, Homi K. *The Location of Culture.* New York: Routledge, 1994.

Bhattacharjee, Anannya. "The Habit of Ex-Nomination: Nation, Woman, and the Indian Immigrant Bourgeoisie." *Public Culture* 1 (1992): 19–44.

———. "The Public/Private Mirage: Mapping Homes and Undomesticating Violent Work in the South Asian Immigrant Community." In *Feminist Genealogies Colonial Legacies, Democratic Futures*, ed. Jacqui M. Alexander and Chandra Mohanty. New York: Routledge, 1997.

———. "Private Fists and Public Force: Race, Gender, and Surveillance." In *Policing the National Body: Race, Gender, and Criminalization in the United States*, ed. Annanya Bhattacharjee and Jael Silliman. Cambridge, MA: South End, 2002a.

———. "Putting Community Back in the Domestic Violence Movement." ZNet, 2002b. [accessed July 4, 2007].

Bhattacharjee, Annanya, and Jael Silliman, eds. *Policing the National Body: Race, Gender, and Criminalization in the United States*. Cambridge, MA: South End, 2002.

Bhavnani, Kum-Kum, and Angela Davis. "Women in Prison: A Three-Nation Study." *Racing Research, Researching Race*, ed. Frances Windance Twine and Jonathan Warren. New York: New York University Press, 2000.

The Blueprint for Safety: An Interagency Response to Domestic Violence Crimes. Praxis International. http://www.praxisinternational.org/praxis_blue_print_for_safety.aspx [accessed July 12, 2010].

Bourdieu, Pierre. *Outline of a Theory of Practice*. Translated by Richard Nice. Cambridge: Cambridge University Press, 1977.

Brownridge, Douglas A. "Violence against Women Post-separation." *Aggression and Violent Behavior* 11.5 (September–October 2006): 514–530.

Bumiller, Kristin. *In an Abusive State: How Neoliberalism Appropriated the Feminist Movement against Sexual Violence*. Durham, NC: Duke University Press, 2008.

Burns, Maryviolet, et al. *The Speaking Profits Us: Violence in the Lives of Women Of Color; El decirlo nos hace bien a nosotras: la violencia en las vidas de las mujeres de color*. Seattle, WA: Center for the Prevention of Sexual and Domestic Violence, 1986.

Cabral, Andrea, and Diane Coffey. "Creating Courtroom Accessibility." *Same Sex Domestic Violence: Strategies for Change*, ed. Beth Leventhal and Sandra E. Lundy. Thousand Oaks, CA: Sage, 1999.

Cahn, Naomi R. "Inconsistent Stories." *Georgetown Law Review* 81 (1993): 2475–2531.

———. "Battered Women, Child Maltreatment, Prison, and Poverty: Issues for Theory and Practice." *American University Journal of Gender, Social Policy and the Law* 11.2 (2003): 355–366.

Calavita, Kitty. "Immigration Law, Race, and Identity." *Annual Review of Law and Social Science* 3 (2007): 1–20.

Carraway, Chezia G. "Violence against Women of Colour." Stanford Law Review 43 (July 1991): 1301–1309.

Cardea, Caryatis. "falling trees." *Sinister Wisdom* 55 (Spring/Summer 1995).

Carter, Sunny. "A Most Useful Tool." *Living with Contradictions: Controversies in Feminist Social Ethics*, ed. Alison M. Jaggar. Boulder: Westview, 1994.

Cecere, Donna J. "The Second Closet: Battered Lesbians." *Naming the Violence*. Seattle: National Coalition against Domestic Violence/Seal, 1986.

Champagne, Cheryl, Ruth Lapp, and Julie Lee. "Assisting Abused Lesbians: A Guide for Health Professionals and Service Providers." London, Ontario: London Battered Women's Advocacy Centre, 1994.

Chaudhry, Lubna Nazir. "Reconstituting Selves in the Karachi Conflict: Mohajir Women Survivors and Structural Violence." *Cultural Dynamic* 16.2/3 (2004): 259–290.

Chrystos. "'What Did He Hit You With?' The Doctor Said." *In Naming the Violence*, ed. Kerry Lobel. Seattle: National Coalition against Domestic Violence/Seal, 1986.

City Pages Staff. "Public Domain." *City Pages* July 2, 1997. http://www.citypages. com/1997-07-02/news/anatomy-of-a-sellout/ (last accessed June 28, 2010).

Coker, Donna. "Crime Control and Feminist Law Reform in Domestic Violence Law: A Critical Review." *Buffalo Criminal Law Review* 4.2 (2001): 801-860.

Code, Lorraine. *Rhetorical Spaces: Essays on Gendered Locations.* New York: Routledge, 1995.

Cohen, Stanley. *States of Denial: Knowing about Atrocities and Suffering.* Cambridge, UK: Polity, 2001.

Coker, Donna. "Crime Control and Feminist Law Reform in Domestic Violence Law: A Critical Review." *Buffalo Criminal Law Review* 4.2 (2001): 801-860.

Conley, John M., and William M. O'Barr. *Rules versus Relationships: The Ethnography of Legal Discourse.* Chicago: University of Chicago Press, 1990.

Coontz, Stephanie. *The Way We Never Were: American Families and the Nostalgia Trap.* New York: Basic Books, 1992.

Coyote/National Task Force on Prostitution. "Coyote/National Task Force on Prostitution." In *Sex Work: Writings by Women in the Sex Industry.* ed. Frédérique Delacoste and Priscilla Alexander. Pittsburgh: Cleis, 1998.

Crenshaw, Kimberlé. "Mapping the Margins: Intersectionality, Identity, Politics, and Violence against Women of Color." *Stanford Law Review* 43 (July 1991): 1241-1299.

Crimp, Douglas. "Right On, Girlfriend!" In *Fear of a Queer Planet,* ed. Michael Warner. Minneapolis: University of Minnesota Press, 1993.

Cuomo, Chris. *Feminism and Ecological Communities: An Ethic of Flourishing.* New York: Routledge, 1998.

Das, Veena. "Violence, Gender, and Subjectivity." *Annual Review of Anthropology* 37 (2008): 283-299.

Davis, Angela. *Are Prisons Obsolete?* New York: Seven Stories, 2003.

Dawson, Myrna, and Ronit Dinovitzer. "Victim Cooperation and the Prosecution of Domestic Violence in a Specialized Court." *Justice Quarterly* 18 (2001): 593-622.

Debra and Carole. "Interview with Debra." In *Sex Work: Writings by Women in the Sex Industry,* ed. Frédérique Delacoste and Priscilla Alexander. Pittsburgh and San Francisco: Cleis, 1998.

de Certeau, Michel. *The Practice of Everyday Life.* Berkeley: University of California Press, 1984.

De Genova, Nicholas. *Working the Boundaries: Race, Space, and "Illegality" in Mexican Chicago.* Durham: Duke University Press, 2005.

DeKeseredy, Walter S., McKenzie Rogness, and Martin D. Schwartz. "Separation/Divorce Sexual Assault: The Current State of Social Scientific Knowledge." *Aggression and Violent Behavior* 9 (2004): 675-691.

Delacoste, Frédérique, and Priscilla Alexander, eds. Sex Work: Writings by Women in the Sex Industry. Pittsburgh: Cleis, 1998.

Delgado, Richard. *The Coming Race War? And Other Apocalyptic Tales of America after Affirmative Action and Welfare.* NY: New York University Press, 1996.

Dietrich, Mary Lou. "Nothing Is the Same Anymore." In *Naming the Violence.* Seattle: National Coalition against Domestic Violence/Seal, 1986.

Dobash, R. Emerson, and Russell Emerson. *Violence against Wives: The Case against the Patriarchy.* New York: Free, 1979.

Dworkin, Andrea. *Letters from a War Zone*. New York: Dutton, 1989.

Eaton, Mary. "Abuse by Any Other Name: Feminism, Difference, and Intralesbian Violence." In *The Public Nature of Private Violence*, ed. Martha Albertson Fineman and Roxanne Mykitiuk. New York, London: Routledge, 1994.

Esteban Muñoz. José "Pedro Zamora's Real World of Counter-Publicity: Performing an Ethics of Self." In *Hispanisms and Homosexualities*, ed. Sylvia Molloy and Robert Irwin. Durham, NC: Duke University Press, 1998.

Erickson, R., and K. Haggerty. *Policing the Risk Society*. Toronto: University of Toronto Press, and Oxford: University of Oxford Press, 1997.

Falcón, Sylvanna. "'National Security' and the Violation of Women: Militarized Border Rape at the US-Mexico Border." In *Color of Violence*. Cambridge, MA: South End, 2006.

Fanon, Franz. *The Wretched of the Earth*. Translated by Constance Farrington. New York: Grove, 1965.

Farley, M. "'Renting an Organ for 10 Minutes:' What Tricks Tell Us about Prostitution, Pornography, and Trafficking." In *Pornography: Driving the Demand for International Sex Trafficking*, ed. D. Guinn. Los Angeles: Captive Daughters Media, 2007.

Farley, M., and Barkan, H. "Prostitution, Violence against Women, and Posttraumatic Stress Disorder." *Women & Health* 27 (1998): 137–149.

Farley, M., and Kelly, V. "Prostitution: A Critical Review of the Medical and Social Sciences Literature." *Women and Criminal Justice* 11 (2000): 29–63.

Farley, M. and Lynne, J. "Prostitution of Indigenous Women: Sex Inequality and the Colonization of Canada's First Nations Women." *Fourth World Journal* 6.1 (2005): 1–29. (http://www.cwis.org/fwj/61/prostitution_of_indigenous_women.htm, last accessed July, 2010).

Felski, Rita. *Beyond Feminist Aesthetics*. Cambridge: Harvard University Press, 1989.

Figueira-McDonough, Josefina, and Rosemary C. Sarri, eds. *Women at the Margins: Neglect, Punishment, and Resistance*. New York: Hawthorn, 2002.

Fine, Michelle, and Lois Weis. "Disappearing Acts: The State and Violence against Women in the Twentieth Century." *Signs: Journal of Women in Culture and Society* 25 (2000): 1139–1146.

Fire Inside. "Editorial: Domestic Violence, Institutional Violence: Making the Connections." *Fire Inside* 27 (Spring 2004). (http://www.womenprisoners.org/fire/000498.html; last accessed June, 2011).

Fischer, Karla, and Mary Rose. "When 'Enough Is Enough': Battered Women's Decision Making around Court Orders of Protection." *Crime and Delinquency* 41.6 (1995): 414–429.

Fleury, R. E., C. M. Sullivan, and D. I. Bybee. "When Ending the Relationship Does Not End the Violence: Women's Experiences of Violence by Former Partners." *Violence against Women* 6 (2000): 1363–1383.

Ford, David A. "Coercing Victim Participation in Domestic Violence Prosecutions." *Journal of Interpersonal Violence* 18.6 (2003): 669–684.

Fraser, Nancy. "Rethinking the Public Sphere." In *The Phantom Public Sphere*. ed. Bruce Robbins. Minnesota: University of Minnesota Press, 1993.

Freire, Paulo. *Pedagogy of the Oppressed*. Translated by Myra Bergman Ramos. New York: Continuum, 1996.

Frohmann, Lisa. "Convictability and Discordant Locales: Reproducing Race, Class, and Gender Ideologies in Prosecutorial Decisionmaking." *Law & Society Review* 31.3 (1997): 531–554.

Frye, Marilyn. *Politics of Reality*. Trumansburg, NY: Crossing, 1983.

———. "On Being White: Thinking towards a Feminist Understanding of Race and Race Supremacy." In *The Politics of Reality*. Trumansburg, New York: Crossing, 1983.

Futures without Violence. "Formas en las que la mujer experimenta el abuso doméstico" http://www.futureswithoutviolence.org/userfiles/file/ImmigrantWomen/Rueda%20de%20poder%20y%20control%20-%20inmigrante1.pdf (last accessed December, 2011).

Galtung, Johan. "Violence, Peace, and Peace Research," Journal of Peace Research 6.3 (1969): 167–191.

García, Martha Lucía. "A 'New Kind' of Battered Woman: Challenges for the Movement." In *Same Sex Domestic Violence: Strategies for Change* ed. Beth Leventhal and Sandra E. Lundy. Thousand Oaks, CA: Sage, 1999.

George, Amanda. "Strip Search: Sexual Assault by the State." In *Without Consent: Confronting Adult Sexual Violence*, ed. Patricia Weiser. Easteal, Canberra: Australian Institute of Criminology, 1993.

Gilmore, Ruth Wilson, and Craig Gilmore. "Restating the Obvious." *Indefensible Space: The Architecture of the National Insecurity State*, ed. Michael Sorkin. New York: Routledge, 2007.

Giobbe, Evelina. "The Vox Fights." VOX, Winter 1991.

———. "Confronting the Liberal Lies about Prostitution." In *Living with Contradictions: Controversies in Feminist Social Ethics*, ed. Alison M. Jaggar. Boulder: Westview, 1994.

Giroux, Henry. *Border Crossings*. New York: Routledge, 1992.

Goffman, Erving. *Relations in Public*. New York: Basic Books, 1971.

Gottschalk, Marie. *The Prison and the Gallows: The Politics of Mass Incarceration in America*. Cambridge: Cambridge University Press, 2006.

Hagan, J., R. Levi, and R. Dinovitzer. "The Symbolic Violence of the Crime–Immigration Nexus: Migrant Mythologies in the Americas." *Criminology & Public Policy* 7.1 (2008): 95–112.

Haggerty, Kevin D. *Making Crime Count*. Toronto: University of Toronto, 2001.

Hale, Matthew. *Historia Placitorum Coronae: History of the Pleas of the Crown*. New Jersey: Lawbook Exchange: 2004[1736].

Hall, Kira. "Lip Service on the Fantasy Lines." In *Gender Articulated*, ed Kira Hall and Mary Buckholtz. New York and London: Routledge, 1995.

Hall, Kira, and Mary Bucholtz, eds. *Gender Articulated*. New York: Routledge, 1995.

Hall, Kira, Mary Bucholtz, and Birch Moonwomon, eds. *Locating Power* Berkeley: Berkeley Women and Language Group, 1992.

Harvest of Loneliness/Cosecha triste. DVD Directed by Gilbert G. Gonzalez and Vivian Price. Films Media Group, 2010.

Harvey, David. 1990. *The Condition of Postmodernity*. Oxford: Blackwell.

Hasday, Jill Elaine. "Contest and Consent: A Legal History of Marital Rape." *California Law Review* 88 (2000): 1373–1505.

———. "Protecting Them from Themselves: The Persistence of Mutual Benefits Arguments for Sex and Race Inequality." *New York University Law Review* (2009): 1464–

Hernández-Truyol, Berta Experanza, and Jane E. Larson. "Both Work and Violence: Prostitution and Human Rights." In *Moral Imperialism: A Critical Anthology*, ed. Berta Experanza Hernández-Truyol. New York: New York University Press, 2002.

Hoff, Lee Ann. *Battered Women as Survivors*. New York: Routledge, 1990.

Hoagland, Sarah. *Lesbian Ethics: Toward New Value*. Palo Alto: Institute of Lesbian Studies, 1988.

Holder, Robyn, and Nicole Mayo. "What Do Women Want? Prosecuting Family Violence in the ACT." *Current Issues in Criminal Justice* 15.1 (Summer 2003): 5–25.

Hondagneu-Sotelo, Pierrette. "The History of Mexican Undocumented Settlement in the United States." In *Challenging Fronteras*, ed. Mary Romero, Pierrette Hondagneu-Sotelo, and Vilma Ortiz. NY: Routledge, 1997.

hooks, bell. "Homeplace: A Site of Resistance." In *Yearning*. Boston: South End, 1990.

Horsburgh, Beverly. "Lifting the Veil of Secrecy: Domestic Violence in the Jewish Community." *Harvard Women's Law Journal* 18 (1995): 171–217.

Hunter, Tera. *To 'Joy My Freedom: Southern Black Women's Lives and Labors after the Civil War*. Cambridge: Harvard University Press, 1998.

Incite! Women of Color against Violence. *The Color of Violence: The Incite! Anthology*. Cambridge, MA: South End, 2006.

———. *The Revolution Will Not Be Funded: Beyond the Non-Profit Industrial Complex*. Cambridge, MA: South End, 2007.

International Committee for Prostitutes' Rights (ICPR). "International Committee for Prostitutes' Rights World Charter and World Whores' Congress Statements." In *Living with Contradictions: Controversies in Feminist Social Ethics* ed. Alison M. Jaggar. Boulder: Westview, 1994.

Jablow, Pamela M. "Victims of Abuse and Discrimination: Protecting Battered Homosexuals under Domestic Violence Legislation." *Hofstra Law Review* 28 (Summer 2000).

James, Joy. *Resisting State Violence: Radicalism, Gender, and Race in the U.S.* Minneapolis: University of Minnesota Press, 1996.

Jameson, Frederic. "On Negt and Kluge." In *The Phantom Public Sphere*, ed. Bruce Robbins. Minnesota: University of Minnesota Press, 1993.

Johnson, Paula. *Inner Lives: Voices of African American Women in Prison*. New York: New York University Press, 2004.

Jones, Ann. *Next Time, She'll Be Dead*. Boston: Beacon, 1994.

Kaschak, Ellyn. "Intimate Betrayal: Domestic Violence in Lesbian Relationships." In *Intimate Betrayal: Domestic Violence in Lesbian Relationships*, ed. Ellyn Kaschak. New York: Haworth, 2001.

Knauer, Nancy J. "Same-sex Domestic Violence: Claiming a Domestic Sphere While Risking Negative Stereotypes." *Temple Political & Civil Rights Law Review* 8.2 (1999): 325–350.

Koyama, Emi. "Disloyal to Feminism: Abuse of Survivors within the Domestic Violence Shelter System." In *Color of Violence: The Incite! Anthology*, ed. Incite! Women of Color Collective. Cambridge, MA: South End, 2006.

Landes, Joan. *Women and the Public Sphere in the Age of the French Revolution*. Ithaca: Cornell University Press. 1988.

Lefebvre, Henri. *The Production of Space*. Translated by Donald Nicholson-Smith. Oxford, UK, and Cambridge, MA: Blackwell, 1991 [1974].

Lerum, K. "Twelve-Step Feminism Makes Sex Workers Sick: How the State and Recovery Movement Turn Radical Women into 'Useless Citizens.'" *Sexuality&Culture* 2 (1998): 7–36.

Leventhal, Beth and Sandra E. Lundy, ed. *Same Sex Domestic Violence: 10 Strategies for Change*. Thousand Oaks, CA: Sage, 1999.

Lindsley, Syd. "The Gendered Assault on Immigrants." In *Policing the National Body: Race, Gender, and Criminalization in the United States*, ed. Annanya Bhattacharjee and Jael Silliman. Cambridge, MA: South End, 2002.

Lobel, Kerry. *Naming the Violence: Speaking Out about Lesbian Battering*. Seattle: Seal, 1986.

Lowe, Lisa. *Immigrant Acts*. Durham, NC: Duke University Press, 1997.

Lugones, María. *Peregrinajes/Pilgrimajes: Theorizing Coalition against Multiple Oppression*. New York: Rowman and Littlefield, 2003a.

———. "Strategies of the Streetwalker/estratégias de la callejera." In *Pilgrimajes/Peregrinajes: Theorizing Coalition against Multiple Oppression*. New York: Rowman and Littlefield, 2003b.

———. "Structure/antistructure and agency under oppression." *Journal of Philosophy* 87.10 (October 1990): 500–507.

Lugones, María C. "On the Logic of Pluralist Feminism." In *Feminist Communication Theory: Selections in Context*, ed. Lana F. Rakow and Laura A. Wackwitz. Thousand Oaks, CA: Sage, 2004.

———. "Multiculturalism and Publicity." *Hypatia* 15.3 (Summer 2000): 175–182.

Lugones, María C., and Joshua Price. "Dominant Culture: El deseo por un alma pobre." In *Multiculturalism from the Margins*, ed. Dean Harris. Westport, CT: Bergin and Garvey, 1995.

Lundy, Sandra E. "Abuse That Dare Not Speak Its Name: Assisting Victims of Lesbians and Gay Domestic Violence in Massachusetts." *New England Review of Law* 28 (Winter 1993): 273–293.

———. "Equal Protection/Equal Safety." In *Same Sex Domestic Violence: Strategies for Change* ed. Beth Leventhal and Sandra E. Lundy. Thousand Oaks, CA: Sage, 1999.

Lynch, Caitrin. "Nation, Woman, and the Indian Immigrant Bourgeoisie: An Alternative Formulation." *Public Culture* 6.2 (1994): 425–437.

MacKinnon, Catherine. *Feminism Unmodified*. Cambridge: Harvard University Press, 1987.

Mahoney, Martha R. "Legal Issues of Battered Women: Redefining the Issue of Separation." *Michigan Law Review* 90 (1991): 1–94.

Marcus, Isabel. "Reframing 'Domestic Violence': Terrorism in the Home." In *The Public Nature of Private Violence: The Discovery of Domestic Abuse*, ed. Martha Fineman and Roxanne Mykitiuk. New York, London: Routledge, 1994.

marino, dian. *Wild Garden: Art, Education, and the Culture of Resistance*. Ontario: Between the Lines, 1998.

Massachusetts Coalition of Battered Women Service Groups, Inc. *For Shelter and Beyond*. Massachusetts: Massachusetts Coalition of Battered Women Service Groups, Inc., 1992.

Matsuda, Mari J. "Public Response to Racist Speech: Considering the Victim's Story." *Michigan Law Review* 87.8 (August 1989): 2320–2381.

———. "When the First Quail Calls: Multiple Consciousness as Jurisprudential Method." *Women's Rights Law Reporter* 14 (Spring/Fall 1992): 2, 3.

McElhinny, Bonnie S. "Challenging Hegemonic Masculinities: Female and Male Police Officers Handling Domestic Violence." In *Gender Articulated*, ed. Kira Hall and Mary Bucholtz. New York: Routledge, 1995.

McLeod, Maureen. "Victim Noncooperation in the Prosecution of Domestic Assault." *Criminology* 21 (1983): 395–416.

Memmi, Albert. *The Colonizer and the Colonized*. Boston: Beacon, 1965.

Merry. Sally Engle. "Gender Violence and Legally Engendered Selves." *Identities: Global Studies in Culture and Power* 2 (1995a): 49–73.

———. "Wife Battering and the Ambiguities of Rights." In *Identities, Politics, and Rights*, ed. Austin Sarat and Thomas R. Kearns. Ann Arbor: University of Michigan Press, 1995b.

Mignolo. "Dispensable and Bare Lives: Coloniality and the Hidden Political/Economic Agenda of Modernity." *Human Architecture: Journal of the Sociology of Self-Knowledge* 7.2 (Spring 2009): 69–88.

Mills, Linda G. "Killing Her Softly: Intimate Abuse and the Violence of State Intervention." *Harvard Law Review* 113.2 (December 1999): 550–613.

———. *Insult to Injury: Rethinking Our Responses to Intimate Abuse*. Princeton: Princeton University Press, 2003.

Minow, Martha. "Words and the Door to the Land of Change: Law, Language, and Family Violence." *Vanderbilt Law Review* 43 (1990): 1665–1699.

Nagle, Jill. *Whores and Other Feminists*. New York: Routledge: 1997.

Negt, Oskar, and Alexander Kluge. *Public Sphere and Experience: Towards Analysis of the Bourgeois and Proletarian Public Sphere*. Translated by Peter Labanyi, Jamie Owen Daniel, and Assenka Oksiloff. Minnesota: University of Minnesota Press, 1993 [1972].

Nell and Priscilla Alexander. "Interview with Nell." In *Sex Work: Writings by Women in the Sex Industry*, ed. Frédérique Delacoste and Priscilla Alexander. Pittsburgh and San Francisco: Cleis, 1998.

Ogden, Stormy. "The Prison Industrial Complex in Indigenous California." In *Global Lockdown: Race, Gender, and the Prison-Industrial Complex*, ed. Julia Sudbury. New York: Routledge, 2005.

Ong, Aihwa. "Cultural Citizenship as Subject-Making: Immigrants Negotiate Racial and Cultural Boundaries in the United States." *Current Anthropology* 37.5 (December, 1996): 737–762.

Paley, Noelle, and Joshua M. Price. "Violent Interruptions." In *Interrupted Life: Experiences of Incarcerated Women in the United States*, ed. Paula Johnson, et al. Berkeley: University of California Press, 2010.

Park, Lisa Sun-Hee. "Navigating the Anti-Immigrant Wave: The Korean Women's Hotline and the Politics of Community." In *Domestic Violence at the Margins: Readings on Race, Class, Gender, and Culture*, ed. Natalie Sokoloff with Christina Pratt. New Brunswick, NJ: Rutgers University Press, 2005.

Pateman, Carole. *The Sexual Contract*. Palo Alto: Stanford University Press, 1988.

Peace over Violence (formerly *the L.A. Commission on Assaults against Women*). "Cómo sobrevivir la violencia doméstica: Una guía para capacitar a mujeres maltratadas." Los Angeles: Peace Over Violence, 2005.

Pence, Ellen. "Some Thoughts on Philosophy." In *Coordinating Community Responses to Domestic Violence*. ed. Melanie F. Shepard and Ellen L. Pence. Thousand Oaks, CA: Sage, 1999.

Pence, Ellen, et al. *In Our Best Interest: A Process for Personal and Social Change*. Minnesota: Minnesota Program Development Fund, 1987.

Pheifer, Pat. "A Voice for Abuse Victims." *Minneapolis Star Tribune*, April 18, 2010.

Pleck, Elizabeth. *Domestic Tyranny: The Making of Social Policy against Family Violence from Colonial Times to the Present*. New York: Oxford University Press, 1987.

Porter, Theodore. *Trust in Numbers*. Princeton: Princeton University Press, 1996.

Power and Control: Domestic Violence in America. DVD Directed by Peter Cohn. Transit Media, 2010.

Prell, Riv-Ellen. "American Jewish Culture through a Gender-Tinted Lens." In *Judaism Since Gender*, ed. Miriam Peskowitz and Laura Levitt. New York: Routledge, 1997.

Price, Joshua. "Difficult Maneuvers in Discourse against Violence against Latina Immigrants in the U.S." In *Cardozo Journal of International and Comparative Law* 7.2 (Fall 1999): 277–313.

———. "Violence against Prostitutes and the Counterpublic Sphere." *Genders* 38 (2001).

———. "The Apotheosis of Home and the Maintenance of Spaces of Violence." *Hypatia* 17.4, (Fall 2002): 39–70.

Ptacek, James. *Battered Women in the Courtroom: The Power of Judicial Responses*. Boston: Northeastern University Press, 1999.

Quan, Tracy. "The Vox Fights." *VOX* (Winter 1991).

Quijano, Anibal. "Coloniality of Power, Eurocentrism and Latin America." *Nepantla: Views from South* 1.3. (2000): 533–580.

Quinn, Mae C. "Anna Moscowitz Kross and the Home Term Part: A Second Look at the Nation's First Criminal Domestic Violence Court." *Akron Law Review* 41 (2008): 733–734.

Rabinovitch, Jannit, and Susan Strega. "The PEERS Story: Effective Services Sidestep the Controversies." *Violence against Women* 10.2 (February 2004): 140–159.

Rafael, Jody, and Deborah L. Shapiro. "Violence in Indoor and Outdoor Prostitution Venues." *Violence against Women* 10.2 (February 2004): 126–139.

Rafael, Vicente. "Domesticity at the Edge of Empire." In *White Love and Other Events in Filipino History*. Durham, NC: Duke University Press, 2000.

Renzetti, Claire M. *Violent Betrayal: Partner Abuse in Lesbian Relationships*. Newbury Park, CA: Sage, 1992.

Richie, Beth. *Compelled to Crime: The Gender Entrapment of Battered Black Women*. New York: Routledge, 1996.

———. "A Black Feminist Reflection on the Antiviolence Movement." *Signs* 25.4 (2000): 1133–1137.

———. "Queering Antiprison Work: African American Lesbians in the Juvenile Justice System." *Global Lockdown: Race, Gender, and the Prison-Industrial Complex*, ed. Julia Sudbury. New York: Routledge, 2005.

Ristock, J. L. *No More Secrets: Lesbian Battering*. New York: Routledge, 2002.

Ritchie, Andrea. "Law Enforcement Violence against Women of Color." In *The Color of Violence: The Incite! Anthology*, ed. Incite! Women of Color against Violence. Cambridge, MA: South End, 2006.

Robbins, Bruce. Introduction to *The Phantom Public Sphere*, ed. Bruce Robbins. Minnesota: University of Minnesota Press, 1993.

Robinson, Amanda. L., and Dee Cook. "Understanding Victim Retraction in Cases of Domestic Violence: Specialist Courts, Government Policy, and Victim-Centred Justice." *Contemporary Justice Review* 9.2 (2006): 189–213.

Roberts, Dorothy. *Killing the Black Body: Race, Reproduction, and the Meaning of Liberty.* New York: Vintage, 1998.

Robson, Ruthann. "Lavender Bruises: Intralesbian Violence, Law, and Lesbian Legal Theory." *Golden Gate University Law Review* 20 (1990): 567.

———. *Lesbian (Out)law: Survival under the Rule of Law* San Francisco: Firebrand Books, 1992.

Rodman, Margaret, and Mathew Cooper. "Accessibility as a Discourse of Space in Canadian Housing Cooperatives." *American Ethnologist.* 22.3 (1995): 589–601.

Romero, Mary. *Maid in the USA.* New York: Routledge, 1992.

Romkens, Renee. "Law as a Trojan Horse: Unintended Consequences of Rights-Based Interventions to Support Battered Women." *Yale Journal of Law and Feminism* 13 (2001): 265–290.

———. "Symposium: Battered Women and Feminist Lawmaking: Author Meets Readers, Elizabeth M. Schneider, Christine Harrington, Sally Engle Merry, Renee Romkens, and Marianne Wesson." *Journal of Law and Policy* 10 (2002): 313–372.

Rosaldo, Renato. *Culture and Truth: The Remaking of Social Analysis.* Boston: Beacon, 1989.

Rose, Gillian. *Feminism and Geography.* Minnesota: University of Minnesota Press, 1993.

Rose, Mary. "When 'Enough Is Enough': Battered Women's Decision Making around Court Orders of Protection." *Crime and Delinquency* 41.4 (October, 1995): 414–429.

Rosen, Eva, and Sudhir Alladi Venkatesh. "A 'Perversion' of Choice: Sex Work Offers Just Enough in Chicago's Urban Ghetto." *Journal of Contemporary Ethnography* 37.4 (August 2008): 417–441.

Ross, Luana. *Inventing the Savage: The Social Construction of Native American Criminality.* Austin: University of Texas Press, 1998.

Rubenstein, Roberta. *Home Matters: Longing and Belonging, Nostalgia and Mourning in Women's Fiction.* New York: Palgrave, 2001.

Russell, Diane E. *Rape in Marriage.* Bloomington: Indiana University Press, 1990.

Sack, Emily J. "From the Right of Chastisement to the Criminalization of Domestic Violence: A Study in Resistance to Effective Policy Reform." *Thomas Jefferson Law Review* 32.1 (Fall 2009): 31–64.

Sanchez, Lisa. "Boundaries of Legitimacy: Sex, Violence, Citizenship, and Community in a Local Sexual Economy." *Law and Social Inquiry* 22.3 (Summer 1997a): 543–580.

———. "Sex/law and the Paradox of Agency in the Everyday Practices of Women in the Evergreen Sex Trade." In *Constitutive Criminology at Work: Agency and Resistance in the Constitution of Crime and Punishment,* ed. Dragan Milovanovic and Stuart Henry. New York: State University of New York Press, 1997b.

Said, Edward. *Orientalism.* New York: Random House, 1979.

———. "Traveling Theory." In *The World, the Text, and the Critic.* Cambridge: Harvard University Press, 1983.

Sanday, Peggy Reeves. *Fraternity Gang Rape: Sex, Brotherhood, and Privilege on Campus.* New York. New York University Press, 1990.

Saucedo, Renee. "INS Raids and How Immigrant Women Are Fighting Back." In *The Color of Violence: The Incite! Anthology,* ed. Incite! Women of Color against Violence. Cambridge, MA: South End, 2006.

Scarf, Mimi. "Marriages Made in Heaven? Battered Jewish Wives." In *On Being a Jewish Feminist,* ed. Susannah Heschel. New York: Schocken Books, 1983.

Schechter, Susan. *Women and Male Violence: The Visions and Struggles of the Battered Women's Movement.* Boston, MA: South End, 1982.

Schmidt Camacho, Alicia. "Ciudadana X: Gender Violence and the Denationalization of Women's Rights in Ciudad Juáez, Mexico." In *Terrorizing Women: Femincide in the Américas*, ed. Rosa-Linda Fregoso and Cynthia Bejarano. Durham, NC: Duke University Press, 2010.

Schneider, Elizabeth. "Particularity and Generality: Challenges of Feminist Theory and Practice in Work on Women-Abuse." *New York University Law Review* 67.3 (1992): 520–568.

Schneider, Elizabeth M. *Battered Women and Feminist Lawmaking.* New Haven: Yale University Press, 2000.

Scott, James C. *Weapons of the Weak: Everyday Forms of Peasant Resistance* New Haven: Yale University Press, 1985.

———. *Domination and the Arts of Resistance: Hidden Transcripts.* New Haven: Yale University Press, 1990.

Sedgwick, Eve. *Epistemology of the Closet.* Berkley: University of California Press, 1990.

Shepard, Melanie F., and Ellen L. Pence, eds. *Coordinating Community Responses to Domestic Violence. Thousand Oaks*, CA: Sage, 1999.

Silbaugh, Katherine. "Turning Labor into Love: Housework and the Law." *Northwestern Law Review* (Fall 1996): 1–86.

Siegel, Reva B. "'The Rule of Love'": Wife Beating as Prerogative and Privacy." *Yale Law Journal* 105 (1996): 2117–2207.

Smith, Andrea. *Conquest: Sexual Violence and American Indian Genocide.* Cambridge, MA: South End, 2005.

Smith, Brenda V. "Battering, Forgiveness, and Redemption: Alternative Models for Addressing Domestic Violence in Communities of Color." In *Domestic Violence at the Margins: Readings on Race, Class, Gender, and Culture*, ed. Natalie Sokoloff with Christina Pratt. New Brunswick, NJ: Rutgers University Press, 2005.

Smith, Kemba. "Modern Day Slavery: Inside the Prison-Industrial Complex." In *Global Lockdown: Race, Gender, and the Prison-Industrial Complex.* New York: Routledge, 2005.

Soja, Edward. *Thirdspace.* Oxford: Blackwell, 1996.

———. *Postmodern Geographies: The Reassertion of Space in Critical Social Theory.* London, New York: Verso, 1989.

Sokoloff, Natalie J., with Christina Pratt. *Domestic Violence at the Margins: Readings on Race, Class, Gender, and Culture.* New Brunswick, NJ: Rutgers University Press, 2005.

Spelman, Elizabeth. *Inessential Woman.* Boston: Beacon, 1988.

Stanko, Elizabeth. *Everyday Violence: How Women and Men Experience Sexual and Physical Danger.* London: Pandora, 1990.

Stanko, Elizabeth A. "Conceptualizing the Target: Trying to Make Sense of Intentionality, Meaning, Context, and Consequences of Racist, Homophobic, and Domestic Violence." Address, Law and Society Association Meetings, Budapest, Hungary, 2001.

Stanko, Elizabeth Anne. *Intimate Intrusions.* London, Boston: Routledge and Kegan Paul, 1985.

Stark, Evan. *Coercive Control: How Men Entrap Women in Personal Life.* New York: Oxford University Press, 2007.

———. "Rethinking Coercive Control." *Violence against Women* 15.12 (2009): 1509–1525.

Stephenson, Marcia. "The Impact of an Indigenous Counterpublic Sphere on the Practice of Democracy: The Taller De Historia Oral Andina in Bolivia." *Working Paper number 279 Working Paper Series. The Helen Kellogg Institute for International Studies of the University of Notre Dame,* 2000.

Sudbury, Julia. *Global Lockdown: Race, Gender, and the Prison-Industrial Complex.* New York: Routledge, 2005.

Sundahl, Debi. "Stripper." In *Living with Contradictions: Controversies in Feminist Social Ethics,* ed. Alison M. Jaggar. Boulder: Westview, 1994.

Takaki, Ronald. *Strangers from a Different Shore.* New York: Back Bay Books, 1998.

Teichroeb, Ruth, and Julie Davidow. "Cops Who Abuse Their Wives Rarely Pay the Price." *Seattle Post-Intelligencer,* Wednesday, July 23, 2003.

Trinch, Shonna L. *Latinas' Narratives of Domestic Abuse: Discrepant Versions of Violence.* Amsterdam: John Benjamins, 2003.

Walker, Lenore E. *Terrifying Love: Why Battered Women Kill and How Society Responds.* New York: HarperPerennial, 1989.

Wang, Karin. "Battered Asian American Women: Community Responses from the Battered Women's Movement and the Asian American Community." *Asian Law Journal* 3 (May 1996): 151–184.

Warner, Michael. *The Letters of the Republic: Publication and the Public Sphere in Eighteenth-Century America.* Cambridge: Harvard University Press, 1990.

———. "The Mass Public and the Mass Subject." In *The Phantom Public Sphere* ed. Bruce Robbins. Minnesota: University of Minnesota Press, 1993.

———. *Publics and Counterpublics.* Cambridge: Zone Books, 2005.

———, ed. *Fear of a Queer Planet.* Minnesota: University of Minnesota Press, 1993.

Websdale, Neil, and Byron Johnson. "Reducing Women Battering: The Role of Structural Approaches." In *Domestic Violence at the Margins: Readings on Race, Class, Gender, and Culture,* ed. Natalie Sokoloff with Christina Pratt. New Brunswick, NJ: Rutgers University Press, 2005.

Weis, Lois, Michelle Fine, Amira Proweller, Corrine Bertram, and Julia Marusza. "'I've Slept in Clothes Long Enough': Excavating the Sounds of Domestic Violence among Women in the White Working Class." In *Domestic Violence at the Margins: Readings on Race, Class, Gender, and Culture,* ed. Natalie Sokoloff with Christina Pratt. New Brunswick, NJ: Rutgers University Press, 2005.

White, Lucie E. "Subordination, Rhetorical Survival Skills, and Sunday Shoes: Notes on the Hearing of Mrs. G." *Buffalo Law Review* 38.1 (Winter 1980): 1–58.

Williams, Patricia. "A Rare Case Study of Muleheadedness and Men." In *Race-ing Justice, En-gendering Power,* ed. Toni Morrison. New York: Pantheon Books, 1992.

Wilson, Margo, and Martin Daly. "Spousal Homicide Risk and Estrangement." *Violence and Victims* 8.1 (1993): 3–16.

Wittner, Judith. "Reconceptualizing Agency in Domestic Violence Court." *Community Activism and Feminist Politics: Organizing Across Race, Class, and Gender.* New York: Routledge, 1997.

Yngvesson, Barbara. *Virtuous Citizens, Disruptive Subjects: Order and Complaint in a New England Court.* New York: Routledge, 1993.

Young, Iris Marion. *Justice and the Politics of Difference.* Princeton: Princeton University Press, 1990.

Zavella, Patricia. "Mujeres in Factories: Race and Class Perspectives on Women, Work, and Family." In *Gender at the Crossroads of Knowledge: Feminist Anthropology in the Postmodern Era*. Berkeley: University of California Press, 1991.

Zorza, Joan. "Woman Battering: A Major Cause of Homelessness." *Clearinghouse Review* 25.4 (1991): 421–429.

Index